Existential Perspectives on Supervision

Widening the Horizon of Psychotherapy
and Counselling

Edited by
Emmy van Deurzen
and
Sarah Young

palgrave
macmillan

First published 2009 by
PALGRAVE MACMILLAN

Palgrave Macmillan in the UK is an imprint of Macmillan Publishers Limited,
registered in England, company number 785998, of Houndmills, Basingstoke,
Hampshire RG21 6XS.

Palgrave Macmillan in the US is a division of St Martin's Press LLC,
175 Fifth Avenue, New York, NY 10010.

Palgrave Macmillan is the global academic imprint of the above companies
and has companies and representatives throughout the world.

Palgrave® and Macmillan® are registered trademarks in the United States,
the United Kingdom, Europe and other countries.

978–0–230–20330–3

This book is printed on paper suitable for recycling and made from fully
managed and sustained forest sources. Logging, pulping and manufacturing
processes are expected to conform to the environmental regulations of the
country of origin.

A catalogue record for this book is available from the British Library.

A catalog record for this book is available from the Library of Congress.

10   9   8   7   6   5   4   3   2   1
18   17   16   15   14   13   12   11   10   09

Printed and bound in Great Britain by
CPI Antony Rowe, Chippenham and Eastbourne

This book is dedicated to all our supervisees and supervisors – past, present and future – from whom we have learnt and will continue to learn what it means to be human.

Ring the bells that still can ring
Forget your perfect offering
There is a crack, a crack in everything
That's how the light gets in.

Anthem – *Leonard Cohen*

Contents

Preface

Existential psychotherapy has been practised for over a century, but it has only become widely known over the past few decades. It is now well established and many hundreds of existential therapists are being trained and supervised each year. Methods of existential supervision have rapidly evolved in an organic fashion, eventually leading to the start of a full training in existential supervision at the New School of Psychotherapy and Counselling in London, around the beginning of the millennium.

Existential supervision is different from other forms of supervision because it views therapeutic work from a philosophical perspective. It does not police, admonish, control or prescribe how supervisees should work, but rather creates a space and time for contemplation and discussion of the way in which particular clients live their lives and view the world and the way in which different therapists make sense of these ways of being. Existential supervisors show trainees and experienced therapists alike how to take therapy seriously and pause for thought. Existential supervision then is about overseeing life and taking stock. It affords us the privilege of finding out more about the human condition and our own position in it.

In practical terms existential supervision has become a necessity. With the professionalisation of counselling and psychotherapy the practice of supervision has generally become more formalised and structured, following the trend of evidence-based and formalised practice. Existential supervision can provide a much needed breath of fresh air and a sense of space in that climate of constriction. For it takes the broad view of human existence and refocuses the salient issues against the background of the paradoxes and real human concerns that our clients are struggling with. So existential supervision is not just for existential therapists, but is the method of choice for a philosophically disciplined integrative supervision. It enhances therapeutic vision and enables practitioners to open their vista to include the wide sweep of human reality.

The existential outlook provides the clarity of philosophical thinking, which clears the obstacles that ordinarily obstruct our point of view on the world. An existential perspective widens the human horizon and brings us back to the rock bottom of what it is that truly matters in life. This clearing begins by setting every problem against the background of the universal givens within which we all struggle. It continues with a sharpening of our thinking about these human issues and ends with a focused and purposeful project for new ways of living.

The existential vision always values the diversity of views that together make up our human approximations of truth. This book therefore has gathered together a multiplicity of existential perspectives which reflect most, though not all, of the facets of existential supervision. We are grateful to the contributors to this book who have been prepared to describe their own way of working and who have helped us to launch the first ever official guide to existential supervision. We would also like to thank Digby and Martin for their patience, tolerance, love and support during the editing of this book.

Emmy van Deurzen and Sarah Young

Notes on Contributors

The Editors:

Emmy van Deurzen is an existential psychotherapist, counselling psychologist and philosopher who lectures internationally on a broad range of existential topics. She was the founder of Regent's College School of Psychotherapy and Counselling and of the New School of Psychotherapy and Counselling (NSPC) in London, which she continues to direct. She is Professor of Psychotherapy with Schiller International University, Honorary Professor with the University of Sheffield, where she co-directs the Centre for the Study of Conflict and Reconciliation and Visiting Professor with Middlesex University, for which she directs two doctoral programmes at NSPC. She founded the Society for Existential Analysis (SEA) in 1988 and co-founded the International Collaborative of Existential Counsellors and Psychotherapists (ICECAP) in 2006 with Digby Tantam. Emmy is the author, co-author and co-editor of seven books on existential psychotherapy, which have been translated into a variety of languages, including the bestseller *Existential Psychotherapy and Counselling in Practice* (2nd edition, 2002) and her recent book *Psychotherapy and the Quest for Happiness* (2008).

Sarah Young is a UKCP Registered Psychotherapist and a BPS Chartered Counselling Psychologist. She has been practising and teaching in this field over the last 20 years. She has experience working in the NHS and private practice and also in the voluntary sector. She was instrumental in setting up the Hans W. Cohn Bursary Fund for supporting existential psychotherapy trainees and acts as its administrator. She has contributed chapters on existential therapy, existential dream work and bereavement counselling from an existential perspective.

Contributors:

Martin Adams is a psychotherapist and supervisor in private practice and also a sculptor. He teaches and supervises at the New School of Psychotherapy and Counselling and at Regent's College School of Psychotherapy and Counselling Psychology, London. He has a particular interest in the relationship of theory to practice, the nature and purpose of artistic representation and the way philosophical themes are reflected in the novel.

Laura Barnett is a UKCP and ECP Reg. Existential psychotherapist and MBACP (Accred.) supervisor working in the NHS and in private practice. She has contributed articles on existential theory in practice and has edited: *When Death Enters the Therapeutic Space, existential perspectives in psychotherapy and counselling* (2009).

Simon du Plock, DPsych(Prof), AFBPsS, is a chartered counselling psychologist, a UKCP Registered Psychotherapist, a Foundation Member with Senior Practitioner Status, BPS Register of Psychologists Specialising in Psychotherapy and Visiting Professor at Middlesex University. Simon is Head of the Post-Qualification Doctoral Department at the Metanoia Institute in London, Programme Leader of the Doctorate in Psychotherapy by Professional Studies and the Doctorate in Psychotherapy by Public Works, both joint programmes with Middlesex University. He lectures internationally on existential therapy and has edited *Existential Analysis*, the journal of the Society for Existential Analysis, since 1993. He is a co-founder of the Centre for Practice-Based Research at the Metanoia Institute and maintains a private practice as an existential psychotherapist and clinical supervisor.

Dr Brijesh Kumar is a third year Senior House Officer currently training in South Yorkshire Psychiatry Rotational scheme. He has some experience of Cognitive Behavioural Therapy and Cognitive Analytic Therapy under supervision and is gaining more experience in psychodynamic psychotherapy. He is currently working with a drug and alcohol team at Sheffield.

Simone Lee UKCP & ECP Reg. is an existential psychotherapist and supervisor working with individuals, couples and groups, face-to-face, online and by telephone. She teaches and supervises at two London based training organisations and runs Avenue Psychotherapy Practice.

Antonia Macaro is an existential psychotherapist and philosophical counsellor. She is the author of *Reason, Virtue and Psychotherapy* (2006).

Greg Madison PhD is a Chartered Psychologist and an EU and UK Registered Psychotherapist. Greg serves on the faculty at St Stephen's College, Canada, is a Senior Lecturer at Regent's College, London, offers NHS supervision and maintains a private practice in London and Brighton UK. He has research interests in 'existential migration', Focusing and the experiential aspects of existential-phenomenological psychology.

Dr Martin Milton is a chartered counselling psychologist, UKCP registered psychotherapist and a BPS registered psychologist specialising in psychotherapy. He is also Senior Lecturer in Psychotherapeutic and Counselling Psychology in the Department of Psychology at the University of Surrey. He has offered supervision in the NHS, in independent practice and for professional training courses.

Diana Mitchell is a UKCP Registered existential psychotherapist and works with long and short term clients. She supervises 'trainees' on existential courses at The New School of Psychotherapy and Counselling and at The School of

Psychotherapy and Counselling Psychology, Regent's College. She has always been interested in the concept and practice of supervision from an existential perspective. Her paper: 'Is the Concept of Supervision at Odds with Existential Thinking and Therapeutic Practice?' appeared in *Existential Analysis* 13(1).

Lucia Moja-Strasser is a Senior Lecturer at the School of Psychotherapy and Counselling Psychology, Regent's College and is Course Director of the Advanced Diploma in Existential Psychotherapy. She works in private practice as a therapist and supervisor and is an accredited mediator. She has conducted workshops on supervision and therapy at several conferences. She has published papers on existential psychotherapy and contributed chapters on existential dream work and on dialogue and communication.

Dr Paul Smith-Pickard is an existential psychotherapist and supervisor in private practice. He is a former Chair of the Society for Existential Analysis and divides his time between West Dorset and Hydra, Greece.

Dr Alison Strasser is the Director of the Centre for Existential Practice in Sydney and she was instrumental in creating the existential curriculum for a variety of counselling and psychotherapy trainings in Australia. She is a practising psychotherapist, coach and supervisor. Her doctorate focused on unravelling the process of supervision which led to the development of a framework for teaching supervisors. Alison is co-author of *Existential Time-Limited Therapy* (1998) and was the founder of the Australasian Existential Society.

Digby Tantam is Clinical Professor of Psychotherapy at the University of Sheffield (1995–present) and was previously Professor of Psychotherapy at the University of Warwick (1990–5). He is a practising psychotherapist, psychiatrist and psychologist. Digby is co-Director of the Centre for the Study of Conflict and Reconciliation in the University and a partner in Dilemma Consultancy in Human Relations (www.dilemmas.org). Digby has been Registrar of the European Association of Psychotherapy (1999–2001) and Chair of the United Kingdom Council for Psychotherapy (1995–8). He is co-founder of the International Collaborative of Existential Counsellors and Psychotherapists (ICECAP). His book, *Psychotherapy and Counselling in Practice: A Narrative Approach* was published in 2002 and he has published over 160 articles in scientific journals many of them on Asperger's syndrome, as well as numerous books, including his recent book *Can the World Afford Autistic Spectrum Disorder?*

Karen Weixel-Dixon Acc. Mediator. UKCP & EAP Reg. is a psychotherapist, supervisor, trainer and mediator in private practice. She works in the UK and France, with individuals, couples and groups. The paradigm she favours is existential-phenomenological and she has a particular interest in how people experience and engage with temporality. She has published several papers and chapters in the field of psychotherapy and facilitates fora for professional organisations. She is the Secretary for the International Collaboration for Existential Counselling.

1

Setting the Scene: Philosophical Parameters of Existential Supervision

Emmy van Deurzen and Sarah Young

Introduction

Existential supervision is a joint philosophical enterprise. It involves going beyond the usual tasks of supervision in order to consider the supervisee's work from the broadest possible perspective. Existential supervision takes a bird's eye view of the client's issues and concerns in order to place them firmly within the context of the client's life and her position in the world. It looks at the therapeutic relationship from a similarly wide angle and again foregrounds life itself, so that all dimensions of the client's and therapist's exchange will be considered in light of the stresses and strains of their human existence.

It is therefore possible to add an existential dimension to any form of therapeutic supervision by extending the work towards a meta-level of philosophical observation and human understanding. The existential perspective on supervision is thus complementary *to* rather than a substitute *for* other forms of supervision. It allows for an integration of other elements of supervision within a consistent and clear philosophical framework. All the chapters in this book attest to the overarching nature of existential supervision. Some authors address it directly, for example in Chapter 10 the author recognises the universality of the 'givens' faced by the young offenders under discussion and Chapter 14 focuses on the existential 'givens' as a framework for supervision.

Building on Life

The strength of existential supervision is that it builds on the solid ground of life itself and therefore makes room to encompass all human paradoxes, dilemmas and contradictions, highlighting both limitations and possibilities. It transcends narrow frameworks to make supervision multi-dimensional.

Rather than simply concentrating on the therapeutic relationship between the therapist and the client, on the client's problems, or the therapist's response to these, or even on the parallel process between client, therapist and supervisor, existential supervision aims for wide angle vision and sets the scene broadly enough to get an overview of a person's life, so that the pieces of the puzzle can fall into place. The diagram below illustrates this. In existential supervision we consider all of the following:

1. <u>The client</u>: what are the clients concerns and what is the client's life situation? (circle top left)
2. <u>The therapist</u>: what is the therapist's take on the client's predicament? (circle top right)
3. <u>The interaction between them</u>: how have they together approached the problems they are trying to understand and resolve? (the space where the client/therapist circles overlap)
4. <u>The supervisor</u>: what does the supervisor know about these aspects of human existence that have come into focus in this therapy? (bottom circle)
5. <u>The client's life</u>: how does the supervisor's vision understand something of the client's life the therapist does not? (overlap between supervisor and client circle).
6. <u>The therapist's life</u>: what does the supervisor grasp of the therapist's life that is relevant to the work that is being done with this client?
7. <u>Life itself</u>: how does all this relate to the wider dimension of human living? (large circle that surrounds all three protagonists in the supervision).

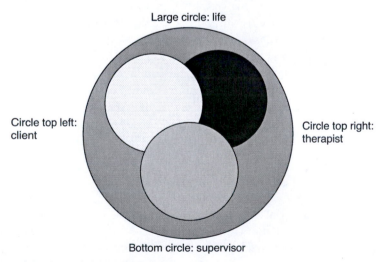

Existential aspects of supervision

Large circle: life

Circle top left: client

Circle top right: therapist

Bottom circle: supervisor

Figure 1.1   Existential aspects of supervision

The supervisee is taught how to look at the client's predicament from numerous angles and to keep experimenting with different views: she learns to literally 'over see' her own work in order to correct and revise it in line with the greater clarity that emerges. Of course this means that the supervisor needs to support the supervisee/therapist in a friendly, calm and robust manner, enabling her to face the fears and blind spots that have previously obscured her view. Supervision is a kind of existential training which goes beyond therapy: we are given the opportunity to imagine what it is like to be all these different human beings and get a glimpse of their different ways of life, as we learn to engage with their otherness and the various problems that emerge from each lifestyle. Supervision affords us the time and place for this reflection and it stimulates and sharpens our understanding of the human condition.

The instrument used for this exercise in human understanding is that of philosophical reflection. The methods used are on the one hand those of Socratic or hermeneutic questioning, bringing out the hidden meanings already inherent in the situation, and on the other hand the principles of the phenomenological method (Husserl, 1925), following the laws of logic and dialectics. Socratic or hermeneutic questioning is fundamental to the work discussed throughout the following chapters and it is alluded to directly and indirectly. The phenomenological method in particular is more fully elaborated in Chapter 4.

All these methods can help us to probe, explore and fathom the depths of life that we ordinarily avoid. The objective of supervision is then to let the light of life and of consciousness shine in the darkest corners of human experience. This will have benefits for all concerned as the exploratory beam of philosophical searching will bring about a growing understanding of the constraints and freedoms in each human existence. This will simultaneously elucidate aspects of the lives of the client, the therapist and also of the supervisor herself.

Widening Circles of Existential Supervision

Of course this journey around the ever widening circles of life has to be grounded in the reality of the client. It begins in the inner circle of the client's world and returns to this for the purpose of verification, over and over again. Tracing the client's worldview and position in the world is therefore paramount. When we start to look at what is happening in the therapeutic relationship it is from an understanding of the client's way of being in other relationships; not just of early relationships to parents or caregivers, but also to siblings, friends, the wider family and colleagues. As we begin to consider the therapist's way of relating to the client the therapist's personal worldview will also come into sight for scrutiny. We can then consider how the therapist's worldview may complement, interfere with or contradict the client's

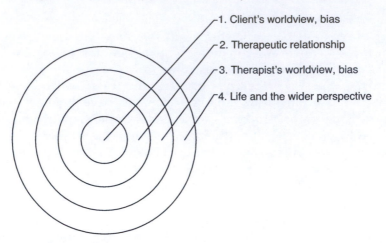

1. Client's worldview, bias

2. Therapeutic relationship

3. Therapist's worldview, bias

4. Life and the wider perspective

Figure 1.2   Existential supervision

position and cause friction or conflict or on the contrary match it so closely that it results in collusion and confusion. The strands of these interactions need to be gently teased out.

Further scrutiny will lead the supervision to penetrate into the inner realms of both the therapist's and the client's grasp of the wider life issues that affect the client's lifestyle and well-being. Now we may need to examine the therapist's assumptions about life and the universe, enabling her to differentiate these from her client's. Gradually blind spots are recognised and brought to light. Figure 1.2 illustrates these four layers of the supervisory task. These layers overlap and intertwine and the work will move organically from one to the other and back again.

Existential Supervision in Practice

Existential supervision acknowledges that all human beings operate from a particular standpoint and that their understanding of reality is always biased. Such bias is the cutting edge of our take on the world. It is what allows us to function and have our own angle on reality. Mostly such bias is transparent and we are unaware of it, taking our own views for granted. But supervision is a time when the client's and therapist's biases are up for scrutiny in order to sharpen or soften their angles and optimise the impact these may have on self and others. Of course by the standards of good phenomenological practice the supervisor's own bias also needs to be accounted for. Clearly not all existential supervisors will work in the same manner. This book will demonstrate the variety of emphases different existential supervisors adopt at different times. Though most contributors to this book would probably agree that existential supervision means to have a wide ranging view that can integrate and include many different ideas, models and approaches to therapy, they would each scrutinise such ideas and models from a different angle. Existential thinking encourages such diversity.

Existential supervision is therefore highly compatible with supervision of trainees who work in a variety of settings. It does mean that existential supervisors need to be particularly aware of the constraints inherent in each setting. The particular difficulties encountered in different settings are addressed by several authors in Part II of this book – for example working in the National Health Service is explored in Chapter 11. Existential supervision is also particularly apt at providing a framework for integration when we supervise practitioners who have been trained in different methods and who have different orientations. This makes it a method of choice in group supervision in voluntary and statutory settings. This overarching nature of existential supervision is implicit in most of the chapters in this book and this in itself points towards existential supervision being a disciplined instrument for methodical integration. Chapter 5 offers a thorough understanding of the supervisory relationship from an existential perspective that can be adopted by practitioners from a variety of orientations. Chapter 7 outlines the fundamentals of the existential practice of supervision and the wheel of supervision described in Chapter 14 provides a specific framework for integration.

Why Choose Existential Supervision?

An existential perspective on supervision foregrounds the human condition in a philosophical manner and this is something that makes sense to most practitioners. All of the authors in this book have in common a philosophical rather than a positivistic or medical outlook on therapeutic supervision. As we have indicated, their supervisory interventions are grounded in a broadly based phenomenological method. This means that they are pragmatic, concrete and descriptive, adhering as closely as is possible to the facts of the client's reality, rather than being theoretically or interpretatively driven. They will encourage supervisees to carefully depict, circumscribe and illustrate their observations and impressions of their clients rather than jump to conclusions or apply immediate interpretations or external meanings to their actions and experiences. They will follow a hermeneutic trail, which investigates many possible meanings rather than attaching ready-made meanings to the phenomena under observation. Therefore they will usually abstain from using diagnostic categories and steer clear of too much certainty about what is ailing the supervisee's clients. Instead they will stimulate a wide ranging exploration of the client's experience, investigating its context and background as carefully and thoroughly as possible. These are elemental aspects of supervision that are relevant to practitioners across the board and that will provide them with a down to earth and workable model for integration.

Philosophical Elements

At the sharp end of existential supervision, specifically trained existential supervisors act as philosophical guides, who provide a clear space for re-thinking and re-experiencing what has happened in sessions and in the life of the client. Existential supervision is a time to take stock and elucidate our usually all too vague understanding of the complexities of human existence. This means that supervisors will ask many questions of their supervisees so as to inspire them to explore, amplify and clarify their understanding of their client's reality over and over again. They will, as we have said, follow Socrates' tracks by hermeneutic questioning, assuming that in doing so it is possible to bring out the hidden knowledge that is already there in the situation. They will freely probe, comment, ask questions and encourage their supervisees to ask themselves further questions and query their initial perceptions of their clients' experiences. The objective is to problematise rather than to rush to solutions. The questions existential supervisors ask will always aim to expand their supervisee's comprehension. Such questioning does not analyse or search for causes and explanations, but it makes clear, reorganises thought and brings things back into a natural order, so that the flow of the therapy and of the client's life make sense and can come back into their own once more. Most, if not all, existential therapists and supervisors will adhere to this Socratic style of questioning. The first three chapters of Part I in particular, discuss the nature of such supervisory dialogue and refer to this process of questioning in supervision.

Such explorations invariably put an emphasis on retracing the client's 'original project' so that they can reconnect with a sense of deeply felt meaning and purposeful living. Sartre (1943) spoke of the original project of each person as that which we have most deeply engaged ourselves with and committed ourselves to, often without reflecting on it. The project is what orientates our thoughts and actions and what makes our lives purposeful. In supervision then we trace the client's original projects, following the path of the 'how, why, when, where and what?' until the client's universe can be sketched and traced with some faithfulness to their experiential reality. Eventually their values and priorities will show the way to what matters at the core of their existence.

The search may now be halted temporarily as our path will have led to the clearing of thought where things come to light and are suddenly seen brightly. In this silent space where all the questions that have been asked bring a new awareness and a new aliveness, now more central, primordial and ontological questions underlying the client's anxiety or depression may be pursued. This is what existential supervision engenders: the sudden 'aha' experience of wonder when we feel reconnected to the source of life which had run dry. Usually this experience touches not only the client but also the therapist and the supervisor. Therapists who work with people who feel out of touch with their lives often become somewhat disconnected themselves, dried up, parched and starved. In supervision they can quench and quell their thirst for new knowledge and understanding and recuperate their vitality, providing supervision generates the wisdom of careful thought that comes from collaborative remembering of the things that matter in life. Existential supervision then needs to go to the source in order to reconnect therapists with the force of life and the power of human awareness. Chapters 3 and 15 emphasise this meditative or evocative part of existential supervision particularly well.

Philosophical Support

One of the most outstanding resources for such meditation and contemplation is the rich heritage of existential philosophies that have been generated over several millennia. This philosophical thinking needs to be engaged with by therapists and supervisors alike if they are to release themselves from the narrow bounds of rational and scientific rigidity and recapture the full depth and breadth of free consciousness. An existential perspective is a perspective that is nurtured by the philosophical tradition and draws not only on its methodology but also on the actual ideas of various philosophers. Part I of this book demonstrates the wide range of philosophy that can be used in this way, though this is by no means an exhaustive picture of the full range of philosophies available.

It is indeed invaluable to be able to stand on the shoulders of giants when we think about the human condition and try to tackle the dilemmas that have long been part of human experience. Existential philosophers have said much about these predicaments and can be consulted for inspiration. Most philosophy is relevant and will sharpen our mind (Howard, 2000). Classical philosophers such as Socrates, Plato, Aristotle or Marcus Aurelius have contributed many insights and gems of understanding into what it takes to live a well lived life. Chapter 2 gives us a flavour of this through the example of the relevance of the work of Aristotle. Unfortunately there was not enough space to include chapters on other classics as well. A Socratic or Kantian or Spinozan or Hegelian chapter would have had much to offer too! But it is of course the philosophers of existence of the last two centuries who stand head and shoulders above the others in terms of inspiring existential psychotherapists and supervisors. And their ideas are woven into all the chapters of this book. Supervisors will be shown the relevance of their ideas at various points. Some examples of this are:

1. Kierkegaard's reminder that anxiety is not something to get rid of or be afraid of (1849). People need to learn to be anxious in the right way: not so little that they live in illusion, not so much that they lose their footing in life. Therapists often forget this and supervision can helpfully explore the importance of facing anxiety in the right way.

2. Kierkegaard's other central contribution is that of the importance of learning to live with paradox: holding the tension between the finite and infinite, between necessity and possibility, between the concrete and the universal.

3. Nietzsche (1883, 1887) can help us to teach clients how to become active and creative again rather than live merely as passive creatures.

4. He also teaches us to be wary of the resentments clients carry. Such lack of zest for life needs to be tackled by a total re-evaluating of all values. Nietzsche's notion of courage and the love of one's life (*amor fati*), no matter what difficulties we encounter, is often a great help in making a new start.

5. Husserl's phenomenological psychology (1925, 1965) is so fundamental to the entire enterprise of existential supervision that his concepts of epoché, or setting aside of our assumptions and bias is practically synonymous with the existential perspective.

6. The phenomenological rules of description, horizontalisation, equalisation and verification are the cornerstones of methodology that no good existential supervisor should be without. These are discussed in Chapter 4.

7. But it is Heidegger's distinction between authentic (owned) and inauthentic (disowned) ways of being that holds centre place in existential supervision (Heidegger, 1927). The touchstone of all existential interventions is whether the therapy is searching for truth and transparency of being.

8. Heidegger's insistence on the importance of facing death and temporality helps us to become real. At the back of every existential supervisor's mind will be the question of how much reality this particular client and this particular therapist are facing and are able to face and how directly they may be able to tackle the limit situations and quandaries of this client's life. It is not hard, with the benefit of the supervisory process of meditative thinking to spot clients' idle talk and avoidance of the real issues. But it is harder to know how to help them move beyond the curiosity and ambiguity that hold them in their sway.

9. We can usefully explore what it would take for clients to live more resolutely. This means living in anticipation of what is and what inevitably will be (namely our death) with a vision of past, present and future. But we need to remember that a balance has to be created and maintained in each life between our active capacity for assertive living in resoluteness on the one hand and for the gentle releasement of letting be on the other hand.

10. Certainly most philosophers, including Heidegger, Socrates, Plato and Aristotle would agree that our search is one of enabling clients to let truth be the guide of their everyday existence, but that great caution has to be taken not to burn our wings by flying too close to the light.

11. Sartre (1943) has contributed much that is of relevance to existential supervisors, including his observation that life is absurd and that meaning has to be created rather than received. Supervision is a good time to remind therapists that the loss of meaning in a person's life need not be seen as a sign of pathology, but may rather be used as the start of a constructive exploration of how new meanings can be created in the client's life.

12. Equally important is Sartre's insistence on the human need to act, lest we fall back into our fundamental nothingness. This is directly linked with his idea that all human beings have an original project which they can choose to pursue, abandon or creatively redefine to make their life work. It is often a salutary reminder for therapists that it is their task to help clients reconnect to this project and show them how new actions will flow from this naturally.

13. The principle of meaningful human engagement is fundamental in existential supervision. Supervisors can re-energise even the most difficult therapy by asking the therapist to wonder what their client's meaningful project actually is. There is always an implied project, even if this is minimal, as in survival, or perhaps even a dignified ending of life. By pinpointing and elaborating the implied but often hidden values that a person treasures their project will emerge and become explicit. This will lead to new avenues of discovery.

14. Merleau-Ponty's understanding of our embodied existence is just as crucial (1962). His work can remind us of the concrete reality of intersubjectivity and the encounter in the flesh that forms the basis of all therapy. Bringing the physical dimension back to life is part and parcel of existential work.

15. Merleau-Ponty shows us how to use the phenomenological method to listen carefully to what clients say and to what they indicate about themselves and their position in the world through gestures and actions: we can gauge how they are embodied and how their existence is connected to its life world.

16. Merleau-Ponty's attention to ambiguity is another, more playful key to sensitivity as we tune into the many sides of the intersubjective connections that interweave and interconnect us with each other.

17. Jaspers' contribution though not directly discussed in many of these chapters needs to be recognised (1951). In the first place his notion of feeling into another person's life, rather than merely using sympathy or empathy is still revolutionary. It is close to identification and can be used to good effect in supervision.

18. His idea of the encompassing and comprehensive nature of what is over the horizon of all human living is an excellent principle to bear in mind when guiding a supervisee to regain a sense of overview of the client's existence. It is very close to Buber's notion of the I-Thou, which also points us towards the infinite. Chapter 5 elaborates on this notion.

19. Jaspers' limit situations are the perfect counterpart to this comprehensive approach. Asking a therapist where or how their clients are up against a limit can be a very productive intervention. It places the therapy directly back in the spotlight of the client's most painful concerns.

20. Tillich's ultimate concerns (1952) are a similar concept and already well known from Yalom's work (1980). Tillich's notion that the more negativity we can take into ourselves the stronger we are, is resonant with Nietzsche's idea that what does not kill me makes me stronger. This kind of staunch

existential stance has moved many a therapy forward, though it has to be used with caution.

There are so many philosophical ideas which enable existential supervision that they are far too numerous to describe here. The above list is of necessity no more than a foretaste of the complex art of existential supervision which is described more fully in the following pages. There are several texts which elaborate these philosophical ideas, as they inform existential therapy (and existential supervision) more thoroughly, for example: Deurzen-Smith (1997); Deurzen (1998, 2002, 2007); Deurzen & Arnold-Baker (2005); Cohn (1997, 2002); Spinelli (1997, 2004, 2007) and Cooper (2003). These texts exemplify the often repeated maxim that there is no one school of existential philosophy any more than there is one school of existential therapy. It has been suggested that any philosopher who is concerned primarily with human existence could be described as existential. We are therefore dealing with a very broad church and within this we shall focus on those philosophers who stand out as specifically relevant to therapy and supervision.

Summary: Reinventing the Reality of Supervision Whilst Learning About Living

It is our intention that this book should appeal to anyone working in the field of psychotherapy and counselling. Therapists, supervisors and supervisees will find something of interest here whatever their orientation because existential perspectives are relevant to all of us. Philosophy is the inspiration for existential therapy and supervision, though its application does not create a new modality or technique of therapy or supervision. Existential thinking becomes an attitude, a way of understanding the human situation that is not just confined to our work as therapists or supervisors. In other words the philosophical underpinnings of our work are not separate from our lives rather they inform how we live our lives. This understanding of the vocational nature of therapy and supervision and this willingness to rethink and relearn what one thought one already knew is a foundation that can underpin supervision whatever the supervisor's particular theoretical orientation.

So, in this book we describe aspects of the supervisory relationship that are rarely addressed. We are offering something entirely different from what is often described in the literature on supervision (where the focus is on: improving the supervisee's knowledge base; the client's assumed intrapsychic processes; parallel process and so on). In existential supervision we are involved in a process in which we formulate ideas, comment on the concerns of another and in so doing refer to our own values, beliefs and ideas about life. The actual process of existential supervision is one in which we learn about human existence in a very direct manner and the supervisor, supervisee and ultimately the client each benefit from this process in turn. Both the supervisor and supervisee are given the opportunity to recognise their assumptions and the values they express – there is time to consider carefully what is usually taken for granted. We take the trouble to tease out our prejudice and to consider our views of the client's world in the round.

Limits and boundaries

All forms of supervision have a responsibility to be aware of ethical issues and ensure that their supervisees work within the professional codes of ethics and do not harm their clients, so that they are beneficent and therapeutic, existential supervision additionally addresses such ethical issues from a slightly different angle. Existential supervisors encourage their supervisees to take a fresh look at the reasons for the ethical codes and they challenge common sense and received wisdom.

In this book we shall therefore not repeat the points about boundaries and ethics that have been made abundantly clear by the professional bodies and by the existing literature on supervision. There are many texts that spell out the problems of duty of care to the client and the ethical tasks of the supervisors (see Carroll & Tholstrup, 2001; Gilbert & Evans, 2000; Hawkins & Shohet, 2000; Dryden & Thorne, 1991). Similarly we shall not belabour the issues that arise in terms of the therapist's personal conflicts and we do not focus on the use of self in therapy, which is so well described in existing volumes on supervision (Horton & Varma, 1997; Scaife, 2001; Wosket, 1999).

Relationship

As far as the relationship between the therapist and the client is concerned, existential supervisors keep careful track of this. They use the phenomenological method of questioning the assumptions of the client and the therapist and of examining these within the context and worldview of each. This is called the exploration of bias (Deurzen, 2009). Earlier, when looking at existential supervision in practice we recognised that bias exists in all of us: we cannot have a take on the world without having a particular lens through which we perceive. The existential-phenomenological concept of bias offers an alternative to the usual notions of 'transference and counter-transference'. All perceiving and relating has an edge, an angle. It is the task of supervision to bring this angle into focus and soften or sharpen it, according to what is appropriate. The bias of both client and therapist can be divided into four aspects:

1. Attitude – the particular stance we have because of the person we are and the character that forms our backbone.
2. Orientation – the way we look at the world because of our belief system and values: these have been shaped by the experiences we have had in the past but are very much related to the projects we have for the future as well.

3. State of mind – the particular mood and mindset we are in at this particular moment because of what is happening in our lives currently.
4. Reaction – the specific response we are having to the other person we are with in this moment.

Being-in-the-world

The existential approach prides itself in taking a revolutionary stance towards the self in bringing out its relational nature. It can be argued that without the contribution of Martin Heidegger (1962, 2001) we would not have this same rigorous attitude to understanding what it means to be human in a physical world with others. It was, in some sense, Heidegger who showed supervision to be about systematic and patient philosophical exploration and deep thinking. It was in his supervisory seminars with Medard Boss' students at Zollikon (2001) that existential supervision first came into being.

In all the chapters that follow Heidegger's concept of being-in-the-world, that is the notion that we are not separate individuals but are always intrinsically connected to and embedded in a world, is present, implicitly or explicitly. Of course Heidegger's way of describing the world would not have been possible without Husserl's method of phenomenology, which is equally fundamental to the practice of existential supervision. But there are many other philosophers who have contributed indirectly to this way of working, from the Athenian discussions of philosophers like Socrates and Aristotle onwards.

Conclusion

There are chapters in this book which are devoted to some of these philosophers, but we are well aware that this is only a first sketch of existential supervision and that there are many authors who have further contributions to make and many further parallels that can be drawn between classical philosophy and the tasks of therapeutic supervisors. Most importantly we hope that reading through these pages you will be reminded of the wisdom of the ages and the ways in which philosophy can guide our explorations of human difficulties. If this means that you will start reading philosophy for yourself and that your supervisory practice will become imbued with a search for truth then the book will have achieved what it set out to do. Enjoy the ideas you will find in the three sections of the book, philosophical, practical and critical, and then set aside what you have read and experiment with your own version of philosophical thinking and existential supervision. For these ideas are not written in stone and when all is said and done the main characteristic of existential supervision is that of its freedom and its basis in individual and original thinking. Existential supervision cannot be done without reinventing it with every supervisee and with every new hour of practice.

We hope you will read this book from beginning to end, but at the same time we recognise that some of you may have a particular interest that leads you to, for example the middle section on Practice. Those of you who are familiar with the philosophers discussed in Part I may be tempted to skip these chapters but be aware you will be doing yourself a disservice since you will find something new here, as each author is discussing their unique under-standing of the philosophers in question and is considering how to apply their ideas to practice. Those who are less familiar with philosophical thinking are encouraged to engage with these chapters however daunting some may at first appear (the glossary of terms will act as a guide). The final part of this book should be of interest to all those working in the field particularly given the move towards registration and regulation. As ever the future is uncertain but we firmly believe the existential perspective has an enormous contribution to make both in terms of integrating seemingly disparate schools of thought and in relation to an alternatively rigorous though liberating way forward for therapy and supervision in this climate of evidenced-based practice.

References

Caroll, M. & Tholstrup, M. *Integrative Approaches to Supervision* (London: Jessica Kingsley Publications, 2001).

Cohn, H. W. *Existential Thought and Therapeutic Practice* (London: Sage, 1997).

—— *Heidegger and the Roots of Existential Psychotherapy* (London: Continuum, 2002).

Cooper, M. *Existential Therapies* (London: Sage, 2003).

Deurzen, E. van *Paradox and Passion in Psychotherapy* (Chichester: Wiley, 1998).

—— *Existential Counselling and Psychotherapy in Practice*, 2nd edn (London: Sage, 2002).

—— 'Existential Therapy'. In W. Dryden (ed.) *Dryden's Handbook of Psychotherapy* (London: Sage, 2007).

—— *Everyday Mysteries*, 2nd edn (London: Routledge, 2009).

Deurzen, E. van & Arnold-Baker, C. *Existential Perspectives on Human Issues: A Handbook for Practice* (London: Palgrave, 2005).

Deurzen-Smith, E. van *Everyday Mysteries: Existential Dimensions of Psychotherapy* (London: Routledge, 1997).

Dryden, W. & Thorne, B. *Training and Supervision for Counselling in Action* (London: Sage Publications, 1991).

Gilbert, M. C. & Evans, K. *Psychotherapy Supervision: An Integrative Relational Approach to Psychotherapy Supervision* (Buckingham: Open University Press, 2000).

Hawkins, P. & Shohet, R. *Supervision in the Helping Professions*, 2nd edn (Buckingham: Open University Press, 2000).

Heidegger, M. *Being and Time*. Trans. J. Macquarrie & E. Robinson (Oxford: Blackwell, [1927] 1962).

—— *Zollikon Seminars*, M. Boss (ed.). Trans. F. Mayr. R. Askay (Evanston: North-western University Press, 2001).

Howard, A. *Philosophy for Counselling and Psychotherapy* (Basingstoke: Macmillan Press, 2000).

Horton, I. & Varma, V. *The Needs of Counsellors and Psychotherapists* (London: Sage, 1997).

Husserl, E. *Phenomenological Psychology*. Trans. J. Scanlon (The Hague: Nijhoff, [1925] 1977).
—— *The Crisis of European Sciences and Transcendental Phenomenology*. Trans. Q. Lauer (New York: Harper & Row, 1965).
Jaspers, K. *The Way to Wisdom*. Trans. R. Manheim (New Haven: Yale University Press, 1951).
Kierkegaard, S. *The Sickness Unto Death*. Trans. H. Hong and E. Hong (Princeton NJ: Princeton University Press, [1849] 1980).
Merleau-Ponty, M. *Phenomenology of Perception*. Trans. C. Smith (London: Routledge, 1962).
Nietzsche, F. *Thus Spoke Zarathustra*. Trans. R. J. Hollingdale (Harmondsworth: Penguin, [1883] 1961).
—— *On the Genealogy of Morals*. Trans. W. Kaufmann and R. J. Hollingdale (New York: Vintage Books, [1887] 1969).
Sartre J-P. *Being and Nothingness*. Trans. H. Barnes (London: Routledge, [1943] 1969).
Scaife, J. *Supervision in the Mental Health Professions: A Practitioners Guide* (London: Brunner-Routledge, 2001).
Spinelli, E. *Tales of Un-Knowing* (London: Duckworth, 1997).
—— 'Hell Is Other People: A Sartrean View of Conflict Resolution', *International Journal of Existential Psychology and Psychotherapy* 1(1) (2004) 56–65.
—— *Practising Existential Psychotherapy: The Relational World* (London: Sage, 2007).
Tillich, P. *The Courage to Be* (Glasgow: Collins, 1952).
Wosket, V. *The Therapeutic Use of Self: Counselling Practice, Research and Supervision* (London: Routledge, 1999).
Yalom, I. D. *Existential Psychotherapy* (New York: Basic Books, 1980).

Part I
Philosophical Foundations of Existential Supervision

Introduction

Emmy van Deurzen and Sarah Young

This first part of the book focuses on the philosophical foundations of existential supervision. Several fundamental aspects of philosophical understanding crucial for existential therapy and supervision are discussed. As we have already said any philosopher who considers the human situation can be described as existential since existence is their focus. But inevitably Heidegger's influence is particularly prominent throughout this book. He was an existential phenomenologist, who, although he distanced himself from it, is 'usually seen as a founder of Existentialism' (Honderich, 1995). His thinking was directly instrumental in the development of the work of Sartre, Merleau-Ponty and also influential on Jaspers, Buber and many other philosophers, some of whom will be referred to in these pages. It may be that some of the concepts addressed in the following chapters are unfamiliar, for example Being, Dasein or the in-between. We have provided a glossary of terms at the back of the book to help you find your way through the philosophy and to enable you to solve your queries quickly and easily.

We begin Part I with an accessible and concise exposition of Aristotle's theory of virtue and its use as a model for supervision. Some readers may be surprised to find Aristotle featured in this section, though he was an inspiration to both Husserl and Heidegger. Chapter 2 is a good example of the use we can make of philosophy in supervision and of the way in which even Athenian philosophers can stimulate our thinking about existential supervision. Aristotle's concept of virtue has universal appeal in that it provides guidelines for working through the dilemmas which confront us all. The importance of context is emphasised throughout which in turn reflects the fundamental attitude of an existential perspective – clients are not seen as isolated beings separated from the context in which they exist but as beings-in-the-world forever in connection with all they encounter. The Socratic dialogue referred to in Chapter 2 is understood as the basis for the interaction between supervisor and supervisee – this is further elaborated in the following three chapters.

Chapter 3 draws on the work of Søren Kierkegaard, frequently described as a forerunner or even the father of existentialism. This chapter provides a unique and profound understanding of Kierkegaard's concept of love and the implications that this love has for the supervisory relationship. The author bravely addresses the complex, intangible subject of soul and spirit – readers are given a glimpse of what the supervisory relationship can become if we are able to open ourselves to this aspect of being human. The author recognises she is describing an impossible ideal but we are given something to strive towards despite our limitations and inevitable failings. Dialogue also figures prominently in this chapter and is understood to be fundamental to the process of supervision. The spiritual world – the *Überwelt* (Deurzen, 2002, 2009) is also addressed in Chapter 5 and is later considered in detail in relation to the 'evocative' in Chapter 15.

The third chapter in this Part (Chapter 4) is a clear and succinct discussion of phenomenology and its implications for existential supervision. As already mentioned phenomenology underpins existential therapy and supervision and provides a framework for both endeavours. In contrast to some authors (see Chapters 3, 5 and 15) the author advocates the use of verbatim reports in supervision (as does the author of Chapter 8 in the context of online super-vision) whilst at the same time recognising their limitations. There is no doubt that verbatim reports, especially when they include full phenomenological descriptions of gestures, features, moods, atmosphere and interactions, are an invaluable source of information for the supervisor. Nevertheless others take the view they interfere with the direct relationship between the supervisor and the supervisee which is paramount. Clearly both points of view are arguable. It is evidence of the flexibility of the existential approach to super-vision that different supervisors will work in different ways. In this chapter we are also challenged to think about the supervisor's responsibilities, some-thing we shall return to in the first two chapters of Part III.

The supervisory relationship is discussed in detail in Chapter 5 by drawing on the writings of three, in some ways quite disparate thinkers, Buber, Rogers and Levinas. The author provides an extremely thoughtful description of the supervisory relationship in the light of the contributions of these authors, acknowledging both potentialities and limitations. The concept of 'mesopathy' is introduced to describe the way of sensing the in-between – the supervisor's sensitivity to 'the interplay of feelings in the room'. As in Chapter 3 there is a concern here with the spiritual and the author acknowledges that whether this dimension enters the supervisory relationship depends on the mesopathy between the supervisor and the supervisee 'in the face of the mystery of exist-ence'. Recognition is given to 'embodiment' – the relatedness to and per-ception of the world and others through our bodies. This important concept is the central concern of the following chapter.

In the final chapter of this section (Chapter 6) we are given a vivid reminder of our ever present existential sexuality and the importance of taking our embodied existence into account both in the practice of therapy and super-vision. The subtle experience of sensing the other's bodily response to us, the reciprocity in every encounter and the felt sense we so often fail to take note of is brought to the fore. So we move from philosophy to embodied existence and are encouraged to bring sensations, feelings and thoughts into awareness in equal measure and to allow them to become an aspect of our work as supervisors (and therapists). Later in Chapter 15, which foregrounds the evocative, we will see this emphasis on embodiment and existential sexuality strongly echoed.

References

Deurzen, E. van, *Existential Counselling and Psychotherapy in Practice*, 2nd edn (London: Sage, 2002).
—— *Everyday Mysteries*, 2nd edn (London: Routledge, 2009).
Honderich, T. (ed.) *The Oxford Companion to Philosophy* (Oxford: Oxford University Press, 1995).

2

Virtue in Supervision

Antonia Macaro

Our account will be adequate if its clarity is in line with the subject-matter, because the same degree of precision is not to be sought in all discussions, any more than in works of craftsmanship. ... So we should be content ... to demonstrate the truth sketchily and in outline, and, because we are making generalizations on the basis of generalizations, to draw conclusions along the same lines. Indeed, the details of our claims, then should be looked at in the same way, since it is a mark of an educated person to look in each area for only that degree of accuracy that the nature of the subject permits. Accepting from a mathematician claims that are mere probabilities seems rather like demanding logical proofs from a rhetorician

(Aristotle, *Nicomachean Ethics*, Book I, Chapter 3).

Introduction

Of the many dangers besetting the path of psychotherapy, dogma is perhaps the most insidious one. Therapists can become excessively attached to the theoretical filters they have adopted to view people and situations and be tempted to stretch the clients to fit their theories rather than *vice versa*. This can and does lead to a subtle form of abuse, in which the clients' own perception of their life predicaments is discounted in favour of the therapist's perspective. Of course it is essential to have theories to guide our work, but in order to avoid causing harm therapists need to be able to balance them with an acute sensitivity to the specific and the contextual.

Related to this is the illusion of clear-cut and universally applicable rules for therapeutic practice: is it appropriate to talk about ourselves in sessions? Is challenge a good or a bad thing? Should we always use the client-therapist relationship as a therapeutic tool? And so on. Of course there are useful rules of thumb that can be applied to these and other issues. But it is important to remember that they are only rules of thumb, and that the answer, almost invariably, is 'it depends'. It would be self-defeating and ultimately dangerous to seek more clear-cut principles than the enterprise of psychotherapy could allow. Instead, therapists need to be able to think through why *in particular situations* it may or may not be desirable to act in certain ways.

While existential psychotherapy[1] is among the least doctrinaire approaches, emphasising the need to become aware of and put aside biases to the extent that is possible, to *clarify* the clients' worldview rather than impose one on them, therapists who subscribe to it are actually as vulnerable to these dangers as those from other schools. In theory these concerns can be addressed in supervision – at its best a space in which theories can be interrogated, their practical applications negotiated, contextual considerations fleshed out and explored. In practice, however, the dogmatism that bedevils therapeutic work with clients often ends up being reproduced in supervision, which then becomes a persecutory space where opinions are held rigidly and questions not encouraged. This kind of supervision is unlikely to foster a thoughtful and safe practice.

What is needed is a model to frame this interchange between theory and practice. If psychotherapy can be conceived of as a kind of Socratic dialogue (Deurzen, 2002), the same can be said of supervision. A useful model to draw on in this respect is Aristotle's theory of virtue, which emphasises the importance of character and context: universally applicable rules for moral conduct are few and far between, and for the most part the rightness or wrongness of an action has to be established in relation to a particular set of circumstances. In the next section I give a brief outline of Aristotle's theory.

His theory is one that has universal appeal and can therefore be employed in a wide variety of contexts by practitioners from a broad range of orientations. The objective is not to stretch the client to fit the theory, nor to stretch the theory to fit the client. By going back to an ancient philosophical discipline of thinking we release ourselves from pet theories and we take a fresh look at the issues that arise in supervision.

Virtue, Practical Reason and the Mean

In ancient philosophy 'virtue' did not mean what we take it to mean today. The pious connotations that may spring to our minds were absent from the Greek term *aretê*, which simply refers to whatever it is that makes something – animate or inanimate – perform its characteristic activity well. At the simplest level, for instance, the virtue of a knife consists in its ability to cut well. But what counts as an equivalent 'virtuous' state for human beings? Human virtue likewise has to involve having and using the abilities that are characteristic of human beings, those that make us who we are, though spelling out what that means is a little more complex.

According to Aristotle, the exercise of the virtues is the main requirement of a good human life. The virtues are particularly necessary in certain areas of life, often to do with pleasure and pain, which human beings tend to find

[1] I use the label 'existential psychotherapy' as shorthand for a cluster of approaches that nonetheless show enough commonalities to justify the use of the singular.

problematic but can never entirely avoid. Being virtuous means becoming skilled at handling these spheres of life in which it is most difficult to get things right: this involves not only being able to make judgements appropriate to the circumstances, but also displaying a harmonious alignment of desires, feelings and intentions. Aristotle thought that the skills and qualities that would allow us to achieve this were of two kinds: practical reason, which is the application of our reasoning powers not to theoretical understanding but to the more imprecise and contingent matters of quotidian conduct; and the virtues of character, which are the qualities and dispositions that make that harmony between reason, emotions and desires possible.

Being virtuous means having a stable disposition to feel and act in accordance with reason, in other words to grasp the right thing to do and do it without too much trouble. One aspect of this is practical reason – the ability to arrive at the right judgement about the best course of action, all things considered, in each situation. This in turn hinges on the ability to identify the ethically significant features of a situation. Sometimes this can be done quickly and easily, in other cases it requires more laborious reflection. Having practical reason includes being able to recognise when a more complex decision making process, involving the application of abstract concepts to particular circumstances, is needed. The other aspect of being virtuous is the motivation to follow our rational judgement, and this is what the virtues of character enable us to do. But the more virtuous we are the easier it will be to make the right decision, and so practical reason and the virtues of character should really be considered two sides of the same coin.

While this is the general structure of Aristotle's theory of virtue, there is also a more specific part, the so called 'doctrine of the mean', which can be put to good use. To characterise the virtues more precisely, Aristotle says that:

> [f]or example, fear, confidence, appetite, anger, pity, and in general pleasure and pain can be experienced too much or too little, and in both ways not well. But to have them at the right time, about the right things, towards the right people, for the right end, and in the right way, is the mean and best; and this is the business of virtue. Similarly, there is an excess, a deficiency and a mean in actions (*NE*, book II, ch. 6).

The virtuous person aims for 'the mean' in feelings and actions and avoids excess and deficiency, which are opposite ways of getting things wrong. For example, courage is the mean between foolhardiness and timidity; even temper the mean between bad temper and placidity; appropriate enjoyment of sensual pleasures the mean between intemperance and insensitivity to pleasure. An important point is that the mean Aristotle is talking about is *relative* to people and situations rather than absolute as in the case of the arithmetic mean.

> For if ten pounds of food is a lot for someone to eat, and two pounds a little, the trainer will not necessarily prescribe six; for this may be a lot or a little

for the person about to eat it – for Milo [a famous athlete] a little, for a beginner at gymnastics, a lot. The same goes for running and wrestling (*NE*, book II, ch. 6).

The mean is not, as is often mistakenly thought, the same as moderation. In the case of anger, for instance, it is clearly not the case that we should always have a moderate amount of anger, since most situations require no anger at all and some situations require great anger. Urmson writes:

> the man whose character is such that he feels only mild annoyance at a trivial slight and is enraged by torture has a character that is in a mean between one that exhibits rage on trivial as well as important occasions and one that can coolly contemplate the greatest outrages (Urmson, 1980: 161).

To sum up, virtue is to be found in a mean between excess and deficiency; the mean is determined by reason; virtue consists not only in knowing where the mean lies, but in a stable disposition to want to do the right thing. But virtue is not acquired overnight: it takes time to develop a harmonious character. The main tool for this task is what Aristotle calls *habituation*. While the intellectual virtues are learned through teaching, training ourselves to acquire new qualities, skills and attitudes is achieved mainly by exercising them. So

> we become builders by building, and lyre-players by playing the lyre. So too we become just by doing just actions, temperate by temperate actions, and courageous by courageous actions (*NE*, book II, ch. 1).

By practising the right responses in situations where knowing what to do is clear we will gradually come to recognise when a process of deliberation is called for. When first implementing a particular change we may have to go against our habitual inclination and control our *behaviour*, but our aim should be to *feel* appropriately rather than just act appropriately. Over time, the accumulated effect of our choices will be the establishment of new habits of acting and feeling. Eventually, self-control and vigilant choice should give way to established inclinations and dispositions. It is our responsibility to do what we can to improve our character, whatever our start in life.

Aristotle realises that hitting the mean – perceiving the right thing to do and wanting to do it – is not always easy, and that sometimes we are just not sure what to do. His advice is that in such situations we should choose the lesser evil. He offers two rules of thumb:

- steer away from the more harmful extreme
- steer away from the extreme towards which we are naturally inclined

Aristotle's doctrine of the mean has been accused of being less than helpful in identifying the right thing to do. It is indeed the case that it does not provide us with off-the-shelf rules for how to act. But this should be seen as a strength rather than a weakness. It is not possible, given human complexity, for any rule to fit all circumstances, and it is only in relation to particular situations and specific examples that an action can be judged right or wrong. The doctrine of the mean provides us with a general framework within which to conduct our enquiries.

Virtue in Supervision

So how can the concept of virtue help to develop a thoughtful supervision practice? The frame it provides certainly works well at all levels of therapeutic work. I have argued elsewhere (Macaro, 2006) that Aristotle's ideas about the good life and virtue can be useful when working with clients who seek therapy to explore how to live. The discussion may explicitly address big questions about meaning and value or it may focus on issues of daily living – achievement, for instance, or taking risks, or love, confidence, autonomy, tenacity, assertiveness, honesty, trust, generosity, the ability to forego immediate gratification, and so on. While the client may not apply the term 'virtue' to these, they can nonetheless be fruitfully explored in terms of the Aristotelian model. Here I would like to suggest that the theory of virtue I have outlined above can also be usefully applied at the level of supervision. This means that both the therapist's work and the supervisor's own responses and interventions can be discussed in terms of virtue and the mean.

In a therapeutic context, we could say that virtue amounts to good clinical judgement.[2] This could be further characterised as the ability to identify the right course of action about clinical matters, to be inclined to follow that judgement and act on it without undue effort, as well as realising when the situation requires more careful deliberation. The fundamental skill is the ability to perceive what, in any given situation, should be foregrounded and acted on. One of the difficulties about psychotherapy is that there are many ways to construe a client's problems: which concepts are most relevant and which should be left aside? A virtuous therapist will not cling to theoretical positions inappropriately, and will know how to apply abstract ideas and techniques to specific clinical situations. According to Fowers, clinical judgement is the capacity 'to recognize and respond to what is most important in a client's presentation' (Fowers, 2005: 55) – an issue that every therapist faces in every session. How do therapists acquire this skill? It is generally believed that clinical judgement comes from experience, but in reality this does not happen simply by accumulating hours, and it requires 'instruction, feedback, and informed practice' (ibid).

---

[2] I take 'clinical judgement' to mean good judgement about therapeutic situations, without implying a medical model of psychotherapy.

Supervision could then be seen as a space in which virtue, or good clinical judgement, is developed. The virtue model would suggest that the ability to see what is most important and choose the best available course of action is initially pursued by training practical reason. This can be done through a joint investigation of the reasons for thinking about the client in particular ways, or favouring certain interventions over others, and the likely consequences of such conceptualisations. It will involve reviewing all relevant considerations – theoretical and therapeutic, ethical, personal and organisational. In this sense the aim of supervision could be to facilitate the therapist's ability to reach the right judgement, all things considered, as a first step towards developing virtue. By regularly talking through our reasons, training the right attitudes and practising the right actions, the ability to perceive and follow the appropriate course of action should eventually become second nature. Of course this is not to suggest that there is only one possible right approach in any therapeutic situation, but a careful consideration of reasons for action should at the very least lead to the exclusion of obviously wrong turnings and to the selection of an approach we could rationally justify.

This conception of supervision as a framework for the development of virtue avoids both a dogmatic application of theory to practice and an uncritical 'anything goes' attitude, neither of which is well suited to protect the client or to further the therapist's wisdom. It is a useful tool to explore the areas of therapy that tend to give rise to dilemmas. Not necessarily big dramatic dilemmas – when to break confidentiality, the challenge of dual roles and so forth – that would call for thorough discussion in the light of professional codes of conduct, but more ordinary, everyday issues of theory and practice, of boundaries and professional responsibility. Furthermore, very similar issues apply to supervision practice, and as well as helping supervisees to reflect on their work, supervisors could use this framework to think about their own practice. In order to illustrate the kinds of topics that could be illuminated by the concepts of virtue and the mean, in the next section I review some issues that are frequently raised in supervision.

Practical Issues

The relationship

Negotiating the exact manner of interaction between therapist and client is one of the areas that often gives rise to questions in supervision. For instance, is it appropriate to start a session by asking a question, say, or should we always leave the responsibility to the client? Is engaging in a certain amount of conversation at the beginning or end of the session to be frowned upon? Should we answer questions about ourselves or always turn them back to the client? Is it ever right to give advice, make suggestions or reassure the client? What should we do if the client wants to hug us at the end of a session? How should we respond to a flirtatious client? What about accepting a wedding invitation? What if we bump into a client in the street?

There is a danger here of reinforcing and perpetuating dogmatic answers that may well have their roots in psychoanalytic thought but have now become detached from it and acquired a life of their own. What are the reasons for believing that we should never initiate a session, for instance? Are they theory-bound and dogmatic? Actually there is no 'one size fits all' answer to this kind of question, but just leaving it at that seems unhelpful. Instead it would be fitting to investigate the reasons for one course of action or another. It is a question of working out what in the particular circumstances would constitute over-rigid or too lax: always rescuing the client could be a form of collusion, but on the other hand not even entertaining the possibility of giving appropriate assistance in order to move the situation on and allow a dialogue to take off at all does seem like avoiding a responsibility that should belong to us as therapists. A definite answer, however, can be given only in relation to a specific context and the potential future consequences.

The more general issue is about maintaining the delicate balance between detachment and involvement that the enterprise of psychotherapy requires. In terms of the excess-mean-deficiency model, it seems easy to fall either into over-involvement or under-involvement. The former would entail things like wanting to be a friend to one's clients, having a 'vision' for them, wanting to give guidance, nurture and look after them, having not only an opinion about their choices but also an emotional investment in the outcome. This kind of attitude is likely to translate into inappropriate behaviour that would encourage role confusion and dependency. The opposite extreme is a lack of engagement with the client that seems unlikely to lead to a satisfactory therapeutic relationship. The mean here lies in what we could call 'appropriate caring' about the client's well-being. It is perfectly alright to care about clients, be friendly to them and have views about their choices, but we must watch becoming overly attached to them or to particular results. Thinking about clients with this scheme in mind could help us to decide what in that particular situation might constitute appropriate caring as opposed to excess or deficiency. This will depend on a number of things, including for example our personality and the client's specific patterns in relation to boundaries and relationships.

Another related set of issues, which can take up a fair amount of supervision time, regards what rules to adopt about practicalities. Supervisees sometimes appear to believe that there are universally applicable rules out there waiting to be discovered. What policies should we have about cancellations, for instance, about replacing or asking clients to pay for missed sessions, about giving out personal phone numbers to clients, receiving texts from clients and so on? The possibilities range from the extreme of being totally rigid about such rules, as a psychoanalytic therapist would tend to be, to that of being entirely *ad hoc* and *laissez-faire* about it. How should we handle it if clients are consistently late or repeatedly miss sessions or are generally erratic in their attendance? Again, the mean will be context related and dependent on the fit between therapist, client and setting. An important distinction to make when thinking all this through is whether any interventions in relation to this kind of issue – such as requesting greater commitment from the client, for instance – have a logistic or a therapeutic rationale. It is perfectly reasonable to attempt to bring some order to a chaotic pattern, but we should be clear about our reasons for seeking to do this.

Another fraught issue is how 'directive' the therapist should be. Does suggesting homework, for example, let alone books to read, somehow 'compromise' the relationship? Is it ever legitimate to take a more 'educational' role with clients? Excessive 'directiveness' would end up getting in the way of respecting the client's autonomy, and a complete lack of it may mean not being as helpful to the client as we might otherwise have been. And when is it appropriate for therapists to bring themselves into the session, or to use the client-therapist relationship as a therapeutic tool? The main thing to stress in this respect is clarity of purpose. One extreme would involve making self-focused interventions without a clear rationale, out of a misplaced sense of our own importance, in a way that diverts attention from where it should be: on the client. The opposite extreme would be to shy away from addressing issues of trusting and relating between client and therapist even when they are clearly the main phenomenon in the room, which if not addressed would probably make work on any other problem impossible. Again, the answer will be relative to each particular situation. Supervision is a time to debate these issues and seek clarification.

Challenging and giving feedback

Another staple of supervision sessions is how much and how to challenge the client. The excess here would involve being confrontational, antagonistic or argumentative. The deficiency on the other hand would involve just providing a sympathetic ear, without attempting to help the client to face any difficult truths. In order to avoid upsetting the client, therapists might avoid any challenge or uncomfortable feedback and settle for a cosy relationship that could be regarded as collusive, while convincing themselves that this is still useful and right for the client. The mean here will be to avoid both inappropriate confrontation and over-protectiveness, challenging at the right level and in the right way (which in some cases might mean not at all). This of course needs to be established in relation to specific situations. Some of the factors that need to be considered are: client's patterns, stage of therapy and kind of relationship established, what the client is able to process at that point and how the feedback is formulated.

Similarly supervisees may be concerned about giving the client *positive* feedback. Complimenting the client could constitute excess, possibly fostering an unhelpful situation in which the client comes to depend on the therapist's approval. On the other hand it seems unnecessarily rigid to withhold all positive feedback, dismissing a potentially useful intervention. The task is to work out the right amount of positive feedback for a particular client in a particular situation. In relation to pointing out the positive threads of the client's narrative, it is a question of avoiding on the one hand stubbornly attempting to convince clients that their life is better than they had realised, forcing a reading of their situation that does not ring true to them, and on the other hand letting them wallow in a globally negative assessment without even addressing the other side of the coin.

Taking appropriate responsibility

Therapists often feel bad if no positive changes are forthcoming, as if unless they were able to fix the clients' problems their performance would be found wanting, or they would not provide value for money, or would be letting the clients down. This could lead to inappropriate interventions, such as attempting to provide quick solutions or give premature answers, and would be an example of taking excessive responsibility. The fact is that as therapists we cannot guarantee 'results': it is a two-way interaction and the client's co-operation is required. We have to accept that we are not omnipotent and that sometimes the client will not change no matter what we do.

The opposite extreme, however – a deficiency of responsibility – is equally problematic, and would involve not even asking oneself the question. The thing is, the question 'am I doing my best as a therapist?' is a fair one and should be asked of oneself, even if it is not easy to answer it. This raises the difficult issue of what a 'good enough' therapist might be, and how we can know we have done our best even when there are no 'results' to show for it. It is too easy to hold as an article of faith that our interaction with clients is therapeutic in itself and no further questions need to be entertained. Instead, if there are no signs of any change, we do need to ask ourselves what the client is really getting out of it, whether we have the expertise to work with the client's particular problem, whether psychotherapy is what the client needs in the first place, or what kind of psychotherapy would be most appropriate. Ultimately, however, there will be cases in which all we can do is deal with our own, understandable, feelings of frustration.

Trust and respect

The importance of trust in the therapeutic relationship is pointed out often enough. Here I want to focus on a different sense of 'trust', which is about taking the client at face value. One extreme in this respect is being routinely suspicious of the clients and their motives and regarding everything they say or do as requiring an interpretation. The opposite extreme is, trusting clients too much, since clearly there are times when scepticism about their narrative is in order. The appropriate attitude seems to be that of keeping an open mind and giving the benefit of the doubt while at the same time being alert to discrepancies and inconsistencies, which can provide useful material for therapeutic work.

But this issue goes right to the heart of psychotherapy, in the sense that the tendency to discount surface meaning for depth interpretation is so well established that it tends to creep in even when, at least in principle, it has been rejected. It would seem an important part of supervision to question the jargon laden comments that are all too often unthinkingly trotted out as if they were in no need of explanation, such as references to 'real self' and 'masks', or 'authentic' and 'inauthentic', not to mention 'defence', 'repression' and a host of other psychoanalytic terms. It is not that this kind of talk cannot be meaningful it is only that it is alarmingly lazy to engage in it without questioning what we really mean. Similar things could be said about automatically interpreting the client's use of humour, or a lack of overt 'emoting', for instance, as a 'defence mechanism'. If we as therapists are convinced that some such mechanism is at play for a client, we may end up directing the conversation in unhelpful ways, whether we realise it or not. This kind of theorising should be addressed in supervision. An appropriately trusting and respectful attitude would first and foremost seek to understand what certain behaviours mean for the client, and avoid being mistrustful unless we have reason to think that things might indeed not be what they seem. But it is excessive to make this our default position, and we should be clear on our reasons for adopting it.

Other ways in which therapists' fascination with theories can lead to a lack of respect for clients is when they assume that particular issues – race, say – are problems even if the clients themselves give no indication that this is the case, or when they make decisions about what topics need to be addressed – their relationship with their mother, say – whether the client likes it or not. This could be seen as a form of bullying. The same applies to interpreting every missed session as betraying the client's hostility towards the therapist, for instance, or to excessive use of parallel processes.

Conclusion

All the issues just discussed also apply to the supervisor's own practice – establishing the right kind of relationship with supervisees, challenging and giving feedback in such a way that it is neither unnecessarily aggressive nor too lenient, taking appropriate responsibility, trusting the supervisees unless there is a reason not to, and avoiding imposing theoretical structures on them. For instance, supervisors would be well advised to reflect on any tendency they may have to push supervisees excessively, hold theoretical positions dogmatically, routinely seek to interpret any supervisees' behaviour – lateness, say, or the order in which they choose to discuss their clients – and so on. Such

reflection would represent an essential part of developing the right dispositions as supervisors.

Finally it is worth emphasising that, as Aristotle himself would point out,
some things are never appropriate. According to Aristotle the excess-
deficiency model does not always apply, and some things – 'spite, shameless-
ness, envy, and, among actions, adultery, theft, homicide' – are just bad. In
these cases it is just not possible to hit the mark – 'committing adultery, say,
with the right woman, at the right time, or in the right way' (*NE*, book II,
ch. 6). Similarly, we could say that there are some things, such as having sexual
relationships with clients, for instance, or otherwise exploiting them, that are
not even up for debate. For these, there are the profession's codes of practice.

References

Aristotle *Nicomachean Ethics*. Trans. R. Crisp (Cambridge: Cambridge University Press,
    2000).
Deurzen, E. van *Existential Counselling and Psychotherapy in Practice*, 2nd edn (London:
    Sage, 2002).
Fowers, B. J. 'Psychotherapy, Character, and the Good Life'. In B. D. Slife, J. S. Reber &
    F. C. Richardson (eds) *Critical Thinking About Psychology* (Washington: American
    Psychological Association, 2005).
Macaro, A. *Reason, Virtue and Psychotherapy* (Chichester: Wiley, 2006).
Urmson, J. O. 'Aristotle's Doctrine of the Mean'. In A. O. Rorty (ed.) *Essays on Aristotle's
    Ethics* (Berkeley: University of California Press, 1980).

3

Deliberations on Supervision

Lucia Moja-Strasser

A deliberation {Overveielse} does not presuppose the definitions as given and understood; therefore it must not so much move, mollify, reassure, persuade as awaken and provoke people and sharpen thought
(Kierkegaard, 1847: 469).

It is in the spirit of the quote above that I will seek to make a contribution towards clarifying what it is to be an existential supervisor. I will be describing what it means for *me* to be an existential supervisor since I can only write about something that is true for me. I do not claim that what I am doing will necessarily have value for anyone else but I hope my deliberations will assist others in clarifying their own perspective on supervision. When I work as a supervisor I abstain from laying down rules for my supervisees. As a supervisor it is not my task to force my views on another human being but rather to throw light on the possibilities they have – at the same time never forgetting their limitations. In so doing the potential consequences for them and their clients, if they are not taking up those possibilities, are highlighted.

There is no one particular way of doing existential supervision, obviously every supervisor brings to the work their own experience and worldview – at the same time there is much that is shared and each approach has something unique to offer that may be of value to others.

Introduction

Existential psychotherapy is a philosophical endeavour that aims to reveal the context in which Being comes to light (Heidegger, 1962). As existential therapists philosophy becomes an integral part of our lives and teaches us how to question the way in which we are. Most importantly this reflection enlightens us to our relationship to the world and to others. This, of course, is also true of existential supervision.

The spirit of existential psychotherapy and supervision involves the ability to care for the person – that is to show compassionate concern. By this I mean a concern that embraces love and understanding and allows the client/supervisee to fully reveal themselves in the knowledge that they are in a safe environment. In *Works of Love* (1995) Kierkegaard discusses the essential characteristics of love that I consider to be fundamental to the process of therapy and supervision. Later we will see how this relates to supervision. The therapist or supervisor facilitates the other paying critical attention to his/her soul – that is to the innate free possibility of reflectively knowing oneself and being able to distinguish between good and evil, truth and lies. This demands a profound understanding: an understanding of what I do and how and when I am doing it. This awareness has direct consequences for my way of being and my relationships with others.

As existential supervisors we need to have clarity about where we are coming from – in other words how we respond to the supervisee's way of being, their concerns and how they relate to their clients and to ourselves. For both supervisor and supervisee this involves a process of unlearning, letting go of previously held assumptions that have been revealed in the interaction. If you are capable of letting go to this extent you can find 'the secret of the art of helping others' – Kierkegaard tells us:

> That if real success is to attend the effort to bring a man to a definite position, one must first of all take pains to find HIM where he is and begin there (1943: 333).

The Supervisor's Attitude

As a supervisor I maintain an awareness of my embodiment and being grounded – grounded in my body. I do not as it were *remain in my head*, rather I respond from my whole being – thoughts, emotions, sensations and so on. This existential understanding of embodiment will be discussed in Chapter 5 and elaborated more extensively in Chapter 6.

In reflective embodiment I strive to be open and at the same time to be aware of my limitations. I need to recognise my vulnerability and be present and I need to be willing to make myself available in the encounter. We are in a side by side dialogue. The supervisor's attitude is akin to the attitude that characterises philosophers. An attitude in which, paradoxically, humility and confidence are both present. Fundamental to this attitude is a constant questioning of myself and of my supervisee. Having a sense of wonder, an intelligent naiveté, will allow me to connect to the mystery of being and recognise that human beings are ordinary and extraordinary at the same time. Being challenging, even sometimes provocative – humour and irony will pepper our dialogue.

An underlying question which is ever present is: Who do I think I am when I say that I am a supervisor? I am a human being with qualities, faults and failings who is in as much need of guidance (being supervised) as my supervisee. What skills or expertise do I have when I call myself a supervisor? I do not believe I am a skilled expert rather I regard myself as a facilitator and a learner, but at the same time I am a 'teacher'. My teaching aims to 'move' the supervisee rather than increase their 'knowledge' – move them from one place of being to another.

> For to be a teacher does not mean simply to affirm that such a thing is so, or to deliver a lecture, etc. No to be a teacher in the right sense is to be a learner. Instruction begins when you the teacher learn from the learner, put yourself in his place so that you may understand what he understands and in the way he understands it, in case you have not understood it before. Or if you have understood it before you allow him to subject you to an examination so that he may be sure you know your part (ibid: 335).

Remaining a facilitator at all times is difficult and it involves constantly letting go of the desire to point out when, for example, the supervisee:

- is lacking awareness of themselves
- is not showing sensitivity to the client's predicament
- is being disconnected from the client's experience
- has an agenda of their own
- is only able to focus on the content of the client's material and ignores the process of therapy
- is reluctant to engage in the process of supervision.

What is the best way for a supervisor to be of any assistance in all these instances without directly pointing out what is missing in the supervisee's interaction with their clients? Through a collaborative exploration these tendencies can be revealed and the supervisee can be rescued from being lost in the content of their client's material or following their own agenda. Irony and humour can often be used to bring about this shift from the above tendencies and open up the possibility of moving beyond the immediate.

It will be seen throughout this book that the existential perspective encourages a collaborative relationship in both supervision and in therapy. If the supervisor is too heavy handed and addresses the issues listed above directly the trust that has been built up in the supervisory relationship maybe undermined and the supervisee's self-esteem eroded. The importance of the supervisory relationship as a place for learning cannot be underestimated – the supervisee takes the experience of the relationship with the supervisor into their relationships with their clients. An authoritarian or bullying stance has no place here or in therapy.

The supervision process will be enhanced by the supervisor's ability to be creative within the interaction. There is no creation of any sort without spirit. By spirit I mean the intangible and invisible aspect of our being. The word spirit, originates from the Latin *spiritus*, which means breath. It is what moves a person. What the spirit tries to grasp is always the same, repetition – not novelty. It involves an awareness of something that is in me and at the same time beyond me and which encompasses everything – Love and God. I can experience this sense of spirit through many different channels: music, therapy, meditation, prayer and so on.

> Even as the rational mind can see that all matter is energy, the spirit can see that all energy is love, and everything in creation can be a mathematical equation for the mind and a song of love for the soul (*Bhagavad Gita*, 1962: 30).

Creativity is manifested in the supervisory relationship, in that this relationship becomes the place where two people bring their respective ways-of-being-in-the-world. As a result of their interaction something new is created: a new awareness, a new perspective, a new understanding of a situation. These emerging insights will affect the respective being of both participants. This creative process could not occur without the conflict and anxiety that is shared by the supervisor and supervisee.

We all live with conflict and paradoxes. Paradoxes are inherent in life and living, they are unavoidable. The two elements of the paradox that form the apparent conflict are inseparable. One of those paradoxes that we constantly come up against in supervision is the recognition that whatever we do, it will always expose us to our possibilities and limitations. Often the limitations are being overlooked and the focus is mainly on possibilities. Kierkegaard reminds us that we are losing out by trying to ignore our limitations – he refers to limitations as the 'negative'.

> The negative thinkers .... always have the advantage that they have something positive, namely this, that they are aware of the negative; the positive thinkers have nothing whatever, for they are deluded. Precisely because the negative is present in existence and present everywhere (because being there, existence is continually in the process of becoming), the only deliverance from it is to become continually aware of it. By being positively secured the subject is indeed fooled (Kierkegaard, 1992: 81–2).

We need to recognise that our humanity entails a constant struggle, a struggle to be alive and face the limitations we all share. A struggle that involves living with uncertainty and contingency: the struggle of being in the process of becoming. It is a struggle that I recognise in myself and am familiar with. Of course the degree of the struggle will vary with each individual. Like conflict, the struggle of being human is a given and it is unavoidable. With understanding and love from another we are able to transcend the struggle rather then be stuck in it and trying to escape from it. As Nietzsche recognised:

> We must learn to love, learn to be kind, and this from earliest youth: if education or chance give us no opportunity to practice these feelings, our soul becomes dry and unsuited even to understanding the tender inventions of loving people (Nietzsche, 1996: 251).

It is important to acknowledge that the journey that is being described here is a life-long struggle and fraught with difficulties – by no means is it something we can ever fully accomplish. Implicit in much of what is described in this book is the recognition that existential supervision is not an easy option despite its collaborative stance. Supervisees are asked to face harsh realities and to show a level of honesty and courage not always expected in such a relationship.

Love and Spirituality in Supervision

> Love is the power that moves the universe, the day of life, the night of death and the new day after death. The radiance of the universe sends us a message of love which says that all creation came from love (*Bhagavad Gita*, 1962: 30).

The supervisor's capacity for love is an essential quality of being without which the quality of the supervisory relationship is in danger of becoming a technical enterprise. What is the nature of this love that is a prerequisite for the relationship between the supervisor and supervisee? What deeds can the supervisor perform to demonstrate his or her love for the supervisee? We need here to clarify what this love is not – it is not directed at the supervisee's specificity: their looks, status and so on, but it is love for their 'beingness' (humanness) – that they *are*.

> To be able to love a person despite his weaknesses and defects and imperfections is still not love, but rather this, to be able to find him lovable despite his weaknesses and defects and imperfections (Kierkegaard, 1995: 57).

The former, 'loving despite', has a condescending tone to it whilst the latter implies: to love someone is to love the person in their beingness and not for some individual qualities that are specific to that individual and in spite of their less lovable traits. It is so much easier to cultivate what Kierkegaard refers to as 'preferential love', where we love one individual above all others, rather than loving another for their beingness in spite of their 'shortcomings'. Preferential love is the type of love recognisable in our friendships and intimate relationships. 'To love people is the only thing worth living for, and without this love you are not really living' (ibid: 374).

Kierkegaard's view of love is vastly different from the romantic, comforting, consoling notion of love with which most of us are familiar. For Kierkegaard loving is living, loving is being fully alive. But words are not a demonstration of love:

> ... just as love itself is invisible and therefore we have to believe in it, so also is it not unconditionally and directly to be known by any particular expression of it (ibid: 13).

Love can only be demonstrated in deeds: 'Love is not a being-for-itself quality but a quality by which or in which you are for others' (ibid: 223). As a supervisor the love I give to my supervisees is unfathomable, 'hidden' but is 'recognisable by its fruits' (ibid: 5).

How can love be communicated in the supervision relationship? – Indirectly. Direct communication can communicate information but it cannot alert the supervisee to their capability and it will not encourage the supervisee's ability to draw out their potentiality. If the supervisor takes on the role of expert and communicates directly what the supervisee should or should not do this will encourage dependency and the opportunity for the supervisee to find their own voice will be lost. Direct communication is not a useful tool in supervision. The existential supervisor will work with the uniqueness of the supervisee and help them to find their own truth, their own way of working and ultimately of living. According to Kierkegaard, for the existing individual, who is always in the process of becoming, truth is inwardness, subjective and secret – 'the entire essential content of subjective thought is essentially secret, because it cannot be directly communicated. This is the meaning of the secrecy' (Kierkegaard, 1974: 73).

I believe that love, the caring of the soul, is fundamental to the process of therapy and supervision. Therefore in supervision I will endeavour to find opportunities for supervisees to reflect on their compassion for their clients. Where does love or lack of love manifest itself in the supervisee's experience of being human? Engaging with this question helps the supervisee move away from what is material (usually connected to content matters) and move into the spiritual realm of their existence.

> .... a human being, even if from the moment of birth he is spirit, still does not become conscious of himself as spirit until later ... The person in whom the spirit has awakened does not as a consequence abandon the visible world. Although conscious of himself as spirit, he continues to remain in the visible world and to be visible to the senses – in the same way he also

remains in the language except that his language is the metaphorical language (Kierkegaard, 1995: 209).

Love and spirituality are expressed indirectly through metaphor rather than directly or literally. The meaning of a word changes in relation to the context in which it is used and from one individual to another. Therefore the meaning of statements must always be clarified and understood within their context. Values and propositions are revealed through words. However as a supervisor I need to pay particular attention to the type of communication that cannot be described in words and which lies outside language.

Life cannot be described by propositions. It has to be lived. When I say 'I am' or 'me', what do I mean by 'I' or 'me'? 'Me' is more defined, more objective, whilst 'I', is more like a process and has to be lived. 'I' is the soul, the mysterious part of my being. Surely, my being, is more than that which is visible to the eye. The soul is not separate from the body but is not the same as the body. It is essential that a supervisor/therapist attends to all aspects of the being of the client/supervisee.

The spiritual, is represented in what is sacred, not necessarily in the religious sense, in the supervisee's life, in what is unique and indescribable in words. By becoming aware of what is sacred, what matters above anything else, what is ultimately meaningful in the supervisee's life gives him/her the opportunity to become a better human being and to develop those human qualities that we all have, which will include the capacity to love and give compassion.

In what way does the supervisor's worldview, including their view of the spiritual, influence and shape the process and outcome of supervision? The spiritual represents the quality of being that has regard for things of spirit as opposed to material or worldly interests. The supervisor's openness to all aspects of human experience, including the spiritual, can enhance the supervision process.

I ask my supervisees questions such as: Who do you think you are when you call yourself a therapist? In what way is your life being enriched by engaging in the activity called 'therapy'? Is being able to be a therapist a gift? Or do we just do it because we have a qualification? What are the possibilities and limitations of therapy? By trying to engage with these questions, we will stumble across the spiritual dimension of their being. This process allows supervisees to recognise and nurture their capacity for love. Even if we deny or overlook the presence of the spiritual dimension it is always present, in one form or another, since it is an inevitable, universal aspect of our being – a given.

The commandment is that you shall love, but ah, if you will understand yourself and life, then it seems that it should not need to be commanded, because to love people is the only thing worth living for, and without this love you are not really living (Kierkegaard, 1995: 375).

Dialogue

Dialogue is fundamental to the process of therapy and supervision:

> A dialogue is the perfect conversation because everything that the one person says acquires its particular colour, sound, its accompanying gesture *in strict consideration of the other person* to whom he is speaking (Nietzsche, 1996: 191).

We stand in the mysterious realm of language. Supervision is important because only in dialogue with another human being can we gain an understanding of ourselves and our work with clients. When we dialogue only with ourselves we can often be deluded in the process. Dialogue is a conversation that by definition involves questioning, challenging and making statements that can facilitate the supervisee's reflection on their own work. Asking questions is a real art. Asking questions in supervision involves tuning in to the other's experience and being guided by the desire to help the other understand their predicament and in the process to increase our own understanding. The questioning can take the shape of a: statement, gesture, look, question or silence. Questions can be extremely powerful as long as they are not loaded questions, whereby we are looking for a specific answer or we believe we know the answer. Hesitant statements made in the full knowledge that they might not be accepted by the supervisee can be equally powerful.

Understanding can also develop through silence which is an integral part of any discourse. During silence, dialogue continues – it is not the absence of having something to say.

> He who never says anything cannot keep silent at any given moment. Keeping silent authentically is possible only in genuine discoursing. To be able to keep silent, Dasein must have something to say (Heidegger, 1962: 208).

The outcome of dialogue in supervision can never be predicted, it can only be grasped in terms of the process of creation that the supervisor and supervisee are a part of. The lasting truth which might emerge cannot be arrived at in any other way, except in dialogue with another human being. Dialogue by necessity will involve conflict and anxiety. The outcome, to a great extent is determined by the supervisor's ability to stand in conflict with the supervisee and bare the anxiety that this will generate.

> In strife, each opponent carries the other beyond itself ... .The more strife, for its part, outdoes itself, the more inflexibly do the opponents let themselves

go into the intimacy of simple belonging to one another (Heidegger, 1993: 174).

Indirect communication will give the supervisee the opportunity to grasp and reach into their experience with heightened self-awareness. With the assistance of the supervisor they can learn from the relationship with the client, as well as the relationship with the supervisor, about themselves and how they are dialoguing with others. They can learn to rely on their own reflections rather than the feedback received from the supervisor. Indirect communication will give supervisees the opportunity to confront in themselves how they are navigating life's uncertainties. Supervisees can also recognise how much they are trying to anchor themselves by creating a false sense of security and in what ways this might interfere with their work with clients. They are given the opportunity to acknowledge how life's uncertainties and fears affect the way in which the supervisor and supervisee relate to each other.

Our way of relating to each other will always be a result of how each of us individually relates to our existence. Our way of being, in other words our style, will emanate from our lived experience. It is often tempting to resort to abstract thoughts and theories which are not necessarily connected to our own existence. Instead of staying with the given phenomena we resort to theorising and intellectualising our experience.

As we have said before, the supervisory relationship is a creative encounter and like any creativity cannot be performed without love and commitment. The key to the supervisory relationship like for any other relationship is listening. Listening allows us to create an environment that engenders trust. Asking supervisees to produce verbatim reports can undermine the trust that has been developed in the supervisory relationship. It may block spontaneity and stifle creativity. The supervision described here relies on dialogue which is in sharp contrast to the type of supervision which espouses the presentation of verbatim reports.

The Supervisory Relationship

Supervision like the creation of any work of art requires craftsmanship. In what way can the supervisor's craftsmanship enlighten the supervisee? Being present in the relationship will include spontaneity, understanding, imagination, attention and intuition, these qualities are present in any form of art. Attention needs to be paid to the impact the supervisor has on the supervisee and *vice versa*. Equally we must not overlook the impact that the supervisee has on their clients. We need to constantly remind ourselves that who and how we are is the result of our interactions and that impacting on each other is unavoidable. The question is how does this affect our way of being?

Surprisingly, giving supervisees a chance to do their own reflecting and allowing them the time to recognise what is missing in their lives is similar to the supervisee coming to terms with what they have overlooked in their interaction with their clients. This is where the inductive type of teaching becomes so important. This entails letting the supervisee find their own truth by engaging with the questions that you as a supervisor provide.

More important however, is the ability to connect to the supervisee's struggles and to recognise that you too have the same or similar struggles. We need to focus on the supervisee's humanity rather than on their faults. The image that comes to mind is that of watching two people playing chess. It is so easy to see where they went wrong and what are the best strategies and moves that they should take. I think this is really strikingly similar to observing and supervising our supervisees.

The role of the supervisor would be an easy one if it only consisted of pointing out what is 'wrong' and how the supervisee ought to go forward. But would this really be of any help and lasting benefit for the supervisee? Could not this be seen as utter arrogance from the supervisor and useless for the supervisee? This is where the parallel between therapy and supervision is so poignant. How often are we tempted to point out to our clients how they could get unstuck or what would be the best course of action for them in order to make their lives 'better'? How long will it be before they are back to square one repeating the same thing again? Humility here becomes a good companion. First of all by not assuming that we can know what is right for another individual and secondly by having faith that we all have the capacity to ascertain what is right for ourselves. Our task is rather to acquaint supervisees with life itself and gain greater understanding of the moves of that particular game and the consequences of each.

Supervision offers the space in which supervisees can freely explore the possibilities and limitations within the relationship with their clients. We understand our supervisees through their relationships with their clients and we understand their relationships by listening to the description of their experience. As we have seen before, the relationship is based on dialogue. The partners in conversation use each other as a mirror expecting to see their 'thoughts reflected as beautifully as possible' (Nietzsche, 1996: 37).

Conclusion

My engagement with philosophy means that my being is always affected and enriched. This occurs if my reading of the philosophical text resonates with me or touches a chord in me. Consequently this will alter my way of relating to the world and others. Some philosophers have had and continue to have an impact on my way of being. My affinity with Kierkegaard has greatly changed my attitude to life and my beliefs about what I can offer someone who is turning to me as a client or a supervisee. His philosophy has influenced me on many different levels.

There are numerous theories and views about the nature of love and they all have some truth in them. However, for me, Kierkegaard's *Works of Love* surpasses them all and his is the voice that truly speaks to me. It opens up and broadens my capacity for love but not in the 'preferential' sense, as Kierkegaard clarifies: 'Love … is not a matter of drives and inclination, or a matter of feeling, or a matter of intellectual calculation' (Kierkegaard, 1995: 143).

The love that Kierkegaard is advocating is spiritual love, which for him is love of God, in other words Christian love. In supervision the concern is not necessarily with spirituality inspired by faith in God but with the spirituality that as human beings we all have, if we open ourselves to that aspect of being human.

Conflict is inherent in any relationship and it is essential for the process of supervision. It is important to recognise where the conflict lies and how in spite of it a constructive outcome can be negotiated that is beneficial for everybody including the supervisee, client and supervisor. The engagement with conflict can lead us to an individual's truth. There is no direct access to truth. We must first understand our 'mistakes' which can then show us the way to truth. 'Truth happens only by establishing itself in the strife and the free space opened up by truth itself' (Heidegger, 1993: 186).

The way in which we engage with conflict and anxiety, to a large extent will colour the outcome of supervision. It is not always acknowledged, but what is essential is to at least be aware of conflict otherwise it will impede the process of supervision. Heraclitus describes this beautifully in his poetic language: 'They do not understand how that which differs with itself is in agreement: harmony consists of opposing tension like that of the bow and lyre' (1962: 28). It is sometimes difficult to believe and accept that opposing views can co-exist and complement each other rather than oppose each other.

The supervisory relationship can stimulate creativity and help supervisees gain confidence and feel valued. There is no basic separation between me, the supervisor, and the supervisee. We are on a continuum and encompassed by something larger than either of us – our love for humanity as a whole. Both supervisor and supervisee need to let go of the desire to help and need to be constantly vigilant of the tendency to lead someone in any particular direction. The paradox here is that when we aim to help we invariably achieve the opposite – like love, helping, can only be known or given, indirectly. 'The eyes and ears are bad witnesses for men if they have barbarian souls' (ibid: 31).

Proper understanding of oneself implies also cultivating the soul – understanding the significance and language of the senses. Words speak not only to our ears but also to our soul. Therapeia, in the Socratic sense of serving the soul, involves encouraging individuals to pay attention to their soul through questioning. This leads to a purification and clarification of their being and to an understanding based on reflective self-examination.

Loving the person of the supervisee, is to show them, not directly but indirectly, what possibilities are there for them that have not yet been realised and also to encourage them towards gaining enough trust in themselves so that they rely more and more on self-understanding. Eventually they will be able to use the learning from the supervision process as a 'method' of self-monitoring.

I offer my supervisees my willingness to listen and attend to their concerns; my ability to be present and sensitive; I make myself available to the way they experience their being-in-the-world, and in turn to the way they are relating to their clients and to myself, the supervisor. I would call all this an attitude towards another human being; a way of relating; an attitude towards my supervisee that is inspired and guided by love. 'Every little work in life, however humble can become an act of creation' (*Bhagavad Gita*, 1962: 32) – if it is done in the spirit of love. All relationships have an element of creativity in them. There are a variety of ways in which we can relate to ourselves, our supervisees and others.

I recognise the way of relating described above is an ideal, which, like all ideals, cannot be fully realised though I constantly attempt to maintain this attitude. It would be rather a God-like stance if I would claim that I am always capable of loving my clients and supervisees in their beingness. I am after all just another human being who fails in my endeavours.

References

Bhagavad Gita. Trans. J. Mascaró (Harmondsworth: Penguin Books, 1962).

Heidegger, M. *Being and Time*. Trans. J. Macquarrie & E. Robinson (Oxford: Blackwell, [1927] 1962).

—— The Origin of the Work of Art? In *Basic Writings*. D. F. Krell (ed.) (London: Routledge, 1993).

Heraclitus, *The Ancilla to the Pre-Socratic Philosophers*. Trans. K. Freeman (Oxford: Blackwell, 1962).

Kierkegaard, S. *Works of Love*. Trans. H. V. Hong & E. H. Hong (New Jersey: Princeton University Press, [1874] 1995).

—— The Point of View for My Work as an Author. In R. Bretall (ed.) *A Kierkegaard Anthology* (New Jersey: Princeton University Press, 1943).

—— *Concluding Unscientific Postscript*. Trans. D. F. Swenson & W. Lowrie (New Jersey: Princeton University Press, 1974).

—— *Concluding Unscientific Postscript to Philosophical Fragments*. Trans. H. V. Hong & E. H. Hong (eds) (New Jersey: Princeton University Press, 1992).

Nietzsche, F. *Human All too Human*. Trans. M. Faber & S. Lehmann (Lincoln: University of Nebraska Press, [1878] 1996).

4

Phenomenology and Supervision

Martin Adams

Introduction

The issue of supervision of psychotherapeutic practice is an example of a more general problem of existence that is: how can any experience be recorded and re-presented? It arises out of a basic difference between humans and other animals – reflective consciousness. Consciousness enables us to reflect and brings up questions like:

What does it mean to be alive?
How should I act and be in relation to other people?

These are summed up in Heidegger's central question as 'Why are there beings at all, and why not rather nothing?' (Heidegger, 1993a: 110).

The problem we face as supervisors is illustrated by the following story (quoted in Hare, 2002). Alfred Munnings – a painter in the classical tradition, the artistic analogue of the natural scientific tradition – commenting on the work of Picasso said, 'Picasso cannot paint a tree'. To which Picasso replied: 'He's right, I can't paint a tree. But I can paint the feeling you have when you look at a tree'.

There is a link which phenomenologists call 'Intentionality', between Picasso and the tree which makes the tree in the painting, simultaneously personal and universal. Picasso did not claim to have painted an objective record of the tree. Intentionality means that we are never separate from the objects that we perceive. Picasso accepted this. By painting the same tree over and over again he was able to get simultaneously closer to the tree and closer to a sense of himself as a perceiving being.

This echoes Cohn's understanding of the phenomenological implications for the therapeutic context: 'Therapists cannot, like scientists, impose their explanatory expectations on the phenomena, with diagnostic labels and reductive interpretations, but keep open to what the phenomena themselves are telling them' (Cohn, 2002: 31).

We must remember that when supervising, presenting for supervision or doing that very specialised task of writing a case study, the starting point is always something that actually happened, but it is not only what happened, it is the sense we make of what happened as well. We can arrive at what supervision in an existential-phenomenological context means if we take 'super' to mean 'over' in the sense of gaining perspective and 'vision' in the sense of the understanding that results from accommodation of alternative perspectives.

Phenomenology as a Research Method

Phenomenology is a research method. It is a way of finding out both about ourselves and the world through a systematic investigation designed to build in consistency and reliability. The word phenomenon is from the Greek, meaning appearance, or that which shows itself. The colloquial phrase 'the things themselves', has been used to refer to these external objects, events and appearances that we have assumptions about.

Phenomenology is therefore a systematic study of these appearances and a correlation of these perceptions with the things as they are. In this way there is no functional distinction between the objective and subjective worlds since they are both equal parts of what is called the phenomenological field and everything we observe and describe is a part of our act of observation and description. We are therefore primarily concerned with investigating meaning rather than simple causation which is the case in the domain of natural science.

We cannot look at anything without first having a way of looking. While phenomenology has assumptions about the nature of human interaction its methodology also accommodates a way of being aware of these assumptions. Every research method has assumptions and those of phenomenology are:

1. we are active interpreters and creators of our world
2. no observation we make can ever be free of assumptions
3. such meanings as we personally create are never totally independent of nor dependent on other people or other meaning systems

To describe and reflect on something as multi-faceted and over-determined as a therapeutic encounter involves trying to do two opposite things – capturing whatever it is about dynamic intersubjective space that makes it so special and translating it through compression, abstraction and selection so that something essential about the encounter is preserved. Phenomenology can help us to do this.

It is one of a number of research methods and it can be compared with the methods of natural science which are also systematic and based on observation in order to determine causal relationships and qualities. This is based on the assumption that the observer does not affect what they are observing. It follows that what is found by one experimenter will also be found by another. What it finds out about the world is taken as being real and fixed.

Another research method is 'Introspectionism'. This is about the observation by an individual of their own mental activity. It pays little attention to events in the external world, and instead emphasises subjective experiences. It also does not put great importance on the context of the experience and is not particularly systematic.

While all research methods have their value, it is important that there be a match between the research method and what is researched. With respect to natural science, the assumption that the observed object is mechanistic and subject to forces beyond its control clearly works very well for an inanimate object, what Sartre describes as a being-in-itself, for example a chair or a stone, but is inappropriate for human beings, what Sartre calls a being-for-itself (Sartre 1943: 617). Phenomenology is therefore the most appropriate research method to investigate human phenomena, of which supervision is one (Giorgi, 1970).

The Nature of Phenomenology

Phenomenology was developed by Edmund Husserl in the early 20th century. Subsequently, both Sartre (1943) and Heidegger (1962) applied phenomenology to the study of existence. Husserl designed it as a method that one person could use to become more aware of their assumptions about what they are involved in. Subsequent writers have modified it for investigating relationships and it has also been applied to research by for example Moustakas (1994) and Colaizzi (1978). In the sense that phenomenology is dedicated to discovering the depth and breadth of the meanings we construct in relation with other people it is a social activity, it is about dialogue.

In supervision the nature and quality of the dialogue *itself* defines the effectiveness of the supervision and hence the effectiveness of the supervisee's work in therapy. We need to distinguish between monologue, duologue and dialogue (Deurzen, 1998: 48). A monologue is when one person is talking and another is listening and the talker's main concern is to talk and has little concern about how he or she is received. The listener's experience is often one of being talked at rather than being talked to or with.

A duologue is when two people are talking to each other and only superficially listening to each other. They may well take it in turns to talk and to listen and even to respond to what each other says but they are not really listening to each other, they are more likely to be listening to what they want the other to say. It is more like two simultaneous monologues.

A dialogue on the other hand is a conversation where the two people attend and listen to each other, not for what they want to hear the other one say, but for what is actually being said and what they can discover. It involves a reflexive openness. A true dialogue is characterised by a certain amount of anxiety, not necessarily unpleasant although it may be, but anxiety in the sense that in a true dialogue we can never know what will be talked about or what thoughts and feelings will be evoked. One can only discover something new if one is open and ready for the possibility of finding a new outlook on the world. This is unsettling because it is not predictable. Dialogue is an exchange between two people in which they find their way through misunderstandings and towards shared truth.

This discussion of dialogue is relevant to all the chapters in this book, for dialogue, in the true sense of the word radically underpins existential supervision.

Husserl proposed several different reductions 'the phenomenological reduction' being the first one (followed by the eidetic, the transcendental and several others). It is a way of becoming aware of our assumptions about our physical, social, personal and moral natures that we put between ourselves and the world. He asked how can we understand anything without first understanding that which does the understanding? He said that by studying the appearance of something, the boundaries of knowledge can be extended in two directions:

firstly, towards the object, to find out about it
secondly, towards the subject, to find out about the process of looking

The correspondence between the subjective and the objective (the external referent) means that we should study them together. We actually make this correspondence all the time in everyday life, but with varying degrees of success. The aim of phenomenology is to increase this success rate and to point out when and how we are mistaken. In supervision the external referent is what actually happened between the therapist and client. The most practical way of re-presenting this is the verbatim record. But even this is not perfect. I will return to this.

Phenomenology as a Framework

In order to be phenomenological, we must also be clear about what we use theory for. A theory can only be an abstract and simplified description of how something was found to be in the past. It can be useful in the sense that we can use it to ground and orientate ourselves but we must not forget that a theory is like a map and that the territory is far more complex and multi-dimensional than any map can ever be. We need to stay alive to the fact that the map is limited and that it may fail to be as predictive as it once was (Deurzen-Smith, 1997: 203). Although theory can help us to generate alternatives, phenomenology can help us to ensure we do not mistake the map for the territory.

Since phenomenology is systematic it follows that there are characteristic actions or skills associated with it and a phenomenological investigation consists of two parts (Ihde, 1986; Moran, 2000). The first part is known as 'bracketing' or 'epoché' (Moran, 2000: 147). It is more passive than the second part, and can be described as having three aspects, attention, description and 'horizontalisation'. It is tempting to think of these aspects in a fixed sequence. This is not only unrealistic but also a mechanistic way of considering a dynamic process. They are best considered as being done simultaneously. The second part is more active and specifies what and how something is to be focused on and is called 'verification'. This has a more hermeneutic, interpretive function. It is where we start to understand the meanings of what has initially been described.

In Chapter 1 the epoché was highlighted as being 'practically synonymous with the existential perspective' and most, if not all, of the contributors to this book would acknowledge its importance. Epoché can serve as a guide for approaching supervision or therapy and encourages an open stance to whatever is encountered. Practitioners who rely heavily on precise theories about human functioning would do well to consider this stance – we saw in Chapter 2 the danger of 'stretching theories to fit clients'. Let us look at the detail of doing phenomenology.

Bracketing

At the beginning of their training all therapists are encouraged to reflect on their experiences with the expectation that having identified their assumptions they will be more aware and therefore better therapists.

Phenomenology informs us that there are three potential pitfalls here. The first is the belief that we can ever be fully aware of our assumptions. Supervision is about discovering the assumptions that constrain and limit the work, within the co-constituted relationship between the therapist and client. The next is that it is not enough to imagine that simply identifying them intellectually will suffice because they will inevitably come back in a manner we are unaware of. Not examining what these assumptions are for, what they mean to us and how they got there is an evasion of our responsibility to ourselves, our supervisees and their clients. Not only that, but we need these assumptions, not just to make sense of the world but to remind ourselves how we usually make sense of the world. Our assumptions inform us and are a creation of our being. The third is the belief that it is a once and for all process. Life is continuous, so reflecting on our evolving assumptions and the way we become unaware of them is continuous. There are many different sorts of assumptions which often interlock. When assumptions combine the belief is that much stronger and therefore more resistant to examination.

An example of a theoretical assumption is: 'Awareness of personal mortality is always a prime motivating force in people's lives'. An example of a personal assumption is: 'The death of my father prompted me to think more seriously about my life'. An example of the two combined would be: 'Unless the supervisee gets their client to consider personal mortality the work will not progress'. It may well be so, but the point is that the *conclusion* is defined by the *assumptions*. A result of assumptions being unexamined is that what is taken to be 'true' and 'obvious' will bear an uncanny resemblance to the assumptions. When this happens, the map has been mistaken for the territory.

Phenomenologically, all knowledge and all conclusions about the world are considered to be tentative. They are simply an imperfect way we have of thinking of the matter in hand, for the time being. A danger of the supervisor's unexamined assumptions is that the supervisee will feel that the supervisor's assumptions are *fact*, with the rule being: 'If you learn my assumptions you will practice properly'. Such an issue is of greater importance when the supervisee is depending on their supervisor to pass a course. It is also more likely if there is some superficial coherence between the two people, for example if the supervisor and supervisee had the same training. Rigorous application of phenomenology will enable us to shine a light on our practice more effectively and more critically.

Attention

When encountering anything we turn our attention onto it. Immediately, we interpret it in terms of familiar objects or experiences. This attention is active and we are doing more than just listening to the supervisee, we are listening to ourselves listening, and trying to put aside, while being aware of them, whatever associations we are having. For the time being these associations just need to be remembered, their significance is not yet known. It is likely to become clear in due course and be used in verification.

Our ability to attend is correlated with our ability to live with uncertainty. If we can, then we are able to see things anew, but if we cannot we are either likely to be muddled and vague or restrictive and dogmatic. In the first we have no map and in the second we mistake the map for the territory. To see things anew has also been described as 'unknowing' (Wolters, 1978; Parsons, 1984, 1986; Casement, 1985; Spinelli, 1997).

On a skills level, we need to be silent. If we insist that what meets our first glance is literally all there is we will not see it in its dynamic multidimensionality. We need to find a way of throwing just enough light in order to see, but not so much that we inhibit, flatten and freeze, bearing in mind all the time that we are, despite our best efforts, influencing the object. By being phenomenological we find out about this influence.

Description

Description is more difficult than it seems, since it requires us to see through the assumptions we have. Explanation attempts to give an account of events in terms other than themselves, and will abstract and attribute causation. Theory as an explanation is a sophisticated form of metaphor, and metaphors can give an illusory understanding, they often obscure more than they illuminate. The temptation for the supervisor to explain is proportional to their anxiety and explanation is invariably given to relieve the supervisor's anxiety or to impress the supervisee with the supervisor's learning.

Although supervision is a dialogue, to concentrate only on the verbal is to put too great an emphasis on language. It can be argued that verbal cues are only obvious to us because we live in a verbal culture and psychotherapy is a symptom of this culture. We cannot assume:

- that what someone says is a complete description of their experience
- that if a supervisee says 'yes' they agree with and think the same way as us
- that the experience can either currently or eventually be verbalised

To hold to any of these assumptions drastically reduces our view of the world.

The dimension of human experience that has the most direct connection with our intentional nature is the emotional dimension. Emotions are what connect us and locate us within our existence. They are the ebb and flow of human experience with currents, undercurrents and cross currents. They are like the weather, and there is never *no* weather. Emotions are the connection between being and doing and are both about dynamic continuity, the impossibility of fixedness in time and space and the impossibility of certainty.

This is why description needs to focus primarily on emotional experience and its context, rather than mediated intellectual or cognitive experience. An acknowledgment of one's emotions will lead to a fuller understanding of one's strengths and weaknesses.

The most useful question to start a descriptive analysis is not 'Why?', because this requests a distancing from present experience by attempting to establish causal links but the questions 'What?' and 'How?', which simply request further description. As in:

- How do you mean?
- What's that like?
- Can you say a bit more about that?

Horizontalisation

On many occasions in supervision we are on the edge of the known world. And we do not know what any of it means. This is why we have to refrain from prematurely coming to a conclusion that one aspect is more important than another. Moreover our ability to identify parts of the story and the experience will inevitably be limited by our own life experience and our ability to convince ourselves of particular ways of seeing things is enormous. It therefore follows that our success at horizontalising is dependent on our ability to identify and understand our assumptions, so if we catch ourselves thinking about our supervisees and their clients in particular ways, it gives a clue that we are not horizontalising well enough, and we may well be mistaken. However, as long as one is describing the elements of the experience if only to oneself, sooner or later certain elements will appear to be more in evidence than others.

If attention, description and horizontalisation are done rigorously, hidden assumptions will gradually come to light and the metaphorical brackets we put round them will remind us they are assumptions and not facts and therefore more likely to limit our field of vision. A supervisor cannot expect to have a sufficiently clear awareness of another person's assumptions unless they are aware of their own. This is not just a good idea. It is a principle of phenomenological practice. In applying epoché to supervision, the supervisor needs to do four things:

1. identify their assumptions
2. bracket them
3. remember them
4. understand them

And if this is done sufficiently rigorously the supervisee will reflexively be enabled to do the same.

Verification

The second part of the application of phenomenology is more active and is sometimes called verification. The activities of epoché can be powerful and can frequently rekindle genuine philosophical perplexity and personal questioning, but on other occasions a descriptive analysis is not enough. The overall aim of verification is to explore and question meanings, both within the narrative, the process, and the relationship between the supervisee and their client. It is about wondering how all the elements and all the impressions and questions accumulated during bracketing are correlated. It is about how content and process are interlinked. It is also an examination of the way intentionality gives meaning. But it is not a questioning-of, rather a questioning-with – a dialogue.

Verification is about distinguishing the 'structural or invariant features', the common elements, from the 'variant structures' (Ihde, 1986: 39), those particular to this situation. In other words how valid are the assumptions that have come to light?

There are two pitfalls here:

Firstly the common elements must of course belong together by virtue of themselves and not be made to fit together by virtue of a currently favourite theory or set of assumptions.

Secondly it is difficult to judge at what point enough evidence has been gathered to justify breaking the rule of horizontalisation and to select a particular item to focus on.

This is something that can only be learnt through experience. Ultimately we only know how useful something is by the effect it has when it is tested – and by the extent to which possibilities are narrowed down or opened out. If a supervisor does not acknowledge that some elements are more in evidence than others it does a disservice to the supervisee and their clients. A reluctance to rely on the authority of your own experience can lead to an idealisation of ignorance. This is the other side of unknowing, when we are determined not to know. Hiding behind ignorance can be as damaging as hiding behind theory.

Verification can be formalised as follows:

Following the supervisee presenting their work, the supervisor presents their reflections on the supervisee's work as items for discussion.
This leads to a discussion that re-examines assumptions hidden within both the therapist's and the client's descriptions.
And this discussion leads dialectically to a preliminary working consensus about the issue under discussion and its consequent re-description (Berguno, 1998).

This sequence, presentation – discussion – re-description, is endlessly repeated and is the essence of dialogue. Phenomenologically we are engaging in 'imaginative variation' (Langdridge, 2007: 19). We are allowing ourselves to wonder out loud what the connections are between elements we previously noticed and bracketed and now seem worthy of further exploration. We are also more actively challenging and interpretative. We are of course always interpreting in the sense that we are always making sense of whatever we encounter – this is the meaning of the term intentionality (ibid: 13) – but the duty of a phenomenological supervisor is to make sure that interpretations are made within the framework of the phenomenological field rather than that of a theory or the supervisor's or the therapist's preoccupations.

If the supervisor is being phenomenological there is nothing that will make supervision intrinsically persecutory. The supervisee can just as easily see the supervisor as persecutory as the supervisor can see the supervisee in need of correction and these are assumptions which need to be examined. Although they may seem 'invariant' they are in fact 'variant'. Phenomenology sees supervision as derived from a developmental model of the person rather than a deficiency model. Assumptions being what they are, we need to acknowledge the possibility, or rather probability if not certainty, that we are deceiving ourselves about our practice, and to take responsibility for the anxiety of this discovery.

However painful it may be to live in a world with other autonomous beings, each of us has a responsibility to acknowledge both our own view and that of the other. The important phenomenological question for a supervisor is not whether we have responsibility as supervisors but what is the nature of the responsibility that we have, and how can we exercise this while simultaneously acknowledging the autonomy of the three people involved, the supervisor, the supervisee and the client.

The implications of this checking of our responsibility are:

- that supervision can only ever be about the last session and not the next session
- that the supervisor should not tell the supervisee what to do next
- for the client's sake the supervisor needs to believe in the supervisee's ability to practice professionally – though obviously if the supervisor has doubts about this they need to be addressed
- the focus should always be on the supervisee's work with clients – which of course does not exclude the supervisee's own experience or the relationship with the supervisor

The nature of responsibility that we have as supervisors will be discussed further in the first two chapters of Part III.

With respect to our co-constituted nature, it must not be forgotten that the supervisor/supervisee relationship is a part of a nexus of baffling complexity. And it is inevitable that how we are in other parts of our lives will be echoed in supervision. This is how we understand parallel process. We exist in a world of other beings that we observe and are observed by. These other beings provide us with valuable feedback about how we are in the world.

Phenomenology and Verbatim Records

Our capacity for self deception should not be underestimated. Or to put it phenomenologically, our ability not to bracket effectively should not be forgotten. Our ability to convince ourselves and other people that something happened in a particular manner when nothing of the sort happened is awesome. Nevertheless we do have effects on each other, mostly on a level beneath awareness but encoded in language (although they can be preverbal).

This is why verbatim records are so valuable. We need to know as much as possible about the 'What' in order to understand the abstraction. Verbatim records are not perfect, nothing is and unless they are taken from a contemporaneous recording they are also subject to revision. No moment can be experienced twice. The second time is never the same as the first if only because it is the second time and not the first. But we need to get as close as we can to the primary evidence. Perhaps the best way is for the supervisor to be in the same room as the therapist and the client. This is clearly not workable although it happens on every training course in the use of 'triads'. In the clinical arena, family therapy is observed directly with the use of one-way mirrors and in live supervision instructions are given as the therapist works (though this clearly changes what occurs).

The use of video and audio tapes is cumbersome and time consuming and can also risk changing the process, although its effect can be minimised by familiarity and discussion. A verbatim account, if not the best, is possibly the least worst compromise.

Psychotherapy is an exchange, a dialogue conducted for the most part in a verbal spoken language. This places constraints on it. Regardless of how over-determined, personal and multi-faceted a language is, we always have to start from the 'things themselves' in order to find out about the 'things themselves'. The 'things themselves' in the context of supervision are the words that were used in the dialogue. The more we start with what the supervisee thought went on in the session, rather than what was said, the more we are not starting with the appearance and are therefore not being phenomenological.

We must also remember that the verbatim record is only an illustration of something, and hence cannot stand on its own. Heidegger reminds us that 'language is the house of Being' (Heidegger, 1993b: 217). By this he means that we do not use language to communicate unambiguous meaning, our use of it reveals our cognitive, existential and embodied relationship with the world (Langdridge, 2007: 161). Therefore the verbatim is just the start.

A metaphor we can use is that of an opera. The libretto is the dialogue, the music is the tone, and the choreography is the movements and posture of the two people. A verbatim account is just the libretto, but at least it is one of the three and from the libretto we can build up an understanding of the other two.

What comes next is learning how what was said was understood or misunderstood, in order to decode the interlocking meanings. As phenomenologists we need to know about the person who does the perceiving as well as what is perceived.

Objectification and Subjectification

There is always the possibility of objectifying the client via the use of verbatim records. Whenever we remember, we do just that, we re-member. We put back together. It is inevitable that this involves an objectification and an abstraction. Objectification is always a danger in any reflection process, and especially so if only the client's words are reported. Indeed we can objectify ourselves by pretending neutrality. A verbatim record that includes the exchanges between the two people reduces inadvertent objectification and returns the focus to one of quality of relationship. The question in supervision then becomes one of: 'How could it be that these two people are having a relationship with these qualities?' Concentration on the dialogue between the two people, rather than simply on what one of the people said will also reduce the tendency to concentrate on individual 'pathology' and enhances concentration on the co-constituted nature of the work.

Regardless of the dangers of verbatim records there is a much greater danger which arises from not using verbatim records, that of subjectification, that is relying on Introspectionism. In subjectification the client becomes a figment of the supervisee's imagination and appears within supervision as a collection of memories, desires and impressions which are hard to tease out from the supervisees own un-bracketed assumptions. As supervisors we need a reliable way of knowing whether, for example, a client actually agreed with something the therapist said (which the therapist would obviously like them to do) or whether the client was merely responding to a covert suggestion (which the therapist would obviously not like them to do). Verbatim records are one of the best ways to ascertain this. Presenting a verbatim record allows us to do this by tracking the subsequent exchanges gaining a more direct sense of process and getting away from speculation.

It is impossible to re-member an entire session so what results will inevitably be selective. But it is a skill that can be learnt through consistent application of particular strategies, for example those described in 'interpersonal process recall' (Kagan, 1984).

As supervisors we need to have a way of knowing if assumptions are bracketed and of ensuring that the therapist's own agenda is not being followed. Practising phenomenologically can ensure this.

Conclusion

This chapter has related the philosophy and the research method of phenomenology to the practice of supervision. It is suggested that phenomenology is the most appropriate research method for studying human interaction of which supervision is one example. This is because its systematic methodology enables the practitioner to accommodate and be open to multiple meanings and possibilities while remaining true to the relational facts. It does this by ensuring that one's assumptions are always to the fore and never accepted without considerable examination.

References

Berguno, G. 'Teaching Phenomenology as a Social Activity', *Existential Analysis* 9(2) (1998) 18–23.

Cohn, H. W. *Heidegger and the Roots of Existential Therapy* (London: Continuum, 2002).

Colaizzi, P. F. 'Psychological Research as the Phenomenologist Views It'. In R. Valle & M. King (eds) *Existential Phenomenological Alternatives for Psychology* (Oxford: Oxford University Press, 1978).

Casement, P. *On Learning from the Patient* (London: Routledge, 1985).

Deurzen-Smith, van E. *Everyday Mysteries* (London: Routledge, 1997).

Deurzen, E. van *Paradox and Passion in Psychotherapy* (Chichester: Wiley, 1998).

Giorgi, A. *Psychology as a Human Science. A Phenomenologically Based Approach* (New York: Harper & Row, 1970).

Hare, D. 'Why Tabulate?' 7 (Oxford: Arête, 2001) *Guardian* 2.2.2002.

Heidegger, M. 'What is Metaphysics?' In D. F. Krell (ed.) *Basic Writings* (London: Routledge, [1947] 1993a).

—— 'Letter on Humanism'. In D. F. Krell (ed.) *Basic Writings* (London: Routledge, [1947] 1993b).

—— *Being and Time.* Trans. J. Macquarrie & E. Robinson (Oxford: Blackwell, [1927] 1962).

Ihde, D. *Experimental Phenomenology* (Albany: Suny Press, 1986).

Kagan, N. 'Interpersonal Process Recall: Basic Methods and Recent Research'. In D. Larsen (ed.) *Teaching Psychological Skills* (Monterey: Brooks Cole, 1984).

Langdridge, D. *Phenomenological Psychology* (Harlow: Pearson, 2007).

Moran, D. *Introduction to Phenomenology* (London: Routledge, 2000).

Moustakas, C. *Phenomenological Research Methods* (London: Sage, 1994).

Parsons, M. 'Psychoanalysis as Vocation and Martial Art', *International Review of Psycho-Analysis* 4 (1984) 453.

—— 'Suddenly Finding it Really Matters: The Paradox of the Analysts Non-Attachment', *International Journal of Psycho-Analysis* 67 (1986) 475–88.

Sartre, J-P. *Being and Nothingness.* Trans. H. E. Barnes (London: Methuen, 1943).

Spinelli, E. *Tales of Un-Knowing* (London: Duckworth, 1997).

Wolters, C. *The Cloud of Unknowing* (Harmondsworth: Penguin, 1978).

5
The Supervisory Relationship

Laura Barnett

Introduction

Starting from the premise of human existence as being-in-the-world, this chapter looks at three people who revolutionised the way we look at the other and at relation, the philosophers Martin Buber and Emmanuel Lévinas, and the psychotherapist Carl Rogers. It then examines the supervisory relationship in the light of their thought. This is, at the same time, a personal work of exploration: until now I have learnt about supervision experientially, while absorbing from training and reading what captured my imagination and suited my way of being. I am therefore curious to see the picture that will emerge from taking these thinkers as my starting point, and to find out whether my own supervisory relationships resemble it.

Being-in-the-world

When Heidegger (1962) says that we are 'in' the world, 'in' does not refer to a place, but to a way of living *within* a web of meaningful connections (as in the expression 'in limbo' – a way of living which is marked by uncertainty). The hyphens express the inseparability of being, world and their meaningful connection. Being-in-the-world entails a view of human existence as being 'in relation': we are always in a relation of sorts with the world and others, for even avoidance of and indifference to others are forms of relating.

From this very rich concept, I would also like to highlight Heidegger's reminder that we are embodied beings and that we are always attuned in a particular way: we perceive the world and others (including our supervisor and supervisees) through our bodies, and our perceptions are coloured by the way we tune into the world, by the mood we are in (and we are never not in a mood). The world and others are meaningful to us: we are always making sense to ourselves of what we perceive and experience. Thus in the supervisory relationship, as elsewhere, we are always constantly interpreting, whether correctly or incorrectly, our perceptions and experience of the other.

Martin Buber (1878–1965)

> The basis of man's life with man is twofold, and it is one – the wish of every man to be confirmed as what he is, even as what he can become, by men; and the innate capacity in man to confirm his fellow men in this way … actual humanity exists only where this capacity unfolds (Agassi, 1999: 12).

Martin Buber had a keen interest in psychotherapy. He studied psychiatry for three semesters and corresponded with such thinkers as Jung, Binswanger, Friedman and Farber. He conducted a dialogue with Rogers before an audience of about four hundred people. Buber 'wanted to know about man… in the *so-called* pathological state' (Anderson & Cissna, 1997: 20) and felt that his 'philosophical anthropology'[1] had something to offer psychology (Agassi, 1999: 195).

Underpinning Buber's anthropology are the two poles of 'distance' and 'relation': we need to set others and the world at a distance to be able to observe, relate and engage. And we can then relate to the other as to an object (observing, experiencing, using), thus maintaining that 'primal' distance; or else we can seek, 'with our whole being', to relate to the other, while affirming him in his otherness. The latter kind of relationship, Buber argues, is what defines us as 'persons' rather than mere 'individuals'. However, 'No man is pure person and no man pure individuality' (Buber, 1996: 87) – Buber is not dealing in absolutes.

Buber encapsulates these two attitudes in the two 'primary words' *I-It* and *I-Thou*. It should be stressed that: *'Thou'* is the 'familiar' form of the personal pronoun (German *'Du'*, French *'tu'*); and that Buber is not saying that we relate as *I-It* towards objects/animals/nature and *I-Thou* towards men. We can relate to anything and anyone as either *I-It* or *I-Thou*. Thus we can relate to our supervisees and their clients in an *I-It* way: we can objectify them, judge them, use them, or we can seek to relate to them 'with our whole being' in an *I-Thou* manner. And the same applies to supervisees toward their supervisor. 'To man the world is twofold in accordance with his twofold attitude' (ibid: 15).

And yet, Buber adds, the basis of man's life with man is one: his wish to be confirmed, as what he is and in his potentiality, and his capacity to offer confirmation. Buber argues that 'actual humanity exists only where this capacity unfolds' (Agassi, 1999: 12). I would add that the supervisory relationship only thrives where the supervisor confirms the supervisee and the supervisee feels thus confirmed. However, 'Confirmation does not mean approval' (ibid: 86); it does not preclude challenging – indeed, it is a necessary condition for successful challenge. Confirmation is the affirmation of the other in his otherness and the realisation that 'no voice is without value, no witness without

---

[1] This is what Buber called his study of 'human nature', his 'ontology' of man and 'the between'.

reality' (Friedman, 1992: 121). Yet sadly, all too often, I have heard therapists recount experiences of having felt shamed, embarrassed, put down, judged, even bullied by their supervisors.

'The essential problem of the sphere of the interhuman is the duality of being and seeming' (Agassi, 1999: 75). Where supervisor and therapist lack personal and/or professional self-confidence and cannot confirm *themselves* as they are, they will develop ways of behaving that reflect how they wish to appear to each other and to themselves. As their behaviour is not grounded in the truth of 'the turning of their being' to the other, but only governed by *seeming*, a distorted dialogue ensues. This is where the authoritativeness of experience can turn into an authoritarian, judgemental and bullying attitude, as the supervisor seeks to 'impose' himself on his supervisees, rather than 'helping to unfold' their potentialities. And the supervisees' trust may then dissolve into dependency or defensiveness. When the relationship between the supervisor and supervisees ('the between') is thus distorted, the latter are more likely to offer a distorted presentation of their clients: 'seeming' then dominates over 'being', lies dominate over truth. Supervisees present 'case studies' to reflect the way they wish to appear to their supervisor or to forestall adverse comments.

For Buber, truth and authenticity arise in the interhuman realm when people show themselves and communicate without putting up a façade or barriers, and genuinely give of themselves. This stance requires a willingness on the part of both supervisors and supervisees to take the risk of opening themselves to one another and of being changed by the encounter. 'Relation is mutual. My Thou affects me as I affect it' (Buber, 1996: 30).

However, Buber adds that, within a therapeutic or educational relationship, such a mutuality of change does not imply full mutuality. He argues that the other has approached the therapist or educator in his professional capacity and therefore requires something from him; there is a non-mutuality of role. Furthermore, the therapist and the educator, to be effective, need to practice 'inclusion' and 'making present' – different ways of seeing and feeling things from the other's perspective. It is not the client's role to do this: if he were to practice inclusion and try to see things from the therapist's viewpoint, the healing relation would end. Besides, at this stage, the client is probably not capable of doing so: he cannot have and give the same 'detached presence' (Anderson & Cissna, 1997: 35) – in other words he is carrying too much 'baggage' into the relationship. While the non-mutuality of role applies to the supervisory relationship, the supervisee's ability to practise inclusion would presumably depend on the stage they had reached in their own personal development. The late June Roberts said that she could always tell 'how well therapped' (*sic!*) her supervisees were (1998): this was not meant in any judgemental sense, but as a reflection on the tone and quality of her supervisory relationships and the way they unfolded, and of what she felt she needed to or could give her supervisees.

Buber's philosophical anthropology is an ontology of man and 'the between' – between man and man, and between man and God. The two, for Buber, are intimately interconnected: for by entering into 'any *I-Thou* relation ... he [man] properly brings them to him, and lets them be fulfilled "in the face of God"' (Buber, 1996: 170). Buber's religiosity pervades his own work: even his concept of confirmation has a religious aspect to it, since 'confirming' a person in his potentiality means: 'I can recognize in him ... more or less, the person he has been ... *created* to become' (Anderson & Cissna, 1997: 91). Yet whether 'the eternal *Thou*' feels present in the supervisory relationship will depend on each supervisee and supervisor dialogue.

Buber's moving words following Hans Trüb's[2] death summarise the qualities he valued in a therapist. He praised his 'way of frightened pause, of unfrightened reflection, of personal involvement, of rejection of security, of unreserved stepping into relationship, of the bursting of psychologism, this way of vision and of risk' (Agassi, 1999: 21). He presumably would have expected similar qualities in a good supervisor.

The above description of Buber's *I-Thou* relation in many respects echoes the description of the relationship given in Chapter 3 which draws on Kierkegaard's concept of love. This is true particularly in terms of relating to others 'with our whole being' and also in terms of confirming a person in his or her potentiality.

Carl Rogers (1902–1987)

> ... a helping relationship might be defined as one in which one of the participants intends that there should come about, in one or both parties, more appreciation of, more expression of, more functional use of the latent inner resources of the individual (Kirschenbaum & Henderson, 1990: 108).

It might surprise some readers to see Carl Rogers described as being 'on the margins of existential therapy'. We are often so busy trying to define ourselves as existential therapists by clarifying what distinguishes us from our person-centred colleagues that we minimise our commonalities (Mearns & Cooper (2005) is a notable exception). Rogers was one of the speakers at the 1959 Symposium on Existential Psychology that explored those commonalities.

Rogers' person-centred therapy is firmly grounded in his image of the 'person': a person is always 'in the process of becoming' (Kirschenbaum & Henderson, 1990: 123) and his natural tendency is to change in 'a basically positive direction' (ibid: 27). 'A person has worth' (ibid: 176) and naturally possesses an invaluable 'total organismic sensing' of what feels right, which is a surer guide than the intellect alone (ibid: 23). Indeed, man is potentially 'one

---

[2]Psychotherapist to whom Buber was a mentor.

of the most widely sensitive, responsive, creative and adaptive creatures on this planet' (ibid: 405), though, sadly, his process of becoming 'can go terribly awry' (ibid: 408).

It follows from this philosophy of man, that the role of the supervisor is one of giving space to and facilitating the supervisee's own 'organismic valuing process' and his 'process of becoming' in general. This is not a matter of techniques (ibid: 233), but of the supervisor's attitude and how the supervisee perceives it (ibid: 113). For Rogers, the conditions for such a facilitative encounter are: 'psychological contact'; client 'incongruence' and therapist 'congruence'; 'unconditional positive regard'; 'an empathic understanding of the client's internal frame of reference'; and an ability 'to communicate this experience to the client' to a 'minimal degree'.

The first condition of 'psychological contact' expresses Rogers' firm belief that 'positive personality change' can only occur in a relationship (ibid: 221). The second condition, namely the client's 'state of incongruence, being vulnerable or anxious' may seem out of place in relation to a supervisee. While this is more likely to be found among trainees, it is sadly not absent from meetings, or rather 'mis-meetings' between some more experienced supervisees and supervisors. This arises, Rogers would presumably argue, either through their being bound by their past (ibid: 123) or through either person's lack of self-acceptance and acceptance of others (ibid: 19, 120). In other words, the supervisee's 'state of incongruence' and anxiety would be either a reflection of their own issues or a response to the supervisor's attitude and issues – or both.

The word 'congruence' replaces Rogers' earlier term 'transparency', yet each offers a different nuance: 'transparency' expresses more clearly the elements of awareness, honesty and sincerity, and an encounter where 'no feelings relevant to the relationship are hidden to me or the other person'(ibid). 'Congruence' on the other hand emphasises my being-with – both with myself in self-awareness and with the other (my supervisor or supervisee).

Rogers also stresses the importance of accepting the other in his otherness and in his potentiality, which he calls 'unconditional positive regard', 'acceptance' or 'prizing'. Although Buber did not recognise it at the time of their dialogue, this concept closely resembles his own concept of 'confirmation' (without its religious element), and the implications for the supervisory relationship are therefore the same as above.

> Can I step into his private world so completely that I lose all desire to evaluate or judge it? Can I enter it so sensitively that I can move about in it freely, without trampling on meanings that are precious to him? (ibid: 121)

'Acceptance' and 'empathic understanding' underpin a non-judgemental and non-evaluative stance, thus facilitating greater 'appreciation' and 'expression' of the supervisees' 'latent resources'. Yet, if a supervisor experiences a supervisee as working unethically with a client, this is an evaluation and in all congruence it cannot be ignored. Similarly, supervising in a college situation will involve evaluating trainees. Transparency in the relationship is what allows for challenge. The art is to 'enter sensitively', offering feedback in such a way that the supervisee still feels prized and heard, and can in turn hear and accept the feedback and 'achieve the maximum possible self-enhancement' (ibid: 180).

Transparency in the supervisory relationship, acceptance of self and others, and trust in the process of becoming will foster among both supervisor and supervisees 'an increasing openness to experience ... the polar opposite of defensiveness' (ibid: 412) and thus enhance, it is hoped, the 'functional use' of the supervisee's 'latent inner resources'.

Emmanuel Lévinas (1905–1995)

> ... the face speaks to me and invites me into a relation that is fundamentally incompatible with the exercise of power, whether the power of using and enjoying, or that of knowledge (Lévinas, 2000: 216).

> Communication is unlocked ... when we take the risk of uncovering ourselves, of ... allowing the other in and letting go of any shelter, when we expose ourselves to traumatism, through our vulnerability (Lévinas, 1996: 82).

Lévinas attended both Husserl and Heidegger's lectures in his youth and although he was not an existential philosopher himself, he engaged in a life-long personal dialogue with Heidegger and Buber's thought. Unlike Buber, Lévinas showed no particular interest in psychotherapy and he himself described his philosophy as a 'philosophy of utopia' (yet a number of therapists have expressed their indebtedness to his work for example: Gans (1999); Loewenthal & Snell (2000); Barnett (2001)).

Lévinas' contribution to philosophy, and I would argue to psychotherapy and supervision, is the concept of 'alterity' – total otherness. The other is totally other, not through any of his characteristics (psychological, physical) but by the very fact of being other. And as such, he is not simply beyond my knowledge – it is not that I cannot fully know him, but that the very idea of *knowing* another makes no sense. Lévinas symbolises alterity through the concept of the 'face', *le visage*, although not the face as one might observe or admire it: for in looking at its features, the face loses its meaning as 'face'. The face, for Lévinas, represents the other in his total nakedness and vulnerability, without titles, masks or fronts, the face of 'the poor, the stranger, the widow and the orphan' as it approaches us – the 'face' of our clients and our supervisees. The other's face calls unto me, it shatters 'my joyful possession of the world' (Lévinas, 2000: 73) and I feel called into question. It *is* 'disquieting', it may even unsettle me to the core. It speaks to me and invites me to relate to it, and I respond. Lévinas is here speaking a language with which we, as therapists, may well resonate.

However he goes further, 'beyond humanism': 'relation without relation', I did not *choose* as such to respond, I was called before freedom of choice ever existed, 'from time immemorial' – I was 'chosen'. In his vulnerability and nakedness the other commands me and I respond: I approach him and give him 'the bread from my mouth', with no expectation of anything in return. Yet the closer I get the further the distance that separates us. And I fear lest I do violence to him, for I am aware that by my very existence I am usurping 'another's place in the sun'. I am now responsible for him unto death, I am even responsible for expiating the sins he commits and no-one can take my place: my responsibility for him individuates me. I am hostage to him: *'human nakedness calls unto me … in its weakness … but … with strange authority, … God's word and Word in the human face'* (ibid: II–III). We cannot speak to God – not after the Shoah[3]; nor can we speak of Him – to do so would be to entrap the mystery of 'the Saying' in the words of 'the Said'. Yet, in the other's face, we can see a trace of this other Other ('illeity'), a trace of God. Lévinas encapsulates this 'asymmetrical relationship' in the two pronouns *je-vous*, I-you (the 'you' of politeness, denoting the other's position of height, as opposed to Buber's familiar 'Thou').

The above offers a glimpse of why Lévinas called his philosophy a philosophy of utopia. However, entering into a personal dialogue with Lévinas' thought can, I believe, open other dimensions for our therapeutic/supervisory work, as well as spell out their dangers and our limitations. The dangers for both our clients/supervisees and ourselves in feeling irreplaceable and responsible for them and their behaviour, hostage to them unto death are obvious. So too are our limitations: we cannot as therapists/supervisors give 'for free'– even where money is not involved, we may be giving for the pleasure of trying to 'help', the reward of seeing the client blossom and open to life, maybe for required contact hours, or our own sense of self-worth. Never 'for nothing'.

How then can Lévinas' thought inform our view of the supervisory relationship? First of all, he reminds us that the other is *'l'inénarrable'* – 'the one whose story can never fully be told', whom we can never capture in 'case studies'. He also reminds us that the relation is other-centred and embodied – no giving of oneself is divorced from the body; and that the other, by his otherness is different, but this difference is 'non-indifference'. As a supervisor I need to be aware of those differences and indeed value them (not simply those of race, sexuality and disability, but also of values, education, financial situation and class). Lévinas warns us against 'bringing the other back to the same': for us, comparing the unknown of our supervisees' experience or of

---

[3] I am following the French custom in using the Hebrew word, to draw attention to the undesirable semantic connotations of Holocaust as 'sacrificial offering'.

their clients' with the known of our own, whether through identification, modelling, interpreting according to text-book theory and so on.

Lévinas tempers his utopia with the concept of 'justice': justice, or 'the wisdom of love', and laws arose, not to prevent warring, but to help us compare and decide between incomparable others, when faced with more than one calling to us. The supervisor also requires such 'wisdom of love' to guide him in dividing his attention equitably between client and supervisee and, in group supervision, between supervisees and their clients.

Finally, Lévinas reminds us of ethical imperatives that precede, underpin and go far deeper than a set of professional Ethical Guidelines.

The Supervisory Relationship: The Emerging Picture

The relation as crucible of change

The picture that is emerging from this dialogue with Buber, Rogers and Lévinas is of a supervisory relationship that is focused, first and foremost, on the relationship itself (supervisor/supervisee and supervisee/client) – as opposed to the wider context[4] or the narrative content. For both Buber and Rogers, the relation is the crucible of change; so too for Lévinas, albeit from a very different perspective, as he was not primarily concerned with the concreteness of human relationships and ethical practice, but with the fundamental meaning of 'ethics'. Buber and Rogers however are not dealing with ideals and absolutes: they stress that *I-Thou* relations and genuine encounters can only be momentary (Buber, 1996: 51; Rogers in Kirschenbaum & Henderson, 1990: 225fn). We cannot sustain such relationships in supervision, but can only aim for moments of genuine meeting and dialogue, and their transformative power.

Both Buber and Rogers advocate 'the person-to-person attitude of a partner' (Buber 1996: 166), which we can oppose to a relationship where supervisor and supervisees put up a screen and privilege 'seeming' over 'being', objectify or use one another in an *I-It* way. In relation to the supervisee's clients, it involves not reifying them and fitting them into theoretical or diagnostic moulds. As supervisors, it means finding the right balance between observing our supervisees and their reactions – keeping a finger on the pulse of our relationship – and drifting into a judgemental or objectifying scrutiny of their mannerisms and the way they present themselves.

Embodiment and attunement

Lévinas' concept of alterity reminds us that we cannot properly fulfil Rogers' core condition of 'empathic understanding' or Buber's 'imagining the real': we

---

[4]Which reference to philosophers such as Foucault or Derrida would have emphasised.

cannot meaningfully put ourselves 'in the other person's shoes'. However, as attuned being-in-the-world (Heidegger) we do not need to try to suffer-*in* the other (*em*-pathise). We can tune into the other's mood, even if this mood lies in the background: we can sense the anxiety behind our supervisees' (or supervisor's) defensiveness, the 'nakedness' and 'vulnerability' behind the 'cover' of – for example, a joking mask. We can pick up the interplay of feelings in the room. I have called this way of sensing the between: 'mesopathy' (*meso* – the middle, the in-between space) (Barnett, 2009).

In supervision, the between can also include something of the client's presence: for the supervisee may carry into the supervision room, in an embodied manner, something of the feel of his sessions with his client and of their relationship. These feelings are now there open to mesopathy, between supervisee and supervisor: the supervisee's embodied sense of, for example, frustration, envy, anxiety, threat, delight, admiration or awe before the client, may be palpable. Distributing verbatim reports of a session for other group members to study is therefore counterproductive: it loses the therapist's unspoken, embodied contribution, as well as potentially leading to unhelpful criticisms – 'why did you say *that*?'

An embodied, attuned relationship also entails a relationship that is open to the sensing of vital energy, sensuality and sexuality in the other. This can be experienced as revitalising; on the other hand, even where that physicality and sexuality are not flaunted, they may be experienced as intrusive, intimidating or 'doing violence'. Congruence here is all important. The following chapter will explore these themes of embodiment and existential sexuality more fully.

Although Buber rejected what he called the 'centaur' view of man (human head and animal body) which devalues the body, he believed that only the unconscious preserved an undifferentiated body and psyche. 'If the unconscious is that part of the existence of a person in which the realms of the body and soul are not dissociated, then the relationship between two persons would mean the relationship between two non-divided existences' (Agassi, 1999: 241). That is indeed the conclusion we have already reached, from a Heideggerian perspective, without recourse to the unconscious. Heidegger's holistic concept of human existence as embodied being-in-the-world implies that there cannot be such a thing as an encapsulated psyche with its intra- and inter-psychic mechanisms, such as repression, transference and so on.

This is not to say that we do not bring our own 'baggage' into the supervisory relationship: according to Heidegger, both our projects and our past affect the way we view the present, and as Rogers points out we may be 'bound' by our past and unwittingly let it affect our relationship. Some people, I believe, carry a deeply rooted, embodied, predominant emotion to which other minor instances of it attach themselves; for example, for some it is shame, for others guilt, abandonment, terror, or loss. Until it is uprooted, that emotion infuses their relationship to the world and others, including their therapeutic and supervisory relationship (as when therapists cannot end with their clients, supervisors, or supervisees). The past that binds us also includes our unexplored values and assumptions.

Truth

Buber and Rogers underline the value of a self-questioning attitude (as indeed do Heidegger and Lévinas). Supervision offers us a place to think out loud, to question our assumptions, values, the projects we have and the past we carry. It seeks to discover what 'binds' us and is an obstacle in the supervisees' therapeutic work with their clients or in our work together.

A self-questioning attitude means allowing ourselves, whether supervisee or supervisor, to shed rigidity of belief and attitude, to be vulnerable and to learn from the other; it facilitates a mutuality of learning and change. Rogers goes further in advocating greater mutual transparency in the relationship (this is a concept that Buber could not understand (Anderson & Cissna, 1997: 38)). It is not about the supervisor's factual 'self-disclosure' – though personal feelings and reactions, where appropriate, may be tactfully divulged as phenomenological feedback. It is about being present, as oneself – rather than as a blank screen, an idealised self-portrayal or playing the role of supervisor. It is also about admitting when we were wrong, not colluding with our supervisees or hiding behind dogma.

Language, according to Heidegger, has its own wisdom; thus *aletheia* (truth) in ancient Greek reminds us that truth is a work of bringing out of concealment. However, he later adds, we can un-cover too much and bring too much to presence; we thereby miss the important interplay with that integral part that remains concealed, we miss the wholeness of truth. Thus in therapy and supervision, there is a danger of shining too much light on one story, issue or quality: we can become blinded by it and miss its interplay with the other stories, issues, traits, within which it is imbedded, as in a hologram in which only one facet ever comes to the fore.

Where difference and the otherness of the other are accepted, where the supervisor is sensitively attuned to his own and his supervisees' embodied presence, where reductionist dogmatism is banished and self-questioning and transparency prevail and where the supervisor is prepared to give of himself, without it being out of his own need, trust can grow and flourish. Trust in turn creates a safe enough space for joint reflection. Supervisees can then voice their perceived mistakes, insecurities, uncomfortable feelings towards their clients or even towards their supervisor, without anxiously seeking to pre-empt criticism, cover up or automatically justify themselves.

Spirituality

Heidegger, Buber, Rogers and Lévinas all abandoned, each in their distinctive way, 'the god of onto-theo-logy'. Yet the spiritual and the sacred retain an important place in their thought. Whether a spiritual dimension enters the supervisory relationship is not simply a matter of how religious either person is, but depends on the 'mesopathy' between supervisees and supervisor in the face of the mystery of existence. This links with and also contrasts with the viewpoint expressed in Chapter 3.

Conclusion

The above picture of the supervisory relationship has not so much surprised me, as led to further questions: what, if anything, do I feel is missing from it? How does it fit in with the literature on the supervisory relation-ship, which focuses variously on its tasks, context, roles, functions and pro-cess? Is there compatibility/incompatibility, partial overlap or is it a matter of different paradigms focusing on the same phenomena?

For instance, the absence here of 'transference' so present in some approaches (for example Hawkins & Shohet, 2000) is due to a philosophical incompatibil-ity (the absence, in existential therapeutic thought of a distinct psyche with its mechanisms); yet, as we saw, an existential approach will also uncover the obstacles (learnt ways of relating, assumptions, feelings carried in the body and so on) that affect the relationship. The context will also be present, as part of our being-in-the-world.

Does the supervisory relationship that has emerged have 'formative', 'nor-mative' and 'restorative' tasks or functions (Proctor, 2000)? The terms 'tasks' and 'function' do not sit comfortably with the above picture. However, both Buber and Rogers stress the facilitative, and hence 'restorative', role of the therapist/supervisor. Buber's insistence on the non-mutuality of role in a pro-fessional relationship opens the door to a formative and normative element within the supervisory relationship: not in terms of 'tasks', 'skills' (Carroll, 1996); 'strategies and interventions' (Hawkins & Shohet, 2000); but in terms of 'helping unfold' the supervisees' self-questioning attitude and awareness in their response to their clients. Less is left to trust in the supervisee's capacity to self-actualise into a 'good enough therapist' – as in Tudor and Worrall's (2003) strong Rogerian approach. Indeed there is a danger for such trust to lead to collusion or manipulation.

My only surprise is the absence of the word 'boundaries'[5] from the picture that has emerged of the supervisory relationship – interestingly it is also absent from the index to the Carl Rogers' Reader. Learning to develop boundaries not bar-riers is, I believe, one of the most important parts of our training as therapists and remains important in supervision: boundaries of time, place, touch and self-disclosure that are clear, firm but not rigid, and boundaries of receptivity that are permeable and do not keep the other out, yet can prevent the sponge effect.

I now feel that, with my own two supervisors, I can own up openly to my mistakes and insecurities without fear of condemnation either as a therapist or

---

[5]Confidentiality, whilst absent, is clearly taken for granted by both Buber and Rogers.

as a person; and, they too have offered me a glimpse into their own vulnerability. Interestingly, I now sense increased mutual warmth and respect. The process of writing this chapter has also spurred me to start revisiting my supervisory relationships with my supervisees.

Rogers was once asked for his description of 'the good life'; he replied: 'a process that is *"enriching, exciting, rewarding, challenging, meaningful"'* (Kirschenbaum & Henderson, 1990: 420). The same could be said of good supervision.

References

Agassi, J. Buber (ed.) *Martin Buber on Psychology and Psychotherapy, Essays, Letters and Dialogue* (Syracuse: University Press, 1999).

Anderson, R. & Cissna, K. N. *The Martin Buber – Carl Rogers Dialogue: A New Transcript with Commentary* (New York: University of New York Press, 1997).

Barnett, L. 'The Other's Eye and I', *Existential Analysis* 12(2) (2001) 336–44.

—— (ed.) *When Death Enters the Therapeutic Space: Existential Perspectives in Psychotherapy and Counselling* (London: Routledge, 2009).

Buber, M. *I and Thou* Trans. R. G. Smith, 2nd (revised) edn. (Edinburgh: T&T Clark, 1996).

Caroll, M. *Counselling Supervision: Theory, Skills and Practice* (London: Cassell, 1996).

Friedman, M. *Dialogue and the Human Image: Beyond Humanistic Psychology* (London: Sage, 1992).

Gans, S. 'What is Ethical Analysis?' *Existential Analysis* 10(2) (1999) 102–8.

Hawkins, P. & Shohet, R. *Supervision in the Helping Professions*, 2nd edn (Buckingham: Open University Press, 2000).

Heidegger, M. *Being and Time* Trans. J. Macquarrie & E. Robinson (Oxford: Blackwell, [1927] 1962).

Kirschenbaum, H. & Henderson, V. L. (eds) *The Carl Rogers Reader* (London: Constable, 1990).

Lévinas, E. *Autrement qu'être et au-delà de l'essence* (Paris: Kluwer Academic, [1974] 1996).

—— *Totalité et Infini, essai sur l'Extériorité* (Paris: Kluwer Academic, [1961] 2000).

Loewenthal, D. & Snell, R. 'Levinas and the Postmodern Therapist', *Existential Analysis* 11(1) (2000) 136–43.

Mearns, D. & Cooper, M. *Working at Relational Depth* (London: Sage, 2005).

Proctor, B. *Group Supervision: A Guide to Creative Practice* (London: Sage, 2000).

Roberts, J. *Personal Communication* (London: 1998).

Tudor, K. & Worrall, M. (eds) *Freedom to Practise: Person-centred Approaches to Supervision* (Ross-on-Wye: PCCS Books, 2003).

6

Existential Sexuality and Embodiment

Paul Smith-Pickard

Introduction

As soon as we mention sexuality and embodiment in the same sentence as psychotherapy or supervision it is perhaps inevitable that the twin ghosts of Freud (1905) and Reich (1983) will appear lurking in the shadows and this poses a slight problem for existential therapists. In subscribing to the notion that we are not isolated egos but embodied beings in a shared world, existential psychotherapy has understandably been defined in opposition to some of the fundamental ideas within psychoanalysis. This is a tradition stemming back to Binswanger (1963) and Boss (1963) and the early days of Daseinsanalysis. Given the central significance of sexuality in the work of both Freud and Reich it is perhaps inevitable that sexuality and the body have not featured strongly in much that has been written on the subject of existential psychotherapy. Furthermore the pioneers of daseinsanalysis took their inspiration from Heidegger and his seminal work *Being and Time* (1962), which has no mention of sexuality whatsoever and, as Sartre (1996) pointed out: his 'Dasein' appears asexual. Conversely for Sartre: 'the For-itself is sexual in its very upsurge in the face of the Other and through it sexuality comes into the world' (Sartre, 1996: 406).

Why should we then bring existential sexuality and embodiment into our thoughts about supervision and the various ways in which we might be engaged in the supervisory encounter? As both Sartre (1996) and Merleau-Ponty (1996) have pointed out, existential sexuality and embodiment are two fundamental elements of existence that lie at the heart of every encounter. If these philosophers are correct it is not then a question of us deciding to bring existential sexuality and the body into supervision because, whether we acknowledge them within the encounter or not, they are always already there as irreducible elements. Sartre and Merleau-Ponty are not alone in their views on sexuality as we find them echoed in the work of Foucault (1990) as well as some contemporary forms of relational psychotherapy (DeYoung, 2003) and analysis (Maroda, 2002), and body psychotherapy (Asheri, 2004).

In this chapter I will attempt to describe how these elements feature in my own practice as a supervisor and also provide some philosophical basis for my work. Hopefully this will take us far away from any confusion of seeing existential sexuality and the body in supervision as being concerned with some sort of 'existential sex therapy' and bring us to an understanding of how existential sexuality is used to co-construct an embodied narrative in the therapeutic encounter and that it needs to be regarded similarly in supervision. This then leads us into seeing existential sexuality as a mutual system that attempts to capture or appropriate the embodied consciousness of the other, whilst at the same time offering one's own body, or embodied self, to be impressed upon by receiving the resemblance and otherness of the other. What I am describing is existential sexuality as a system of reciprocity whereby we fascinate and are fascinated by the other, appropriate and are appropriated by the other, and desire the other's desire for us. I will begin with some thoughts about supervision.

Meeting 'Myself' in Supervision

My work as a supervisor has mainly been developed from my personal experience of supervision – distilling from this what I have found both helpful and unhelpful. This includes my experiences both as a supervisee and as a supervisor. It is also informed by my experience as a psychotherapist and is underpinned by certain philosophical ideas that I would describe broadly as existential and post-modern. Looking back over my own experiences as a supervisee, I feel fortunate to have had two long-term supervisors both of whom allowed me to explore the thoughts and feelings that I had about myself in relation to my clients. They did this without judging me and yet helping me to be aware of ethical and professional boundaries. They both shared my interest in metaphor and were widely read in professional texts and in literature generally, all of which they brought into our work. I felt that they both cared deeply about the work I was doing with my clients and in turn I felt a huge amount of respect for both of them. I remember one of them saying that in therapy people sometimes hear themselves as if for the first time. And if they are really lucky they get to meet themselves as if for the first time. This idea has remained with me as a potent image of psychotherapy in the sense that the presence of another person provides us with the opportunity to encounter ourselves differently. As I will show, it is through other people that we know who we are, and it is also through us that they find a sense of identity: 'One recognises *oneself* in that old smile of recognition from that old friend' says Laing (1990: 87).

It was in supervision with these two supervisors that I began to meet myself as a psychotherapist in ways that were just not possible from the experience of working with my clients alone. It was the way in which I was able to speak to them which was significant. Needless to say that the way I spoke was directly related to the way they listened. Their listening encouraged, in the sense that it gave me the courage to speak my thoughts as they were without too much reserve or editing. I was listening to myself speak and meeting myself at the same time whilst observing my supervisor respond to my words in a sort of mutual reciprocity. I do not want to give the impression that our encounters were always harmonious and that there was no dissonance between us. There were times when I felt that I was unable to communicate what I had experienced in my client work and times when they both seemed to have made unhelpful assumptions about the interaction between my clients and myself. Frequently my descriptions of my experiences seemed to fall short of the feelings within the actual experiences themselves. I often wanted to address what was happening in the room between us but at that point in my career I felt unable to do so and neither of them seemed to be inclined to explore it.

Was I aware of existential sexuality and embodiment in the room? First of all I have to confess that I had a strong desire to be approved of by both of them. It was not so much that I wanted them to like me. It was more that I wanted validation and legitimating from them. It was as if I gave them the power to tell me if I was an adequate therapist or not. The supervision definitely suffered because of this as it meant that I was not always as open as I could have been about some of the feeling content around desire between my clients and myself. It was not the verbal content of what had taken place that I was editing in supervision but the non-verbal felt senses and interaction. Certainly the experience of working with these supervisors was a significant factor in my becoming interested in the ideas expressed in this chapter. I would not have called it existential sexuality at the time but in hindsight there was often a powerful embodied narrative going on between us during supervision. There was also a sense of bodily disturbance with one of them that was at times linked to a level of erotic desire on my part. I felt a bodily disturbance in her at times but it was never brought into the supervision.

My interactions with these supervisors helped me to make sense of my experience with clients, and then later with supervisees whilst at the same time helping me to allow a picture of myself as a psychotherapist to emerge. My self-identity as a professional, both as a therapist and a supervisor, has been deeply forged through the process of supervision. However this self-identity is not something that is fixed.

As Cohn (1997) has pointed out: from a phenomenological perspective if two therapists meet the same client it will not be the same client. Similarly I would suggest that I am a different psychotherapist with each of my clients and a different supervisor with each of my individual supervisees or supervision groups. I would even go further to suggest that despite what Jaspers (1969) calls 'a relative constancy' in myself as either a therapist or a supervisor, my clients and supervisees basically meet a new 'me' and a new 'them' in each separate encounter. It is as if we have to re-find ourselves in each encounter with each new person and a fundamental way in which we negotiate this is through the deployment of existential sexuality.

This fundamental understanding that in every encounter we are different people and are in turn experienced differently, neatly captured in the phrase 'I have as many personalities as I have friends', is clearly a position shared by all the authors in this volume. They would also recognise that inevitably the way in which we experience someone is as much about ourselves as it is about the other.

Existential Sexuality

> The question is not so much whether human life does or does not rest on sexuality, as of knowing what is to be understood by sexuality (Merleau-Ponty, 1996: 158).

I have deliberately used the phrase 'existential sexuality' rather than just the word 'sexuality' in an attempt to distinguish it (however incompletely) from some of the unhelpful assumptions within the various colloquial uses of the word where sexuality becomes an object. An example of this is when people talk about 'my sexuality' as a defining characteristic of identity. In the context of this chapter, it is also important to state that we are not *specifically* referring to supervising work with clients who are presenting with issues of gender confusion, sexual orientation, sexual difficulty, body image, or even an 'existential sex therapy' (although these may well be issues that emerge within the course of therapy). What we are referring to here is an existential image of sexuality, as an interpersonal phenomenon that is always present, as Merleau-Ponty says: 'like an atmosphere' (1996: 168).

One of the difficulties of working with a concept like sexuality is its relation to sex and the frequent conflation of one term into the other. The relation of sex to existential sexuality is more of the order of figure to ground where sex is simply an aspect of existential sexuality where the deployment or articulation of existential sexuality is not dependent on a genital focus or sexual maturity. As the deployment of existential sexuality exists throughout the lifespan and is not simply focused on sex, we might ask, what is the intention behind existential sexuality, and how might we recognise it? In his notion of '*complementarity*', Laing showed us that by focusing on sexual acts or sexual instinct and orgasmic satisfaction alone, we are ignoring; 'the erotic desire to make a difference to the other' (Laing, 1990: 85).

'Complementarity' is that function of relationship where self-identity is achieved through an Other. We exist in a shared world where the image and presence of the Other is constantly with us as a horizon and also as a threat to our existence. The Other can both existentially validate us and negate us. We need to both give and receive in order to be able to make a difference to another, and to do so is to be existentially validated by them and they by us in a form of mutual reciprocity. If what we give is not received or accepted then it leaves us feeling empty, especially if what we are giving is some aspect of ourselves.

The fundamental way in which we attempt to preserve or maintain our self-identity in this mutual encounter is through the deployment of existential sexuality. Strange as it may seem, a useful key in understanding existential sexuality as an interpersonal phenomenon, (rather than an instinctual libido), is the phenomenon of desire. In desire, what we desire is to be desired by the Other, and in our attempts to make a difference to another, to be existentially validated by others, we use existential sexuality to attempt to capture their consciousness. Obvious examples of this would be to flirt or to charm, although the seduction of consciousness is generally less blatant and we learn to do this in varying degrees of sophistication or even desperation from earliest childhood.

Desire is communicated through the whole body and in particular through the eyes and what Sartre (1996) calls *'the look'*. We experience desire as a troubling moment of self-consciousness, an upsurge of the world that reveals our embodied presence to both ourselves and to others. We experience desire as a bodily disturbance but what we desire is not simply another's body but a body alive with consciousness that can desire us back in turn. The self-consciousness of desire helps us to recognise the ambiguous dimensions of the body that we simultaneously experience as being both a subject and an object for us. What can become confusing here is that although I may claim that existential sexuality is co-extensive with life and exists much of the time without a sexual content (that is not orgasmically focused), any sexual encounter that is orgasmically focused will be an articulation of existential sexuality. It is not an either/or situation and desire can easily become erotic and possibly sexual when the possibility of sex emerges as figure from the ground of existential sexuality.

These thoughts become interesting and challenging if we relate them to the way we might be with supervisees or with clients in a consulting room. Ideas of 'eye contact' and 'body language' take on a different meaning or bias when we relate them to existential sexuality and desire.

In a post-Cartesian world there is no mind without a body and similarly there is no existential sexuality without other people or embodied subjects with whom I share a world. Existential sexuality is played out around this ambiguous phenomenon of embodiment and one of the places that it is played out is in the consulting room. Supervision is not a meeting of two minds but of two incarnated consciousnesses embedded in a shared world where sexuality 'spreads forth like an odour or a sound' (Merleau-Ponty, 1996: 168). Let me now turn to the body and examine some different aspects of embodiment.

Aspects of Embodiment

The world is experienced through our bodies and embodiment points to the fact that our bodies are the site of our experience. But our bodies also function as a repository of experience, and a residue of our experience is evident in the ways in which we articulate our body. In other words we embody our histories. For example, we can all recognise familiar idiosyncratic gestures in other people whom we know, and we all have our own personal repertoire of movements and gestures, which are as distinctive as our facial characteristics. They are aspects of our identity for others, and have been shaped by our lived relationship with the world. This repertoire of our *habitual body* reflects our history in as much as it contains all the learnt structures of behaviour and our customary ways of relating and interacting.

These idiosyncratic articulations, which provide each of us with our own 'embodied vernacular', are for the most part, outside of our awareness. That is not to say that I am unaware of my body. As Merleau-Ponty has pointed out, at any given moment I experience ambiguous subjective and objective dimensions of the *phenomenal body* as the 'body I am' and the 'body I have'. My *phenomenal body* is both subject and object for me and for anyone else who encounters me. It is the experience of my body interacting with the world in the present moment. My *phenomenal body* has a powerful element of self-consciousness arising from the fact that in the act of perception there is reversibility where I become a perceiving/perceivable. By this I mean that I can see Others in the knowledge that I also can be seen by Others and this makes me self-conscious as I can never escape my awareness of the Other. This persisting self-consciousness means that subjectivity is always intersubjectivity.

I project myself into an imagined future and world with others through my *virtual body*, which is derived from the possibilities and limits discovered in the *phenomenal body* and my history stored within the *habitual body*. The *habitual body* has much in common with Bourdieu's (1990, 2000) concept of *habitus*, which attempts to bring together the embodied and embedded (in-the-world) nature of our existence. He says that we feel at home in the world because the world is also in us.

Habitus

Bourdieu's notion of *habitus* is one that permeates both my therapeutic practice and my supervision practice. *Habitus* is something that gives substance to our existential predicament of being-in-the-world-with-others and specifically locates us within an intersubjective and unified field of existence. *Habitus* is both personal and shared, in the form of cultural schemas and ideological conditions that we embody personally, and then use collaboratively to construct the conditions for a consensus of common sense that functions below the level of awareness and language. *Habitus* is more than simply the context of our lives. It is also the repeating patterns and structures of relationship that we embody, as well as our worldview, our *cultural capital* (a set of cultural experiences, values, beliefs, norms, attitudes and so forth that equip people for their life in society), and the relatively constant sense we may have of ourselves as a differentiated self.

In supervision an exploration of *habitus* encourages the principle of reflexivity and supervisor transparency because I have to accept that my practice will contain certain habits that I am unaware of, or take for granted, in the form of self-evident dispositions and styles of perception, thought, and action. These out-of-awareness habits have been acquired through my history and the life of my body. They are habits of my lived body and they in-habit me.

As a supervisor and as a therapist I am vigilant about challenging my habitual ways of functioning and my commonsense attitudes concerning the practice of psychotherapy. I also challenge them in my supervisees and encourage them to do the same for themselves and with their clients. In this way supervision becomes a three-way process through which all participants benefit and gain understanding.

Existentially Informed Supervision

As a supervisor myself I have provided supervision to people from different therapeutic orientations as well as existential therapists. I offer my supervisees 'existentially informed' supervision. The reason for this is that I do not consider that there is a comprehensive or single definitive body of thought and practice that can be called existential psychotherapy. There are only existential approaches to therapy that occasionally collect around a person, an institution, or set of ideas that are informed by a body of philosophical thought, and by the wider field of psychotherapy. This being so, it is perhaps obvious that there will inevitably be different views as to what constitutes supervision from an existential perspective, as is evidenced by the present volume. This is a reflection of the discussion in Chapter 1 where it was suggested that existential supervision provides an opportunity for integration and offers an overarching philosophical framework for work whatever the orientation.

All I can offer in this chapter is an understanding of my own experience as both supervisor and supervisee in the full awareness that what I say has the potential to be read at some future date by colleagues with whom I entered into a process of supervision. I trust that what I say has some recognition and meaning for them based upon our co-constructed supervision encounters where I have attempted to dissolve the scholastically constructed boundary that Bourdieu (2000) warns us about, between the 'world in which one thinks' and the 'world in which one lives'. He describes a scholastic world where the act of speaking and thinking about practice actually separates us from practice. I regard the tension between these two worlds as a fundamental challenge in supervision when we are attempting to work within a philosophically informed framework. Especially when we are trying to make sense of both practice and experience, which is, after all, a large part of what I consider supervision to be about.

This distinction is also reflected in the structure of this chapter where I am using a scholastic framework (the world in which one thinks or writes) in an attempt to illuminate practice (the world in which one lives). This may be seen perhaps as an artificial distinction but it is a device or metaphor to help us have some clarity about the way that we embody our therapeutic practice. A practice for which it is sometimes difficult to find a perspective that might challenge our assumptions about what we have done and what we think we are doing. Again this is another of the challenges of supervision for me.

And so how do my thoughts on supervision relate to the topic of this chapter? Let us return to Merleau-Ponty to throw some light on how what I have already said about supervision might be connected to existential sexuality and embodiment.

Embodied Inter-Experience

> Since sexuality is relationship to other persons, and not just to another body, it is going to weave the circular system of projections and introjections, illuminating the unlimited series of reflecting reflections and reflected reflections which are the reasons why I am the other person and he is myself (Merleau-Ponty, 1998: 230).

This quotation may at first glance seem somewhat cryptic but what Merleau-Ponty is describing here is sexuality as a form of what I would term 'embodied inter-experience'. He is describing sexuality as a shared embodied presence and mutual or consummate reciprocity within an encounter. Embodied inter-experience is I believe a phenomenon that we may all experience or sense, but which is difficult to put into words. It is not simply the embodied experience of two people meeting, which may lead to an implicit knowing or co-constructed 'felt sense' that is shared, but, what Sartre describes as, 'an upsurge in the face of the Other' (Sartre, 1996: 406). For Sartre this upsurge is an attempt to capture the consciousness of the Other in a bid to grasp the Other's 'free subjectivity'. Merleau-Ponty however does not share the same linear view of intentionality, for him there is always a sense of reversibility where I can only touch in the knowledge that I too can be touched, I perceive in the awareness that I too can be perceived.

Working with existential sexuality and embodiment in supervision is not simply about reporting information or analysing a verbatim account. It is about developing an awareness of the subtle ways in which we engage and disengage with each other, along with learning to listen with our whole being. Existential sexuality operates at the level of an embodied narrative running alongside or independently of any spoken narrative linking us to each other through our bodies. It is like a dance where we become something or someone we never could have become by ourselves. Who we meet in this dance may not be who we thought we were or who we could be. We may be delighted or disappointed, but whoever and whatever we find can be used to develop our practice and ourselves as well as give us insights into our clients. Understanding sexuality from an existential perspective can help us understand the articulation of the 'in-between' and the ambiguous reversibility in the meeting with the other and through that, the meeting of oneself in ways that are unexpected and unplanned.

When I am working with another person I am constantly attempting to be aware of the strength of their impact on me as well as trying to judge my impact on them. Mostly I experience this in the form of a bodily awareness in the ebb and flow of contact and loss of contact. Often when I concentrate on my bodily felt-senses, words come to me in the form of questions, comments, or interventions that are spontaneous. Sometimes these tacit words are insightful and accurate, sometimes not. If not, supervisees will quickly correct me and this in itself opens up new avenues for exploring my misperception and my tacit bodily felt sense. In other words my bodily felt sense of the embodied presence of the other person becomes a tool in our exploration of the supervisee's experiential recall of their experiences with their client and the experience of recollecting those experiences in the present moment of supervision.

How can I trust these intuitive senses? The answer lies in my openness to the other person's body and in trusting what it tells me. As I have already indicated earlier, our bodies have various aspects to them some of which are tied to the pre-personal life of our *'habitus'* in the form of the *'habitual body'*, then there is our *'phenomenal body'* which allows us to anticipate and participate in a world of possibilities, and then the *'virtual body'* that allows us to transcend our immanence into a speculative future of possibilities. This focus on the body is surprisingly informative in supervision as all of these aspects come into play.

If we offer our phenomenal body into the space of the supervision we can allow the other person to impress themselves upon us in ways that cannot be linguistically articulated. We can listen and communicate with our bodies. One of my supervisees described to me the sessions of active and involved silence that he shared with one of his clients where so much was 'said' that was outside of language. Our habitual bodies, that is the supervisee's and my own, offer all sorts of clues and understandings that reveal both our histories and our structures of behaviour in a co-constructed embodied narrative.

This is similar to the experience of the in-between discussed in the previous chapter and also echoes the 'mesopathy' introduced by the previous author. In Chapter 15 the 'bodily felt sense' referred to here will be expanded upon and developed further.

Conclusion

For my part as the supervisor in the encounter I try to model the same level of awareness of embodied inter-experience and existential sexuality as I do with my own clients. I attempt to share my experience of what is taking place in the encounter through self-involving statements about my perceptions surrounding the current interaction in a collaborative spirit of curious enquiry.

To begin with I encourage my supervisees to try and develop an awareness of how their client is impacting on them at a bodily felt sense level. I also try and bring an awareness of what is being experienced between us in the room currently as bodily felt senses, what I have already referred to as embodied inter-experience. By this I mean how do their clients invite their therapist to see them through their clothes, gestures, and speech? I often ask questions such as: How do you feel when you are with this client and after they have gone? And how do you want this client to see you? What are you doing to try and get this client to engage with you? How important is it for you that this client likes you? Do you like them? Do you find them attractive, helpless, irritating, manipulating, unreachable, repulsive or seductive? How comfortable do you feel in the room with them? Do you feel skilled/deskilled? Do you look forward to seeing them or do you dread it? How much of the time do you feel that you are 'in contact' with this client? What does it feel like to lose contact with the client?

These are questions designed to disclose the way in which existential sexuality and embodiment are deployed in my supervisees' work with their clients. Along with this I encourage self-reporting on the immediate experience of supervision, especially instances of bodily disturbance. In short, I see my existentially informed supervision as a reversible system of mutual reciprocity within a unified field where I invite my supervisees to dance in the awareness 'that I am the other person and he is myself' (Merleau-Ponty, 1998: 230).

References

Asheri, S. 'Erotic Desire in the Therapy Room. Dare We Embody It? Can We Afford Not To?' (Talk given at the UKCP Conference on 11th September 2004).

Binswanger, L. *Being in the World: Selected Papers.* Trans. J. Needleman (New York: Basic Books, 1963).

Boss, M. *Psychoanalysis and Daseinsanalysis.* Trans. L. B. Lefebre (New York: Basic Books, 1963).

Bourdieu, P. *In Other Words: Essays Toward a Reflexive Sociology.* Trans. M. Adamson (Cambridge: Polity Press, 1990).

—— *Pascalian Meditations.* Trans. R. Nice (Cambridge: Polity Press, 2000).

Cohn, H. W. *Existential Thought & Therapeutic Practice* (London: Sage, 1997).

DeYoung, P. A. *Relational Psychotherapy: A Primer* (Hove: Brunner-Routledge, 2003).

Foucault, M. *The History of Sexuality: Vol. 1 An Introduction* (London: Penguin, 1990).

Freud, S. *Three Essays on the Theory of Sexuality.* Standard Edition, Vol. 7 (London: Hogarth Press, 1905).

Heidegger, M. *Being and Time.* Trans. J. Macquarrie & E. Robinson (Oxford: Blackwell, [1927] 1962).

Jaspers, K. *Philosophy.* Trans. E. B. Ashton (Chicago: University of Chicago Press, 1969).

Laing, R. D. *Self and Others* (London: Penguin, 1990).

Maroda, K. *Seduction, Surrender, and Transformation* (Hillsdale: Analytic Press, 2002).

Merleau-Ponty, M. *Phenomenology of Perception*. Trans. C. Smith (London: Routledge & Kegan Paul, 1996).
—— *Signs*. Trans. R. McCleary (Evanston: North Western University Press, 1998).
Reich, W. *The Function of the Orgasm* (London: Souvenir Press, 1983).
Sartre, J-P. *Being and Nothingness*. Trans. H. E. Barnes (London: Routledge, 1996).

Part II

Existential Supervision in Practice

Introduction

Emmy van Deurzen and Sarah Young

This second part of the book concentrates on the actual practice of existential supervision and focuses on particular client groups and particular settings. The first chapter (Chapter 7) introduces us to the aims of existential supervision with an emphasis on the pursuit of truth. This chapter provides some concrete and practical parameters to guide the work of existential supervision – giving us both a map and compass. A vivid and engaging description of a supervisee's struggles with a depressed client brings the process of existential supervision fully alive. The process is shown to be a collaborative search for understanding and truth in relation to the client's experience which inevitably involves and impacts on the supervisee's worldview. Numerous examples of questions with which to challenge ourselves and our supervisees and ultimately our clients demonstrate that existential supervision is both eminently practical and at the same time a passionate endeavour which can be life changing for all those involved. This chapter provides a paradigm for the practice of existential supervision.

The second chapter (Chapter 8) in this section gives a clear and lively description of the procedures and practices of the real-time live discussion which is online existential group supervision. Supervisees are encouraged to prepare presentations and think about their underlying prejudices and assumptions. Working online provides a unique opportunity for the use of transcripts of actual online exchanges and for the detailed discussion of verbatim reports (as advocated earlier in Chapter 4 on phenomenology), which are considered an essential aspect of online supervision. The author highlights the unique advantages of working online and acknowledges that unlike some existential supervisors/therapists she regards 'leaping in' as the cornerstone of the process (see the following chapter for a contrary view and also Chapter 13) The work is exhilarating, 'different but not worse than face-to-face' and supervisees have an opportunity to learn about themselves, their work and ways of being.

Chapter 9 explores existential supervision in the context of work with addiction. By adopting a philosophical perspective, the author questions the way we conceptualise supervision, addiction, and the supervision of addiction.

Whether people presenting with problems of addiction can be clearly distinguished as a sub-set of those who present with other life problems is also questioned. The reasons why this distinction is frequently applied are discussed and it is shown how the assumptions that underpin this distinction may limit our ability to encounter our clients. A specific way of conceptualising existential supervision is proposed. While non-dogmatic it recognises the foundational status of relationship in existential therapy and the inclusion of an 'existential focus' function to clarify the nature of the co-constituted therapeutic alliance.

The next chapter (Chapter 10) echoes the previous one in focusing on a specific group, namely young women offenders. The author demonstrates that the existential dilemmas these women face are the same as for us all, though their situations are more acute – hence their experience is the 'same and different'. Despite the limitations imposed on these young women the assumption that their futures are determined by their appalling past experiences is challenged. Again, as elsewhere in this text, relationship is seen as central, it is suggested that most, if not all human difficulties manifest in the relational realm of existence. The importance of our worldview is also recognised and is seen as fundamental to our experience of life. The same process of dialogue discussed in previous chapters is seen to underpin the supervisory relationship. Most importantly it is emphasised that the existential attitude serves as a foundation for all our engagement with the world – it is not something that is merely applied: it is real. Existential supervision is shown to be particularly suited to the prison context discussed in this chapter.

Existential supervision in the NHS is the focus of the final chapter in this part (Chapter 11). While the existential approach is not normally the method of choice in the health service, this chapter argues that it has an important contribution to make, especially in terms of supervision. The particular relevance and appropriateness of existential supervision in the NHS in working with trainee psychiatrists is discussed. An extended case vignette demonstrates how the more medical stance, which is usual in this context, can be extended to include a more descriptive and heuristic narrative approach. It is clear that existential supervisors may be able to contribute a new dimension of understanding to an otherwise rather pragmatic setting.

7

Aims of Existential Supervision: Truth as a Guiding Light

Emmy van Deurzen

But all things excellent are as difficult as they are rare (Spinoza, Ethics: V: XLII).

Introduction

The aims of existential supervision are multiple and diverse. But they are always to:

1. Help therapists and clients to tell the truth about their lives and their relationships: this means first of all teaching them to recognise their own bias and personal worldview.
2. Enable therapists to become more open, more understanding, more calm, steady and strong in relation to their clients and their therapeutic work.
3. Learn new things about self, other and the multiple connections and aspects of human living.
4. Throw new light on human issues and difficulties, elucidating and clarifying what was obscure, secret, unknown or confused.
5. Enable therapists and clients to live a better life in tune with their values, making the most of their situation, talents and experience.
6. Monitor the ethical and moral issues that may threaten clients' or therapist's safety.

Four Dimensions of Existence

In order to achieve some of these very general and abstract objectives we need to formulate concrete and practical parameters to guide our work. We need a map and a compass to show therapists how to understand where clients are lost, and how they might find themselves. The map is not that of personality theory or psychopathology but that of the overall territory of life itself.

83

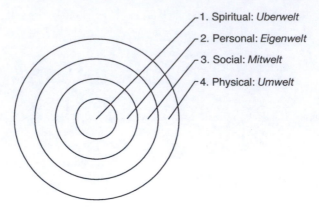

1. Spiritual: *Uberwelt*
2. Personal: *Eigenwelt*
3. Social: *Mitwelt*
4. Physical: *Umwelt*

Figure 7.1   Four dimensions of life

If we consider the four dimensions of life (see Figure 7.1) to be arranged in a spherical constellation, a three dimensional model of an individual's world is generated. At the core of this sphere is the spiritual dimension, where meaning is created. This is usually experienced as the centre of our world. It is the most intimate dimension of existence and close to the heart of our inner being. But it is also the most hidden and often taboo aspect of life. It is also from this core that we find direction in our lives and that we feel connected to a kernel of truth. In the next layer from the core, the personal dimension, we still feel very private individuals and it is here that we think about ourselves and define our narrative history, our character and temperament. We like to keep much of this hidden, fearful of judgement, though considered and caring feedback invariably gives this sense of self a boost of energy. Much of our interactions remain reserved on the next layer, the social dimension, where we relate to others from a carefully constituted social persona, or ego, which others can like or dislike and argue with, praise or challenge. The outside layer of our existential reality is that of our physical presence in the world, the body self or the flesh that forms the skin that actually touches the world of objects and other bodies and is touched by the world in return.

Supervision can be a good moment for sketching a picture of the ways in which the client is engaged with the world, on physical, social, personal and spiritual levels and to pinpoint where her strengths and weaknesses, discomforts and confidence lie. It allows us to get a better sense of values and beliefs. The same also applies to the supervisee, for it is impossible to help a therapist think about another person, without clarity about herself. So, as we sketch a picture of the client's worldview, we compare and contrast this to the therapist's own.

Passions, Values and Emotions

But it is not enough to have this rational and intellectual grasp of the client's and the therapist's perspectives. As supervisors we need to put our finger on the issues that the client and the therapist are most emotionally concerned about. We ask ourselves what it is that drives the client to distraction and despair and how this resonates or 'dissonates' with the therapist. This means of course that supervisors need to feel secure in their personal understanding of emotion so as to provide the wisdom and stability to explore strong feelings from a position of calm presence.

Emotions are a response to the gain or loss of a person's values. They indicate where we find ourselves in relation to the things we value or scorn. The compass (Figure 7.2) of emotions can therefore help us locate and understand our position on the map of existence. It helps us navigate in troubled waters, or find our way out of the woods (see Deurzen, 2002; Deurzen & Arnold-Baker, 2005). The emotions at the top of the compass feel like a high, whereas those at the bottom feel like a low. The emotions on the left hand side are those of anxiety, indicating engagement with what we value and want, whereas the emotions on the right hand side are emotions of depression, indicating disengagement. As we move from highs to lows and vice versa, each notch on the way up or down has a specific flavour or atmosphere. So anger, for instance, is an emotion that is generated as we try to retrieve a value that is currently under threat. Envy, as another example, is an emotion of aspiration, where we know what we want but still think of it as out of reach. Our emotions may attach to any value on the fourfold dimensions of our existential world, thus complicating our experience. Supervisors can use the compass to help therapists locate the experiential world of their clients. The following vignette will illustrate how these instruments can be applied in practice and in the pursuit of truth in supervision.

Figure 7.2 Compass of Emotions

Supervision of Work with a Depressed Client

The client's story

Wendy was an experienced and well trained therapist who worked in primary care. She usually brought lots of positive material to supervision, sometimes enthusiastically and confidently discussing the many ways in which her clients improved. Generally she resonated easily with her clients and learnt quickly from mistakes, frequently getting new ideas from our discussions and applying these with alacrity. So when she introduced her stagnating therapy with her client Cara with a sigh and a frown, it was clear that some serious work was required.

Wendy, herself in her early 50s, had been working with this client of 42 for several months. The client was a single woman who had been in a relationship with a married man for close to ten years. Cara had come to counselling for severe 'clinical' depression. She had made several suicide attempts in the past and was still tempted to end her life. She had told Wendy that she had lost the will to live. Everything seemed meaningless since the end of her relationship with her lover Jim. She had hung onto him for dear life for a decade, hoping against hope that he would eventually leave his wife for her. When she became pregnant by him two years previously, she had thought this was her moment. It had been a make or break situation and she had announced the pregnancy to her lover with great panache. He had strung her along for weeks, making her think it would all work out for them. Then, at the eleventh hour he had decided that he wanted her to have an abortion since he had realised he could never leave his family.

Cara had been disbelieving and went into a state of denial. She had postponed having an abortion thinking he would come around eventually. She had started to show and had her first scan. She had told others of her pregnancy and had formed a bond with the child in her womb. She thought she would have the baby anyway and that Jim would change his mind after the birth. Their relationship became very tense during this time as Jim resented her 'disobedience' and did not want 'to be lumbered with another child'. He had three teenage children with his wife Liz, who was his childhood love. Jim, also close to 40, was looking forward to a time when his kids would leave home and he could take it a little easier. He was not about to embark on starting a new family. He then chose to break off the relationship for these reasons, though Cara thought it was actually because she had begun to refuse to have sex with him. She had been in her 20th week of pregnancy and was sure he was trying to pressurise her into having an abortion before the legal time limit was up.

Cara knew that Jim was desperate to avoid his wife finding out about the clandestine relationship and so she decided the moment had come to force the issue, since she was now determined to have the baby anyway. She wrongly assumed that his wife would have sympathy with her in her pregnant state and she arranged to meet Liz, without telling Jim, to disclose the situation to her. Not only did Liz not believe that Jim could be the father of her child, she accused her of being a callous liar and a slut. That night Jim came to see her and beseeched her one last time to have a termination. He was very angry with her for having spoken to Liz. He belittled her and treated her like an unruly child. He said that she was behaving very irresponsibly and should get rid of a baby she could not look after. There was a terrific scene and Cara screamed and shouted as she never had in her life. She felt assaulted though Jim did not actually hurt her physically. That same night she started bleeding, was hospitalised and the baby was stillborn. She felt absolutely devastated and drained of all life. Jim and Liz did not visit her in hospital where she remained for a week with complications. Jim sent a daft card with a picture of the seaside town where they had often conducted their affair with just five words on the back: 'it was not to be'. She felt outraged at his callousness and deeply hurt.

After she came home from hospital she was off work for many months. She felt empty and ashamed and profoundly bereft for the child she would never have. It was some time into this sick leave that she first took an overdose. Jim had been true to his word and had not been in touch. He had told his secretary to deal with her calls so that she had to give up trying to reach him by phone. Her letters and emails remained unanswered and when she had gone to meet him at his office he had coolly turned her away, joking with his colleagues about his 'stalker'. This had enraged her further and she had pursued him to his house where another humiliating scene with Liz had finally brought home the reality of the end of the relationship.

Existential supervision

When Wendy had suggested that there was a fair amount of aggression in her actions towards Jim and Liz, Cara had claimed that she had not felt angry but 'gutted'. Wendy had argued with her about it, trying to demonstrate to her how hostile her behaviour had been and Cara meekly acknowledged she might be right, but said this realisation only made her sadder, since all she had done was to protect her unborn child. She reiterated that her life had been destroyed and that ending it would be by far the best solution. She had only agreed to see a counsellor to please her GP, but was determined to die.

Wendy felt under tremendous pressure and had no idea how to reach Cara. She had worked with suicidal people before but never with anyone who was so set on ending her life. She felt incapable of reasoning with Cara as 'there was nothing one could say to ease her pain'. When I asked her to explore this inexpressible pain and describe it to me, she told me of her own abortion and miscarriage. 'So, you know about such pain, in principle, but in practice, are you allowing yourself to experience some of the same pain that Cara is feeling right now?'

I then sketched for her the picture that had formed in my own mind: that of a woman who has put all her hope in one man and has thrown herself completely into the yearning for her one irreplaceable and unique baby. She fights for these precious possessions tooth and nail and not only loses the man, but also the child and then her self-esteem as well, having been humiliated and scorned by her lover and his wife. Wendy could see how devastating this would be and she looked thoughtful and hurt. She had just remembered that in the aftermath of the stillbirth Cara had gone into early menopause. So she had also lost her fertility and any hope of having her own child in the future. By tracing the multiple losses that Cara had suffered the experience of her existential predicament became obvious. It was not hostility or aggression but despair, defeat and grief she was contending with. Wendy knew immediately that she had so far failed to touch this bottomless pain.

In fact, she admitted shamefully as we explored further, she had made all sorts of judgements about Cara's position in the world. She had assumed she knew the situation, having herself had a daughter with a man who had also been previously married. She had assumed this gave her extraordinary sympathy with Cara but could now easily see how this had made her feel somewhat smug and superior for having succeeded where Cara had so clearly failed. She could see her own bias and realised she must have come across as wanting to better Cara and set her straight. She was happy to explore this further by answering my question about where she thought Cara had gone wrong. Cara, she said, had not played her cards well and had been much too aggressive and desperate in pursuit of her lover. In some ways she had herself to thank for her predicament.

Re-engagement with the client's issues

Wendy knew and felt how this judgement had stopped her being truly with Cara. She could also appreciate that Cara might fear just such condemnation from others in her isolated position. Wendy was gradually grasping something of Cara's universe and she could sense how restricted her world had become. She could now allow herself to imagine herself in Cara's position, rather than imagining that Cara was in the same position she had once been in. For the first time she felt tearful at Cara's plight. She realised what a total failure Cara must feel for having gambled herself away and lost everything. In thinking about the loss of her unborn child some deep and hitherto unacknowledged emotions about her own termination arose and led to an even warmer understanding of her client's predicament.

We now traced the many ways in which Cara had suffered losses. She had indeed lost on all dimensions of existence. She had lost her physical confidence in her body by being unable to bring a child into the world and also by not being sexually attractive to her lover any longer. She had lost her social pride by having humiliated herself in front of her lover and his wife and also for having lost her job. She had lost her self-esteem by having stooped so low to beg for her lover's love and make herself emotionally dependent on him. Finally she had lost her sense of spiritual meaning, as all the objectives that had given her life purpose had faltered and failed. People who feel suicidal frequently experience this kind of total bankruptcy of their values on all fronts. However the strength of Cara's anger and subsequently of her despair told us of her great vitality and of the force of her longing for the values that had been threatened and lost. We agreed there was much hope in this.

Therapy begins in earnest

Wendy took all these ideas on board and she was able, in her own way, to bring the universal human questions that we had debated to her next session with Cara. She asked her what it meant for her to have been unable to bring a child into the world and was stunned at Cara's response, as she wept for a long time before starting the work that she had postponed till this point. At the end of their session she said to Wendy what a relief it was to finally feel understood and see a glimpse of light. The gap between them was bridged and the therapy moved on steadily after this. After some weeks Cara came to appreciate her experiences as of some value. Later on she acknowledged the role of her suffering in learning about herself and about life. She felt that Wendy had validated her experience instead of seeing it as catastrophic. This had made it valid and worthy. In supervision Wendy thought the key had been to dare to truly meet Cara's despair and face it down.

The role of existential supervision was to allow Wendy to go into the grief and set aside her own position of strength and judgement, whilst acknowledging these were hers to keep. She also found a way to comprehend and gain a concrete sense of the collapse of Cara's entire worldview and this made her feel confident in relation to Cara's situation rather than afraid of it, as she had been before. It also gave her several ideas about ways in which Cara could reaffirm her values. She helped Cara to do so over the next months.

Progress was made possible because Wendy was able to stand steady with her client and could show her that there was at least some safety and human understanding even at the rock bottom of her life. This allowed Cara to discover that this low point was a good place from which to count her losses and start rebuilding a different world from the one she had so desperately wanted to leave behind. Unsurprisingly, there was a great renewal of energy in both Cara and Wendy's lives after this. She became able to live with all the most extreme polarities and paradoxes of life (see Table 7.1).

	Desires	Fears
Physical	Life pleasure	Death pain
Social	Love belonging	Hate isolation
Personal	Identity integrity	Freedom disintegration
Spiritual	Good purpose	Evil futility

Table 7.1   Dimensions and Tensions of Human Existence

Passionate Pursuit of Truth

One of the things that Wendy learnt from supervision was that the client's truth must guide the therapy and remain its source and inspiration throughout. Therapists often need reminding of how they can make themselves more fully available to their client's life struggle and engage with it in such a way that clients feel able to re-engage with their own truth and bring their life back on track in line with it. Supervision provides the broad vision to encompass such truth, as well as the capacity to rise above apparently impossible obstructions on the path.

The philosophical nature of existential supervision means that it often leads to open and wide ranging discussions with the supervisee about the human issues that preoccupy their clients. In such discussions the objective is not to use rhetoric to argue a point or to convince, but rather to use all the tools and comprehension at the disposal of supervisee and supervisor to gain a better and more accurate picture of the client's experience in particular and of life in general. It is a joint venture and an existential adventure which can be most enjoyable when conducted with openness and generosity. This pursuit will be the more passionate as each of the people involved in it can perceive clearly how an understanding of the client's issues will clarify something new about life.

It is this mutual puzzling out of human existence that makes supervision such a fascinating experience. If this search for truth, both universal and specific, is undertaken with verve it transfers new vibrancy and dynamism to the therapy and usually translates rapidly into new progress. The supervisee will begin to ask different questions and remark on hidden aspects of the client's words and experiences that were left unseen. They will become increasingly expert at un-snagging the client from the troubles they were caught up in.

Resonance and Verification

Allowing the therapist to resonate with her client's experience and feel into the client's world is crucial at the beginning of the process. This is in line with

Jaspers' notion of *Einfühlung*, which is literally a feeling into the other's internal world (Jaspers, 1968). It is often helped by the use of dramatic devices, such as the supervisor or supervisee speaking as if they were the client. It may also help, as in this example, for the supervisor to paint a colourful verbal picture of the existential world that is emerging, rather like a director of a play or a film might do to inspire an actor to feel into their role. For in-depth therapeutic work to happen we first need to get the feel for the client's world and truly engage in their universe. This is not a theoretical or easy task, but an intimate, demanding and difficult one. It means picking up their worries, letting ourselves resonate with all that really matters in their world and allow ourselves to be touched by these. So, as we enable the therapist to pick up the scent, we plunge them into a new experience of living, extending themselves towards the client's world. We teach the supervisee to engage, not in mere role play, but by capturing the precise tonality and exact keys, rhythms, moods and atmospheres that define the client's reality. We teach therapists to let themselves be affected before they become understanding and wise. To do so we use the phenomenological method of constant description and verification until we have hit the spot and it feels just right.

We might say: 'so, your client is heartbroken, is wiped out by her lover's betrayal', as a descriptive.

Then we wait for confirmation by the therapist, who might hesitate and say: 'I am not sure she is exactly heartbroken. She seems rather eager to show him he is in the wrong. Taking her own life seems to me more about anger than about being heartbroken, but yes, the betrayal is a huge issue for her'.

We do not argue, but continue to probe and call the therapist to further thought and feeling. We may say: 'Is it more then as if she can't tolerate the betrayal because it took her by surprise? You said she felt gutted, which conjures up a sense of having been attacked and emptied of all one's internal integrity: a sense of total failure.'

The supervisee might reflect for a moment and say: 'Yes, I think so. It is almost as if she can accept that the relationship has broken up but she can't accept that her life has been broken into pieces. She would rather chuck it in than mend it'.

The supervisor responds: 'That may seem the right thing for her if she cannot trust herself to get her life right. How would *you* feel if you had wanted to start a new life with your lover and felt you deserved it because you had patiently waited for him for ten years and now were pregnant by him? Only to find that all of this is ripped away from you and you are treated as if you do not deserve this happiness after all? Would it not seem as if everything had come to nothing and you had somehow failed to make it work?'

'I would feel pissed off and humiliated!' the supervisee shouts out.

'Is that how your client comes across?' Asks the supervisor.

'Yes, I think that might be closer to the truth'. The supervisee confirms.

'So her determination to kill herself may well be a last ditch attempt at being in charge and getting back at the people who have humiliated her, whilst ridding herself at the same time of the shame of having failed so totally? It may be worth checking with your client whether any of this makes sense to her.'

At this point the supervisee is reminded of the importance of verification. Each speculation about her client's experience has to be checked and verified with the client until the understandings we arrive at in supervision actually fit the client's reality as well as the truth of human existence and the therapist's own sense of truth.

Tackling Secrets and Taboos

In this process we will invariably come across all kinds of ideas and experiences that were kept hidden from view. Therapy often comes to a halt when it is going down paths that are too familiar and well trodden. When these paths are left behind interesting insights ensue. We have to dare to float new and radical ideas sometimes. The client who was heartbroken and who assumed she needed mainly support and empathy from her therapist, may turn out to be quite robust enough to cope with her situation, if only she can make sense of it and find purpose in her plight. Her willingness to gamble on a secret affair may need to be reviewed but it may also need to be acknowledged as a kind of personal bravery. Her misunderstanding of her lover's weakness and her underestimation of his commitment to his family may need to be challenged but it may also be seen as an expression of a kind of unexamined faith, a naïve belief in love.

Was self-deception involved here? Why was she so sure she could hurt the other woman when she is scandalised about the other woman hurting her? What are the secret thoughts and assumptions that have come to grief and how can an acknowledgement of these prejudices make for a better life almost immediately? The partner's capacity for deception and cowardice may not really have come as such a big surprise but the client's willingness to put up with it may teach her something new about herself. Similarly her willingness to fight for her survival may have revealed new strengths like tenacity and intensity, on which she can draw now. There are many gems to be taken from each experience of grief and suffering and there is much merit, meaning and progress in the hardships from which we have to learn.

Supervisors are in a position to show supervisees how to take a closer look at life and how to perceive it from a new angle. They know from their own therapeutic experience that clients' broken illusions might give birth to a new and stronger phase of life. This is why supervisors need to have acquired substantial gravitas and practical wisdom. Supervision is about inspiring the courage to look at life candidly and courageously, with wonder and awe for the human capacity to face up to suffering. Supervisors need to be strong, calm and present enough to stand in a place from where such vision in the round is possible.

Victimisation, Suffering and Immoral Behaviour

They also need to be capable of having a questioning attitude. Debate with the supervisee about the bottom line of life will lead to moral and ethical considerations. Was that abortion an option? In refusing the termination was the client truly prepared to raise the child alone? What does it mean to experience oneself as a victim of others? Is that a credible viewpoint or is it more complex than this? The therapist is encouraged to think through the issues. What is abortion in the first place? What is miscarriage? What is stillbirth? What does it mean to give up on a lover? On a baby, much wanted? What can possibly replace this? What is the loss, but also what is the gain? What are the life implications of having come to suffer such things? What doors are opening after such an experience? What lessons can be learnt? How can the suffering become purposeful? How will the client live with the things that have happened with honour and dignity? How can they get a taste for making new and better decisions about life in future? Predictable responses are queried and arguments are unravelled. Supervision is a time to think from scratch.

Faith and Purpose in Life

It is also a time to help supervisees to think through taboo issues like that of religious convictions and to examine the nature of faith or intuition. It is a time to bring up some of the fundamental human questions, like why we live the way we do and what we think life is about in the first place. A client can be brought back from the brink of disaster by the realisation that their trials and tribulations may be a stepping stone towards a greater project. Nothing is ever just what it seems and supervision is a time to allow for another look and for some careful and playful speculation. Therapists become more effective when they have been willing to tackle controversial issues for themselves. Of course illogical thinking may need to be queried too.

Finding the Way

Supervision works best in a climate of collaboration. Existential supervisors do not need to be directive (unless perhaps in their work with trainees), nor particularly non-directive (unless they work as peers), but they are direct and speak clearly about all that is at stake. They do not beat around the bush but ensure that the therapists they mentor learn to think more carefully about their attitudes, assumptions and interventions and the impact these have on their clients. As supervisees become more aware of the directional nature of all therapeutic interventions they will learn to use their authority and influence gently and respectfully in the best interest of their clients.

Supervision is an unpressurised space and opportunity to work out how this can be done, for there is room for experimentation. If supervision is enthusiastic and engaged all protagonists benefit: the client who is helped to reconsider her life in a new light and the therapist who has become more deeply committed to her client's struggle and who is also learning to apply the newly discovered principles to her own life. But the supervisor benefits most of all, for it is a huge privilege to create space and time for the consideration of so many diverse and varying facets of human living. From the safe distance of the supervisory relationship we can learn to articulate things that we may miss as therapists since we do not always have the presence of mind to catch them in flight.

Conclusion

In conclusion then, existential supervision allows us to create a deeper and more intense understanding of human living. All dimensions of existence (see Figure 7.3) are thoroughly and exhaustively explored. To work with therapists on their clients' dilemmas and quandaries generates a philosophical outlook that is also eminently practical. The sense of solidarity that is created between supervisor, therapist and client is a unique example of collaboration. It allows us to realise that we all share the burden of the human condition and that we

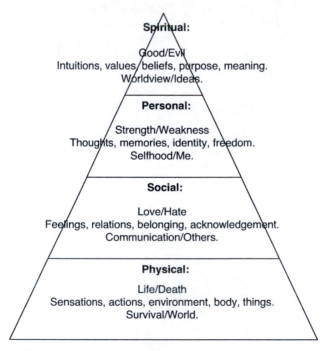

Figure 7.3   Dimensions of existence

can help each other in getting a little closer to its hidden secrets and truths by being honest and candid in our appraisals. Doing existential supervision is to find out how people can carry their troubles with greater gusto and vitality and how to recover the zest for life when it is lost. The sharing of these insights with fellow human beings is a tremendous and gratifying experience.

References

Deurzen, E. van *Existential Psychotherapy and Counselling in Practice* (London: Sage Publications, 2002).

Deurzen, E. van & Arnold-Baker, C. (eds) *Existential Perspectives on Human Issues* (London: Palgrave, 2005).

Jaspers, K. 'The Phenomenological Approach in Psychopathology', *British Journal of Psychiatry* 11(4) 13–23 (1968).

8

Online Group Supervision

Simone Lee

Introduction

Online supervision is an activity where the worlds of cyber-technology and psychotherapy[1] converge. In this chapter I describe and reflect on my online work as a training supervisor[2] for a college based in London, which offers existential-phenomenological psychotherapy training programmes and specialises in distance learning. I will consider existential aspects that emerge in this context.

Context

Once on the professional pathway, students see clients in a placement; whose clinical accountability, culture and policies will influence the in-house supervision. Training supervision, while having some inevitable overlaps, has the primary purpose of viewing the supervisees' therapeutic work and all this encompasses through an existential-phenomenological lens. Each online group module comprises ten weekly two hour sessions and has up to five student participants, who can be located anywhere globally, whose range of experience, personal development and training can vary widely. They will all have the equivalent of a foundational training in psychotherapy and are typically in their 30s and 40s with a rich life experience. To enrol online, they will, of course, need to have access to a computer, be able to type and to communicate in English.

Although the context of this work is that of an existential-phenomenological training programme such online supervision undoubtedly has cross-theoretical potential. Whichever orientation is espoused it is possible to supervise online and the existential concepts emphasised here can be usefully employed by any practitioner, since they refer to universal experience.

---

[1]'Psychotherapy' is used as a catch-all for psychotherapy and counselling.
[2]To research this paper I polled the views of past online supervisees who generously offered very full feedback. I extend thanks to them all.

Chat Room Environment

The cyber-supervision takes place in a secure chat room and is synchronous: a real-time live discussion. Students do not see or hear one another. Enrolled students enter the chat room through a series of menus, using their personal passwords and logins. In lay terms, a chat room is a dedicated screen display dominated by a large window which shows the 'chat'. There are other windows and menus variously scattered on the screen. 'I-Chat' is simply the online conversation which has been typed into a separate window and 'posted' to the chat-window. Each posting is displayed prefaced with the sender's name and sometimes the sender's local time.

Supervision Structure

The supervision session has a simple two part format. For the first hour, after initial greetings, supervisees share questions or professional issues emerging from our previous meeting or which have occurred in the intervening week. Online supervisees have been particularly receptive and active in these discussions. The second hour is similar but uses a verbatim report from a psychotherapy session as a springboard for a hermeneutic discussion and analysis; this activity focuses on the actual language of the reported dialogue to see what inferences and meanings are revealed therein.

During our sessions, we explore meanings, values, biases, paradoxes and human dilemmas. We consider any correspondence with the thinking of existential philosophers and therapists. We talk about what it means to be an existential therapist and if there is a slide towards a 'medicalised', idealised, mechanistic or behavioural approach this is examined. Characteristic of most existential supervision is the focus on the 'way of being' of the student and the client; the therapeutic relationship itself, the client's 'story' being secondary. Throughout our discourse, I actively encourage supervisees to resonate personally with material and to contemplate the meaning and relevance for their own practice.

At the end of each online session, with students' consent, I email a copy of our online discussion to all group members. Periodically during the module we review our work.

Clearly it is possible to conduct online supervision without the use of verbatim reports though this author finds they are an extremely useful starting point for discussion. This viewpoint concurs with the position taken by Adams in his discussion on phenomenology in Chapter 4. Online supervision is an excellent vehicle for phenomenological work.

Welcoming

Before we convene for our first meeting, I link up with the group members by email. Drawing on my knowledge and experience gained as a cyber-supervisor and bearing in mind especially those students new to chat rooms and group supervision, I attempt to set expectations comprehensively for the forthcoming term, and to advise on practical details such as different time zones and emergency helpline numbers. I ask students to send each other brief training and personal biographies in advance of our first session and also statements of what they seek from the supervision. Interestingly, even for students who have already met face-to-face or online, these biographies seem to be valued and foster a sense of connection. It is different to see your life story in writing and to have it validated by others.

To the email, I attach an outline of how to prepare their presentations, suggesting ways of finding a focus that will lead to an unfolding in our existential-phenomenological supervision:

> Think about a piece of work you are trying to make sense of, an untameable bias/prejudice, a session or a situation in your practice which for some reason or other you have found particularly difficult or challenging. Prepare an anonymous typed verbatim, which encapsulates something of the issue you are grappling with. The group will enter into an examination and discussion of the work and the chosen verbatim in the spirit of exploration and discovery, making it a creative and constructive forum.

I see this first communiqué in its entirety as integral to the supervision and not merely an appendage. Within are explicit and implicit messages. It welcomes. It invites resourcefulness. It forewarns. It sets the shape, tone and mood for the work and, conveys something of the potentiality, fun and richness. Not least, I legitimise and encourage students to share their experience of the online supervision:

> If at any point in the session anyone feels unhappy, lost, misunderstood, cross or upset, I strongly encourage you to let us know. I consider our process as a group to be very important.

Heaton reminds us that:

> … both Heidegger and Sartre teach that if we approach a subject in order to discover what it is and merely look at it from the outside as it were then we cannot comprehend its 'being-meaning' (*Seinssinn*), we must first get into its 'implementation-meaning' (*Vollzugssinn*) to really understand its being-meaning (1999: 21).

Since existential supervision, like existential therapy, is a philosophical practice, to practise the philosophy, to make meaning from the enterprise, we need to be fully involved.

Commitment

Marcel names 'availability' as the interpersonal stance where we willingly open and transcend ourselves towards the other (Macquarrie, 1972: 111). Complementary is his notion of 'fidelity': 'Community is built on the basis of fidelity, our faithfulness to the engagements we have taken upon ourselves' (ibid: 112).

Fulfilling our commitment to a supervision group can be even more demanding than other group situations, since we are not only disclosing how we make relationships with clients (whom we often feel fiercely protective of); we are also exposing ourselves to earnest self-reflection. Online factors can intensify this.

> **Supervisee:** For me there is more risk taking because I did not have web cam or anything like that so you are putting your thoughts and feelings into a void in a sense and there is the suspense of what will happen, how it will be received, it requires a lot more work cognitively, because there is less body language.

Notwithstanding, committed and authentic participation in online supervision can engender a welcoming, safe and fertile forum for learning, for some if not all participants, for some, if not all of the time.

> **Supervisee**: My experience of relationships formed online is very positive in that I feel you can really *'know'* a person without seeing them and get a good sense of them.

Another student, speaking of a point in her early experience of online work alludes to alienation and misunderstanding saying: 'It felt a very lonely and painful place at times'. She found courage and confidence to continue and remarked, 'I am so glad I did because I really flourished in the environment and it was so enjoyable'.

While it is not desirable or conducive to learning to feel continual estrangement, there have been times when engaging with pronounced discomfort has delivered the group and individuals to a place of profound enlightenment. Here is an edited reproduction of a dialogue illustrating this phenomenon. A student was trying to present and the group kept digressing. Eventually, I shared my difficulty with the group. Different yet uncomfortable responses were evoked in us all. We addressed what had happened, but the tension was still reverberating.

> **Supervisee A:** I'm not sure how helpful this is becoming for me. I am afraid that this will be seen as avoidance (maybe it is) but could we move on.

Supervisor: At various points during this discussion, I have thought about moving on, Supervisee A then I have thought that some really interesting things are happening that reveal us and how we communicate, how we respond to control/lack of control, being with others. Using ourselves as touchstones of experience can be very useful. I notice how you Supervisee A are now finding it unhelpful and the others have different responses.

I invite the group to stay with the process and there are further revelations.

Supervisee A: Yes. I think that I have stood back and processed what my responses are to this and why and then it lost its power. I guess that I would like to bring it back into some focus so that I can process and learn more. Perhaps there is something to be learned from your facilitation, in that if we as therapists challenge the client who is diverging from the 'stuff' of therapy then we will meet with something of them and their way of being in the world? Scary.

I guess this is what happens in therapy too? Even when it is time-limited therapy with goals??? So what I wanted to explore has been explored but not in the way I anticipated ... Hey good stuff isn't it?

Supervisee B: It is really open communication with the exposure of our own feelings.

Supervisor: My attunement is jarred with the group – being with others and that creates anxiety. I could ladder that to a prevailing low-level sense of the threat and uncertainty of others.

Supervisee C: I see it as a clash of understandings and meanings that have created the way for more open communication, it is just the stuff that happens in relationship all the time.

Supervisor: Isn't it hard to stay with the anxiety?

Supervisee A: Yes, the important thing was that it could be spoken in the group and not ignored.

Supervisee B: It is hard to stay with the anxiety, very good stuff. I think this is very good training for the therapeutic dialogue for example when something needs to be said in the relationship which is tough. Perhaps revealing our own feelings about the client.

Supervisor: A big part of our work is to work with the uncomfortable, whatever the uncomfortable is for us. I have a theory that if work doesn't go to difficult places for us then we should be looking at what is it that is going on. After all, as Supervisee C seems to say, relationships are multi-faceted.

Supervisee B: Uncomfortable for me is about courage.

Supervisee A: Uncomfortable for me is a message that I need to listen to and work out the meaning.

Supervisor: 'You must bear a chaos in yourself in order to bring a dancing star into the world'.[3]

Supervisee A: Sometimes I need to have courage and take it on and sometimes I need to look after myself. The important thing for me is listening to the message.

Supervisee B: The key for me is in relaying my own feelings which are real and can't be questioned. Perhaps their perception differs, but if I am relating my own feelings about what has transpired, that doesn't seem to cause much confusion.

This dialogue epitomises the stuff of existential practice for it shows that '… existence cannot be described by propositions which are then grasped. […] it has to be awakened as it concerns our own freedom' (Heaton, 1999: 22).

Also conveyed is how a willingness to stay with uncertainty can liberate us to learning. Kočiūnas captures this when speaking of groups in general: 'Authentic participation […] is possible only when the participants are sincere and sensitive to all that […] is going on around, when they are constantly and willingly reacting to changing situations of the group life' (2000: 107).

Idiosyncrasies of Online Supervision

For online initiates there is no need to attempt to bracket the world, as a lively chat room can, like the Husserlian epoché, serve as 'a device for breaking the bonds of familiarity we have with things, in order to see those things anew' (Ihde, 1986: 120). Readers will recall the discussion of bracketing in Chapter 4 – here we find that bracketing of the world is, in a sense, unnecessary since being online in and of itself breaks the bonds of familiarity. It is not surprising therefore that many feel 'at sea' early on in their first experience of online supervision.

---

[3]From Zarathustra's Prologue (5) Nietzsche, F. *Thus Spoke Zarathustra*. Trans: R. J. Hollingdale (London: Penguin, 1961).

Entering the chat room, an ancillary window lists those logged in, but unless you see active chat, in spite of the indicators, you may be quite alone. You can infer that those *not* named are not there, however there is no guarantee that listed fellow cyber-supervisees are there either. They may not be at their computers, or they may have recently signed out or may even have been disconnected. The suspense is similar to arriving at an empty house and calling out 'Is anyone there?' When you walk into an embodied supervision group, while there may certainly be other tensions, this is not one of them. Online, even when the group is in mid-conversation, a quieter member of the group can have been jettisoned out into the ether before their absence is registered. It is bad 'losing' a fellow-supervisee, though many agree the worst is when it is *oneself* who is disconnected.

Online little of the process is transparent. One student, speaking of the face-to-face situation, said she had keenly relied on seeking to interpret the nature of her connectedness or disconnection: 'Tiny visual clues help me remain open, engaged and "alongside" the other'. Given the limitations of cyber-supervision, one needs to get used to being with and 'hearing' conversation through reading and tuning in. Unseasoned cyber-nauts find the irregular rhythm and the different cadence between postings confusing. And the multiple conversations taking place can 'sound' like a 'din': 'It feels like a cocktail party with small groups and one-to-ones'. The chat room screen refreshes regularly which cannot only be disconcerting; but can also hamper keeping up with the chat, since little time is available to scroll up and read earlier postings before the screen is 'whooshed' away. Those who have minimal keyboard dexterity or have computer problems have to negotiate those difficulties too.

These difficulties, which are mainly encountered at the beginning of the online experience, can preoccupy supervisees and can bring a disproportionate focus onto the computer and the screen, hindering a fuller engagement with the group. This was remarked on by one student: 'Joining the online supervision group somehow elevated the "online" nature of the enterprise above the group aspect of it and affected my ability to use my own judgement and wisdom to guide me along'.

Some find adaptation easier. One supervisee, adept at typing at speed, reported: 'I enjoy expressing myself through writing so this particular mode suited me well'. She used the term 'writing' and not 'typing', which suggests the transparency of her relationship with the hardware (ibid: 141). Other students found having to rely on typing to communicate enforced a new discipline. 'The medium encouraged me to distil my thoughts and express them concisely, as typing words takes more time than speaking them', said one, adding how this translated into her actual therapy practice: 'This helped me develop my ability to express myself in fewer and more carefully chosen words in the therapy room'.

For another, condensing language, in an environment he experienced as risky, came at a cost: 'Richness can get pared down and this can be a disadvantage, especially if trust about one's work (in one's own mind as well as in others') isn't established first'. And even if one is used to expressing oneself through the typed or written word, many find, at some time or another, there is the pressure of keeping up with the group. 'Communicating considerable complexity is hard in the written word, especially when trying to do so, on the fly and at high speed'.

Adaptation

Eventually, most supervisees become accustomed, even endeared to the eccentric music and interflow of conversation and hardened to the vagaries of encounter in a cyber-environment.

Chat room discourse is not linear. Side-exchanges occur where students support and acknowledge each other or have little jokes. Transitions between conversations are rarely seamless. Supervisees eventually abandon the looser style of formulations, which work well face-to-face, such as 'Can you say more' and evolve a more explicit style: 'Can you say more about "being in bad faith", Jean-Paul?' This mode of dialogue gives text easier legibility even when conversations are interwoven. And people develop warmer online personae as they find their way around this ethereal territory. So while postings are literally meant for silent reading, they have an oral, noisy, inflective, conversational quality and are aerated with spaces, ellipses and 'smilies'. Dynamic and in the moment, meanings become discernible in spite of the actual order of postings. As one supervisee encapsulated it: 'The rhythm, timing or rate at which the sentences appeared on the screen became a crucial phenomenon in terms of the meaning of the interactions'. This accounts for why sometimes texts lose in the reading – they have a 'you had to be there' quality.

And there is a strong possibility too of falling into a shared natural attitude within the online group; this can itself be shaken up. One supervisee, when asked to name what she liked least about the supervision, said the following:

> When the chat room indicated 'doors shut' on our last session this brought with it the rude awakening that intimacy created as result of real, genuine encounters was in the end a temporary illusion – unreal in terms of every day human-ness. The intimacy was with the computer, with silent text in cyberspace.

Evolving as an Online Supervisor

Kasket states that: 'the absence of a physical space that is shared, facilitates the clearing of another kind of space' (2003: 66); this new territory has compelled me to adapt as a supervisor. I present below some areas where my style of working and attitudes have shifted in response to and as a result of working online.

Since people appear 'cooler' online (Wallace, 1999: 15), even before we actually start sessions, through the 'welcoming process', I actively promote the development of warm, communicative relationships. During supervision, I model an informal and approachable style tailored to the environment, experimenting with the available tools such as 'smilies', coloured texts and different fonts. (In spite of all my prejudices against such frivolities prior to supervising online, I cannot deny the effectiveness of a well placed, well timed 'emoticon'). Addressing the fascinating phenomenon of meeting online and being simultaneously in another place has brought about some warming and atmospheric exchanges. Here is one:

> **Supervisor:** I thought we could start by briefly describing where we are. I'm at home in my office. It's grey outside and I can see trees through my window. It's quiet in the house.

> **Supervisee A:** I am in my office at work. The blinds are closed and I have three lamps so it feels really cosy. The team are all having lunch in another building so it is very quiet.

> **Supervisee B:** I am in the study with afternoon sunlight streaming onto the garden which is in full flower and looking absolutely gorgeous. The house is quiet but soon to erupt with everyone coming home.

> **Supervisee C:** I'm at home in the sitting room. I can hear children playing outside and there's background traffic noise from City Rd, a street over from the flat.

Fun, even hilarity and joy, have been experienced in these fora; these connections are important, because a bonded group generates enthusiasm and energy for the real work of supervision.

At times, however, it has been confusing for some to recognise the boundaries of the 'friendly supervision'. I surmise this may partly be due to the reliance of online work on email, an accessible yet informal conduit, to keep sessions ticking over. On the occasions when students try to engage me in lengthy email exchanges, I usually ask them to bring their manifest issue or concern to the group. Sometimes, if the situation merits, I will arrange an online one-to-one with the student. From an existential perspective, how we respond to the parameters of any environment reveals how we respond to limit situations *per se*; this itself points to a rich source of meaning.

Being constrained by limits and being free are existential tensions. In spite of its 'bad press', 'leaping in',[4] has become a cornerstone of my practice,

---

[4]Whether or not one believes Heidegger (1927: 156–60) privileges 'leaping ahead' over the other possible mode of concern 'leaping in', 'leaping ahead' has become a sound bite for 'good practice' in existential circles.

especially since time is voracious online. An interventionist style of facilitation and management does, I proffer, benefit online supervision:

> **Supervisee:** What I found most productive, in that it facilitated relevant communication and learning, was a supervisor who held the group firmly so that we did not waste valuable time digressing up less useful paths, at the same time as actively encouraging an opening up and an examination of our experience.

The concepts of 'leaping in' and 'leaping ahead' are defined in the following chapter and we will see (also Chapter 13) 'leaping ahead' is usually understood as the right mode of relating in existential practice. But in the unique setting of online supervision 'leaping in' might be more facilitating of the supervisory process.

When a supervisee is presenting his or her verbatim report, I often lead the enquiry, asking basic phenomenological questions – encouraging description of the chosen session and the therapist's experience and understanding of the encounter. This allows space for the dialogue to find its own momentum before I invite the group in. Our duologue may last longer if the group is less experienced; if there is a sensitive or key area that needs to be focused on; if the client's story is particularly emotive or has 'juicy' and potentially diverting anecdotal detail; or if the group is large.

Groups, especially larger ones, can become unwieldy particularly when the pace accelerates. In this situation I may copy the entire chat into a document giving me a current and accurate snapshot of our conversation; this permits me to verify our actual exchanges and to scan for postings stranded unacknowledged in the ethereal relay. From this I can then summarise the main threads of discussion and process and note overlooked postings. Feeding back helps the group take stock. This activity is pastoral too; never sure how supervisees are construing their situation online, be they quiet or verbal, I intend by this intervention to invite quieter, straggling or struggling supervisees into the discussion.

Lateness is not uncommon online and it provokes particular difficulties. Intermittent arrivals tend to propel the group into a continual round of salutations and cordialities which slow the start of the supervision. For a late-comer, it is harder to pick up midstream when clues about atmosphere and sensitivities are sparse. For those already online someone arriving mid-flow of something intricate or delicate can be experienced as intrusive. Typically I intervene by ushering latecomers (and returners from the ether) into the group, updating them with what is going on and asking them to try to pick up the thread.

Working with text offers many benefits. Students email their verbatim reports to the whole group in advance allowing time for preparation of questions and observations. This advance preparation frees me to facilitate during the actual session. Text being the online means of communication allows one to see the dialogue unfolding, which brings into greater focus the choice of words used in the discourse – this often prompts interesting discussions. The greatest benefit of working with the written word is that the dialogue can be saved and read after sessions; in this knowledge, I sometimes post points and questions about philosophy, practice and process that we have not had time to explicate together; squeezing them in like 'footnotes' to the supervision. I also ask supervisees to do the same when time is limited and ideas are abounding, or to divert pressure away from an individual student:

> **Supervisor**: Group, while C is responding, I invite you to think about partiality and impartiality. Although C is working with couples, you don't actually need to have more than one person present in the consulting room to 'take sides', as it were, or to want a particular outcome between people. Any thoughts about this either philosophically or practically or both from an ex-phen perspective? Thanks.

Supervisees generally remark how useful they find the transcripts; one commented: 'I have used these scripts time and time again to strengthen my own practice'. I, too, have honed my style of working as a result of looking over these transcripts.

Silence has manifold meanings; online there are different possible manifestations many of which are not always identifiable, rendering silence uncertain and sometimes puzzling. One example is the unnoticed disappearance into oblivion, thus, when a student is silent for while, I tentatively monitor whether they are still there, or not. Another type of silence, more frequent when students are presenting their work, comprises not only thinking time but also reading, re-reading and typing time too – these are busy active silences. Supervisees sometimes retreat into silence when they are confused or have missed the cues to enter the dialogue. There can also be times when the group is unified and tuned in to a full and pregnant silence, these are rarer. Other silences have their own emotions and characteristics; some find full expression, others do not.

One student recounted to me a significant event in our work when I shared my speculations about her being silent:

> What I have learned about myself is that in a person-to-person situation, I tend to observe a lot. I initially reacted to online supervision in the same manner, and it was not until a session in which you related to me that you were wondering if I was bored, that I understood a misperception I was capable of giving in this particular mode of learning. It was surprising for me to comprehend that I had been perceived as lacking interest, but I also understood your response. I had been quiet because I felt unsure of the topic ... can't remember exactly ... but it made me aware that this was a new opportunity to challenge myself. It feels doubly important online to be

sure others are aware of my interest in the topic at hand, otherwise my quietness is easily misinterpreted.

Ihde (1986: 139) posits that the 'world' which is developed using a mediated, indirect means of access modifies our perception significantly and yet, in spite of inaccurate perceptions, overwhelmingly it appears that we can understand one another, especially when we take greater pains to explain ourselves and share our interpretations. I was glad for this supervisee's elucidation, which served also as a humbling reminder to be even more assiduous online in questioning my assumptions; and to facilitate safe ways for the group to find expression, especially for difficult feelings such as shame, doubt, vulnerability and isolation. I need also to consider how *my* way of being online might be experienced and interpreted.

Working online, I have questioned further the benefits of different supervision formats. Supervisees with personal maturity, rounded abilities, reflexivity, a responsible work ethic, an ability to focus and co-operate have great potential to adapt to and flourish in any supervision environment. Even so, since supervision is predicated on challenging ourselves and our work, all supervisees need to be nurtured and, online, extra support may be called for to help students adapt to the cyber-environment. Paradoxically, because perspectives *are* unsettled online, it can be difficult to form a connection with someone who is disoriented. When evaluating an individual's suitability for this mode of supervision, I believe it is important to consider the broader group needs. One student said that what worked less well online was 'working with (new) colleagues who are at very different points in their professional, inter-personal, and dare I say personal journey'. The student added: 'At times this felt like a burden; it felt frustrating and disengaging'. Research reveals the cyber-environment to be a surprising dis-inhibitor, and one where shy people can become very open and those who consider themselves reasonable and cool-headed can flare up more easily as they interact with others (Wallace, 1999: 2). Whilst one obviously cannot predict how new online supervisees will fare, I propose the following be included in selection criteria to help recruit appropriate students:

- to have some experience of supervision
- to be already established in work as a therapist
- to have demonstrated a co-operative attitude with foregoing training

Conclusion

Since it is a mystery that: '… we never have direct experience of the mind, thoughts feelings or motivations of others. Yet we often feel that we do' (Owen, 1999: 24); surely it is less of a mystery that we *can* relate to others online. Husserl spoke of 'primal institution', that is the 'sense of another person as a human being with an immanent life-stream of consciousness "like me"' (ibid). Paradoxically, much as people are 'like me,' they are also not like me, in the sense that their responses to many situations are often different. This leaves room for misunderstanding in any context, but online, there not being actual physical presence, the challenges to understanding are stepped up. We humans, however, are highly developed natural communicators (Pinker, 1995) and have an astonishing capacity to understand 'in the breach' (ibid: 229), to draw inferences from what is not said and seen; we are well equipped to master and manoeuvre the boundless and speculative space online. And online, in the absence of certain cues and information, we are hyper-attentive to the information we do have; perhaps it is this that intensifies the online relationship. When absorbed in dialogue, it is as if the computer *does* indeed extend my sense of embodied intentionality into the supervision forum and I feel myself to be in that space, there, with them (Ihde, 1986: 141).

I believe supervising online provides a unique opportunity for existential exploration. At its best online supervision enters a realm of learning, sharing and intimacy that is palpable, alive and real, in a different, but not worse or diluted way than face-to-face supervision. Cyber-supervision, for some, requires time and commitment to settle into and some supervisees miss the proximity of the other. In spite of this, I suggest that all cyber-supervisees, as a result of the medium, are able to learn something additional and important about their way of being which is significant for their therapeutic practice. I therefore urge therapists interested in existential phenomenology, whatever their orientation, to be experimental, to 'bracket' their prejudices, to be prepared to break through their natural attitude and take that plunge headlong into cyberspace for online existential group supervision.

References

Heaton, J. M. 'Is Existential Therapy Just Another Approach?', *Existential Analysis* 10(1) (1999) 20–6.

Heidegger, M. *Being and Time*. Trans. J. Macquarrie & E. S. Robinson (Oxford: Blackwell, [1927] 1962).

Ihde, D. *Experimental Phenomenology: An Introduction* (Albany: University of New York, 1986).

Kasket, E. 'Online Counselling', *Existential Analysis* 14(1) (2003) 60–8.

Kočiūnas, R. 'Existential Experience and Group Therapy', *Existential Analysis* 11(2) (2000) 91–112

Macquarrie, J. *Existentialism* (London: Penguin, 1972).

Owen, I. 'The Special Hermeneutic of Empathy', *Existential Analysis* 10(2) (1999) 21–40.

Pinker, S. *The Language Instinct* (London: Penguin, 1995).

Wallace, P. *The Psychology of the Internet* (Cambridge: Cambridge University Press, 1999).

9
The World of Addiction

Simon du Plock

Introduction

In considering the nature of existential supervision as it relates to therapeutic work with problems of addiction, we must begin by establishing the meaning of existential therapy of addiction – and addiction itself. We cannot, either, ignore the significance of the word 'existential', since it is this which sets the tone for such supervision. As Deurzen states:

> The existential approach is first and foremost philosophical. It is concerned with the understanding of people's position in the world and with the clarification of what it means to be alive. It is also committed to exploring these questions with a receptive attitude, rather than a dogmatic one: the search for truth with an open mind and an attitude of wonder is the aim, not the fitting of the client into pre-established categories and interpretations (1990: 1).

The distinctive character of existential supervision is to be found in the way it supports therapists to maintain a philosophical attitude in their work with clients.

There is a dearth of literature which specifically addresses working existentially with addiction. This is not, in fact, surprising, since this approach does not tend to promote specific treatment modalities for specific client groups. We are, typically, concerned to engage with process and with blocks to process and strive to avoid seeing clients in terms of treatment labels. I will argue in this chapter that these concerns form the core of existential supervision, and that they are of particular relevance when considering ways of supervising work with addiction.

Re-conceptualising 'Addiction'

Why look at supervision of addiction? Because this area has been considered as a specialist area of therapeutic practice by approaches other than the

109

existential, it has therefore received greater attention than has work with most other client groups, and has generated a literature which tends to promote the world of addiction as a relatively clearly delineated world. Existential therapy is well placed to offer a critique of these assumptions, while providing insights into ways of working with addiction. Though existential therapy and supervision critique rather than employ treatment labels, clarification of meaning is central to this approach since it leads us to ask what we mean when we, or our clients, use the term 'addiction'.

There has been a significant movement in the British and North American literature on addiction in the past decade, away from concentrating on addiction as a state characterised by a sharp reduction of the capacity for voluntary behaviour in relation to specific substances (generally termed 'drugs'), towards the notion that people can get caught up in quite ordinary activities when they become invested with special meaning. Following Shaffer's (c.f. Baker, 2000: 10) contention that 'anything can be addictive which powerfully and quickly and predictably changes how you feel', I would argue that the addict is one who self-medicates. The addiction can be to a substance or an experience; shopping, gambling or eating (or abstaining from eating), may equally fulfil this definition.

Perhaps as many as half of my clients present either directly or indirectly with problems related to substance use, another quarter present with issues around 'obsessive compulsive' behaviour, such as obsessive exercising. Others present because they are using pornography obsessively or find themselves sitting at their home computers every moment of their 'leisure' time, cruising chat rooms and virtual reality websites. If I also include those clients who complain that they are caught up in emotional situations in which they experience themselves as externally determined and unfree, then I am talking about the great majority of my clients.

The degree to which they fit the classical notion of addiction varies, but I find myself drawn to Walters' definition of addiction as 'the persistent and repetitive enactment of a behavioural pattern' which includes four elements:

> progression (or increase in severity)
> preoccupation with the activity
> perceived loss of control, and
> persistence, despite negative long-term consequences
> (1999: 10).

Implications for Existential Supervision

Such a re-conceptualisation of addiction has a profound impact on how we think about therapy of addiction and, in turn, how we regard the supervision of this therapy. This work begins to look less like a specialisation, requiring concomitant special interventions and monitoring of interventions, and rather more like our everyday practice. I find that the most facilitative way I can explore issues of addiction with supervisees is via the concept which Spinelli and Strasser have termed 'the self-construct'. This notion of self-construct is valuable for the way it directs our attention to the way in which each of us assembles, over time, a set of beliefs, values and aspirations about who we believe ourselves to be. An integral component of this is that we also make judgements with regard to who we cannot permit ourselves to be. This construction of a self in the face of nothingness, the attempt to create an essence, is not necessarily problematic. It is, rather, an inevitable part of human being. As Sartre famously expressed it, man is a 'useless passion' (Sartre, 1943: 615). In attempting to make ourselves fixed and substantial, though, we inevitably deny something of our freedom and human nature.

Much of my work with supervisees focuses on the particular ways in which the unique self-construct of their client both opens up and limits their way-of-being-in-the-world. I undertake this process of clarification with the supervisee not with the intention of helping them 'move the client on' in some way, but to enable them to engage as fully as possible with the client so both of them can 'see what is there'. When the client truly sees how they have constructed their 'way-of-being-in-the-world' they may elect to modulate it. (This is not, though, to underestimate how difficult this is likely to be, nor the degree of support they may require from the therapeutic alliance).

Supervisees frequently object that they are duty bound to direct the client towards accepting that their present behaviour is injurious or dysfunctional and that, particularly when a client presents seeking to free themselves from an addiction, they must 'do' something to bring this about. I counter that when the client appreciates their role in creating their self-construct they may also reflect on any changes they wish to make. The therapist will then be faced with the challenge of journeying with the client as they recover (or even discover for the first time) their freedom, and its attendant existential anxiety. There is a temptation on the part of therapists, as Heidegger (1927) describes it, to 'leap in' (*Einspringen*) to rescue clients in distress, rather than 'leap ahead' (*Vorspringen*) to return them back to their responsibility for their self. The former, which I think of as the 'lifeboat' approach to therapy, *may* pull the client out of deep water, but does not enable them to reflect on how they navigate their way through life in order to avoid future perils. It may, worse, suggest to the client that there is an 'ultimate rescuer' at hand, and that they do not therefore need to strive to recover their own agency.

In drawing the therapist's attention to the importance of 'being with' rather than 'doing to' the client, the existential supervisor urges a qualitatively different encounter with the client's being, compared with that which is generally the case in working with addiction. It is more common for the therapist to relate to the client as an expert rather than enter directly and whole heartedly into a relationship. The existential therapist must accept the obvious but, sometimes, discomforting fact that they are a part of the client's relational world.

The therapist offers the possibility of a reparative relationship in which the client may find both the space and the safety in which to reflect on their sense of self. This form of challenging engagement demands much, perhaps as much, from the therapist as from the client. It is at this point that the role of the supervisor takes on a distinctively existential character, since the supervisor is called upon to support their supervisee in a reciprocal encounter with difference. This encounter will almost inevitably lead them to question their own way of being and their own 'sedimented' (Spinelli, 1989: 51) or fixed beliefs about the world. It is crucial that the therapist finds the necessary support in the supervisory relationship to maintain an openness to exploration of the way they attempt to limit or deny this challenge. Still more radically, we can say that therapists need, if they are truly to enter the lived world of the client to the greatest extent they are able, to accept the significance to the client of values and beliefs that they may find disturbing. Because this is so, and may particularly be so when we meet with behaviour which seems purely negative and destructive, as is often the case when working with addiction, the therapeutic enterprise presents the opportunity for clarification for both parties. Therapists who seek to enter the client's world via the acceptance of such beliefs and values *in the context of the client's worldview* open themselves to the clarification of their self-construct in a process which is remarkably similar to that which the client attempts. The temptation to withdraw into the illusory safety of an expert role is strong at these times, and supervisors need to be adept at empathic challenging and appropriate self-disclosure.

The therapist cannot experience the experience of the client. That we can never stand in the place of the other is a basic tenet of existential and phenomenological thinking. It is certainly not the case that the therapist can (or should) give up all their own beliefs and values in order to reflect only those of the client. Sometimes the phenomenological method which underpins existential therapy is misunderstood as being almost a 'merging' of therapist and client, but such a merging would be an anathema since it would destroy the distance required to challenge the client to clarify their meaning world. The supervisor should, though, encourage the supervisee, however imperfectly, to suspend their judgements and wishes to change the client's way of being in order to hear them and provide more focused challenge. For the challenge to have any meaning for the client, beyond a demand, entreaty or instruction, I would argue, it must emerge out of an understanding of the uniqueness of the client's relational field. It is this uniqueness that the supervisor should foreground in their work with the therapist: the client is not just a representative of some phenomenon conveniently labelled 'addiction'.

Such demanding, but rewarding, encounter is particularly indicated with clients who present with addiction related issues, since it provides the possibility for the client to clarify the purpose and meaning of what is often 'explained away' as being a disease accompanied by psychological and physiological 'cravings', over which the client can argue they have no sense of their own agency. Such an encounter offers the client the possibility to clarify the meaning of their behaviour – behaviour which they may be all too ready to dismiss as the outcome of a physiological condition over which they have no control. I resonate with Spinelli's argument about what can facilitate clients to clarify these meanings. He states that clients are far more likely to do so if they fear that their exposure will trigger demands – however subtle – on the part of the therapist for the client to relinquish the behaviour (1997: 140). The supervisor needs to be vigilant and challenge any attempt to unilaterally bring about change in the client. Such unilateral attempts to alter the client's behaviour are anti-therapeutic since they ignore the fact that so called 'dysfunctional' behaviour is both meaningful and purposeful – in this regard it is salutary to recall that defence mechanisms defend against anxiety and cannot, therefore, be discarded until that which they defend against has been addressed.

A common sense approach might urge that a therapist, consulted by a client who states that they wish to break out of some 'addictive' pattern, has an ethical duty to help them achieve this goal, but a moment's thought – once we have put physiological 'cravings' into perspective – will indicate that the client is caught in a tension between, on the one hand a genuine desire to change their habits and, on the other hand, an equally strong wish not to change, or fear of the consequences were they to change. The *conflict* between these two attitudes keeps them where they are. Davies provides a remarkably clear demystification of the notion of craving and withdrawal symptoms in his text *The Myth of Addiction*:

> Put simply, craving is an alternative word which we can use to describe an experience of discomfort, and an accompanying desire to curtail or avoid it ... The use of the word 'craving' is an interesting exercise in attribution, and its primary purpose is to convey how we are intended to perceive the addiction process. It refers to the fact that sometimes people feel a strong desire to use, or use more of, their preferred drug, but it gives the impression of an autonomous force whose power cannot be resisted; hence its attraction. In fact, whether people resist the experience depends on whether they have good reasons for doing so. People in the dentist's chair have a craving to get up and leave; but by and large they stay put (1997: 50–1).

What Actually Happens in Existential Supervision of Addiction?

Existential supervision is a piece of practical research into our openness to, and limitations on, being in relationship with clients. In such an approach the supervisor and supervisee become co-researchers of the phenomenon 'relationship'. The labels we employ to indicate the life problems clients present are subordinate to the relational ground on which the therapist and client attempt to meet.

Our knowledge and understanding of the world is derived through an irreducible grounding of relatedness. We can never understand human being – including our own being – in isolation. The world is a *Mitwelt* – or 'with-world'. In existential supervision the supervisor is intimately enmeshed within a particular type of relational field. They cannot choose to focus only, or even primarily, on the therapist who sits with them; or on the physically absent client. Nor can they take the client-therapist dyad, as reported by the therapist, as their primary focus. Instead, their focus is required – if it is to truly acknowledge the foundational principle of relatedness – to encompass the particular ways in which relatedness expresses itself. This focus comprises three linked aspects:

1. The client's narratives of the experience of being, *as they are reported by the supervisee.*
2. The narratives of the experience of being in relation with the client, *as they are reported by the supervisee.*
3. The supervisor's and supervisee's currently lived experience of related-ness as it unfolds, and enfolds them both, in the space of the supervisory encounter.

We are led to conceptualise the supervisory alliance in terms of a triad: client-therapist-supervisor, rather than three separate individuals and their res-pective roles. This distinctive way of attending to relatedness distinguishes existential from other forms of supervision. While I have, for ease of discussion, posited it as a specific dimension of existential supervision, it would be a mistake to view this as a separate activity in any given supervision session any more than, say, a concern with ethical practice or with the therapeutic contract, which will be addressed only in a particular part or stage of supervision. This attention to relatedness is, rather, as fundamental to supervision as it is to therapy. The content will vary but the form (which is relationship) is a constant.

The world of therapy, as of the professions in general – is increasingly one of 'manualisation' – the requirement to set down the exact steps involved in often very subtle and complex activities. Trainees are often anxious to know what they should 'do' with clients presenting with addiction. Clients them-selves, particularly those who have experience of directive treatment regimes such as the 12 step programme, raise similar questions. With regard to existen-tial supervision it will be apparent that there is considerable attention to the 'being' qualities of the supervisor, and their role in reflecting with the super-visee on how they are 'being' in their work. The attention to relationship which distinguishes existential supervision is more usefully modelled than taught. The supervisor needs to keep in mind – perhaps even more than with other 'client groups' – that they are not 'therapping' the client. The client is not in the room. The-therapist-who-meets-the-client is in the room (c.f. Cohn, 1997: 33). So the situation is co-constituted: the world created by the supervisor who meets the therapist who meets (or fails to meet) the client. While this may seem an elaborate way of thinking about the situation, I would argue that it is in fact helpful and even liberating, since it foregrounds the particular type of relatedness with which we are concerned, honours the 'reality' of the pattern of relatedness, and frees the supervisor from the temptation to instruct the therapist about how to 'cure' the client in a manner akin to the 'apprenticeship' model of supervision associated with psychoanalysis.

This model of the relationship instead foregrounds the fundamental concern: how the therapist opens up or closes down their availability to encounter the lived world of the client. The therapeutic relationship holds the promise of a reparative experience for clients, since it offers new ways of being in relationship. To the extent that existential supervision focuses on the identification and removal of blocks to engagement with the client's world, it shares more in common with existential therapy than most other forms of supervision share with the therapeutic orientation to which they are a correlate. This is not to say that other aspects of supervision, such as providing emotional support, mentoring, and monitoring ethical practice (Feasey, 2002) are ignored. The core, though, of existential supervision, must be attentiveness to the quality of relatedness which the supervisee is able to offer their client. Existential supervision is only 'existential' provided it includes the dimension which is concerned with the quality of the therapist-client relationship, and the ways in which both client and therapist create a space in which to encounter each other.

The great majority of therapeutic work is concerned with ways in which clients experience themselves as free or unfree in their worlds, determined or possessing agency – 'addicted' or not. The notion that it is possible or desirable to demarcate a specific area of therapy as about addiction treatment, or supervision – by extension – of therapy with addicts, is thereby *problematised*. Common sense may initially rebel when confronted with such an assertion – probably all of us have viewed 'addiction' as a special, and perhaps especially challenging area of practice. When we do this we find our ability to encounter the client is altered in subtle but powerful ways. I have noticed that supervisees respond to the notion of working with 'addicts' in ways not dissimilar to working with 'borderline' patients. There is a stock response (it does not initially appear entirely negative) which draws on a number of preconceptions about working with addiction. Exploration and challenge of these preconceptions is the first stage in building an existential supervisory alliance. Preconceptions therapists have brought into supervision with me include:

- The therapist needs special skills. A particular mental capacity often conceptualised as toughness, resilience, ability to hold boundaries.

- The therapist should be experienced, rather than a recent graduate of training.
- The therapist needs to be alert and quick witted.
- The therapist needs to be able to 'dance' with the client if they are not to be led a dance by the client.
- The client is likely to play 'games', push boundaries, reject or, paradoxically, become dependent.
- The client will need 'holding', a 'safe container', or, paradoxically, they will need the therapist to demonstrate flexibility.
- The therapist will need to demonstrate 'wider' knowledge of addiction and of major treatment programmes such as the 12 step programme if they are to gain the trust and confidence of the client.
- The client will sabotage, as well as be deceptive about their habits.
- The 'addiction' is out there – in the client. The therapist does not personally 'know', though they 'know about', addiction.

These preconceptions suggest that addicts are special clients who need special therapists, who, in turn, will require special supervision. If we think about the goal of therapy to open up a space for reflection, we can see that this multitude of preconceptions fills the space and prevents the therapist from encountering the client with a naïve and open attitude. Rollo May's seminal work on relationship provides supervisees with an alternative way of engaging with clients. The 'Here-is-a-new-person', and 'I-Am' experiences which he discusses in *Existence* (1958) constitute, I believe, the necessary, though not sufficient, conditions for distinctively existential supervision. These necessary conditions can be modelled in the supervisory alliance if the supervisor maintains a supervisory style in which they:

- Are curious and naïve, and do not assume privileged knowledge of the client's or therapist's world.
- Strive to focus on the *noetic* (how the supervisee experiences their work with the client) rather than the *noematic* elements of discourse (the story the supervisee reports) (Spinelli, 1989: 11), which is attended to in the other three dimensions of the supervision (see p. 114).
- Attempt to be a fellow traveller alongside the supervisee, and in the process concentrate on the journey rather than pre-agreed destinations or outcomes of therapy.
- Enter into dialogue with the supervisee, rather than providing instructional interaction.
- Are courageous in their willingness to offer and receive challenge, and in so doing encourage the therapist.

The emphasis of supervision is thus firmly on the importance of the relationship. This emphasis on relationship enhances the cross-theoretical and integrative possibilities inherent within the existential perspective.

An Example of Existential Supervision: 'Celine', a Recently Qualified Therapist

I often ask therapists to reflect on their personal and professional identity with the assistance of the following questions:

1. Who do I think I am, when I say that I am a therapist who works with addiction?
2. What does working with addiction allow me to do that I would not otherwise be able to do?
3. What would I loose if I ceased working with addiction?
4. How might my relationship to myself and others be altered if I no longer identified as a therapist of addiction?
5. When I say 'I am a therapist who works with addiction', what words immediately follow from this statement?

This can be a particularly useful exercise when working with therapists contemplating work with clients presenting with addiction issues, since it assists them in identifying their own agenda in entering this field. It is not always helpful to ask supervisees to undertake the exercise above; it is often as productive for me to hold these questions in mind in my conversations with them. Interestingly, these questions are similar to the ones borne in mind by existential supervisors in other settings or contexts (see for example Chapter 3). Existential supervisors are never adverse to questioning and challenging their supervisees – particularly to reveal un-reflected upon assumptions.

In my first session with Celine I noticed that 'helping others' was a theme in her relationships with her family, her partner, and with her friends and work colleagues. I wondered how this 'attunement' would assist or hamper her in her work with clients and decided to invite her to reflect on her own 'addictions'. She was initially appalled by this idea, and especially so when I gently encouraged her to think about ways that her 'helper' self-construct might provide both a resource and an obstacle in her relations with clients. Having introduced the idea, I decided to move on to another aspect of supervision in the hope that Celine might voluntarily return to it in a future meeting. It is important, I feel, to be mindful when supervising, that haranguing the supervisee with what you may suppose to be a valuable insight is almost always detrimental to the formation of the supervisory alliance. In therapy sessions I often run verbal interventions through my mind before speaking in order to reflect whether the words are for the client or are simply something I wish to say. If the latter is the case I generally leave the intervention unspoken. I find the same strategy useful in supervision: the supervisee will often feel confused or will be deflected from their own reflections by inopportune comments.

On this occasion I was pleased that Celine introduced the topic of her 'addictions' at our next meeting, saying that she had felt quite irritated by my attention to what she thought of as personal material. In the intervening period, though, she found herself returning repeatedly to the topic and was surprised to find that she opened a kind of Pandora's Box. Nearly all her inter-actions with others, on reflection, seemed to be designed to maintain her sense of self as a person who helped others, and did so regardless of the cost or inconvenience this might entail. While she was able to look at this further in her own therapy, it was also important for us to consider how the centrality of 'selfless helper' in her self-construct led her to choose to work with a 'special' client group, one which is often considered to be in particular need of help. These reflections moved her, over the course of a number of sessions, to come to a greater sense of awareness with regard to what she would gain and what she would loose if she permitted herself to relinquish her sense of self as 'helper' and allowed herself to be more open to whatever clients brought to sessions.

An Example of Existential Supervision: 'Rudi', An 'Addict in Recovery'

An existential-phenomenological perspective on supervision which critiques the status of 'addiction' as a specialist category of client work requiring special techniques raises questions about the characteristics of therapists working in this field. In the United Kingdom and North America it has long been the case that a large proportion of therapists are drawn from the group of 'addicts in recovery'. Alcoholics Anonymous and Narcotics Anonymous function as ther-apeutic communities and there exist established routes from these to volun-tary work and formal training. We might ask whether this recruitment pattern has helped to keep the disease model of addiction at the centre of therapeutic work, despite the relative absence of support for it from academic psychology research (Schaler, 2000). We might also wonder whether addiction itself can become addictive – it may be that work as an addiction counsellor provides some individuals with the structure and meaning which was formerly pro-vided by the status of 'addict' and the structure of a therapeutic community. That this might be so for some practitioners is not a particularly novel notion – the concept of the 'wounded healer' (Jung, 1983) has been prominent in the therapeutic literature for many years – but it does lead us to ask how a shift in the way we view work with addiction might impact upon the self-constructs of the therapists themselves.

In this regard, I recollect my work as a supervisor for a number of years with 'Rudi', a middle-aged drug and alcohol therapist who held a senior post in a prestigious private clinic. The story Rudi told me about himself when we first met reminded me of religious conversion. Having used various sub-stances – primarily alcohol – from his teenage years until his late 30s, serious illness and the break up of his marriage led him to give up drug use and, via

AA mentoring, he found his way onto a drug counselling training. A decade later, he had forged a career for himself in this field and, subscribing to the disease model of addiction, identified himself as an 'addict in recovery'. This way of being led him to be on intimate terms with the high-status and often famous clients of the clinic, and he took obvious pride in his ability to diagnose and treat musicians and film stars, and encourage them to admit their 'sins' and sometimes bring their whole families into therapy.

While I found his enthusiasm attractive, and his stories about famous personalities beguiling, I was led to wonder with him whether it was possible for him to 'see' the individual beyond the 'addiction' since his world seemed to consist almost entirely of just three categories – 'addicts', 'addicts in recovery', and the 'casualties of addiction', as he referred to the families of his clients. Rudi was initially disturbed by the thought that he might not be as available to his clients as he had supposed. He found this particularly worrying because his identity as a therapist coalesced around the notion that as an 'addict in recovery' he had privileged access to the world of his clients, and could help them reject their damaging behaviours. That he persevered in supervision with me was a testament to his interest in phenomenology and he clearly found himself both attracted and challenged at the level of his self-construct by the possibility of adopting it in his work. Perhaps the most useful thing to emerge from our work together was that Rudi found he was increasingly able to 'stay with' the unfolding stories of new clients, rather than reflecting back to them through an expert lens. He always found it hard to relinquish the 'expert' role, but as he was increasingly able to understand the way it both protected and distanced him from clients he made the decision to, as he described it 'be Rudi' with them.

Conclusion

While I have not propounded specific skills and techniques for the supervision of addiction, I hope I have indicated some of the ingredients which can contribute to an existential-phenomenological *attitude* when working with such problems in living. All clients – all of us – experience a multiplicity of problems in living which we may address in numerous ways on a range from fairly comprehensible to possibly bizarre and apparently 'meaningless' responses. If we wish to enter the lived world of the 'addict' we need to adopt, preferably embody, an attitude of curiosity and care, just as we attempt to do so with other clients with other presenting problems.

I have suggested that it might be helpful to consider what we mean by 'addiction' and whether it applies to a relatively small sub-group of clients or whether the behaviour which is sometimes given the label 'addiction' is widespread throughout the population. I find the concept of self-construct helpful when considering this possibility. This perspective is also helpful in supervision, since it reminds us that addicts are not necessarily a special group requiring specialist therapy supported by specialist supervision. There is no 'them' and 'us'; no radically distinct categories of healthy and sick – we all have the propensity to be addicts and few of us will have really lived who have not had the experience of whatever we mean by 'addiction'.

References

Baker, A. (ed.) *Serious Shopping. Essays in Psychotherapy and Consumerism* (London: Free Association Books, 2000).

Cohn, H. W. *Existential Thought and Therapeutic Practice* (London: Sage, 1997).

Davies, J. B. *The Myth of Addiction* (London: Harwood Academic Press, 1997).

Deurzen-Smith, E. van *Existential Therapy* (London: Society for Existential Analysis, 1990).

Feasey, D. *Good Practice in Supervision with Psychotherapists and Counsellors* (London: Whurr, 2002).

Heidegger, M. *Being and Time*. Trans. J. Stambaugh (Albany: University of New York Press, [1927] 1996).

Jung, C. G. *Memories, Dreams, Reflections* (London: Fontana Books, [1961] 1983).

May, R., Angel, E. & Ellenberger, H. F. (eds) *Existence: A New Dimension in Psychiatry and Psychology* (New York: Basic Books, 1958).

Sartre, J-P. *Being and Nothingness*. Trans. H. Barnes (London: Routledge, [1943] 1969).

Schaler, J. *Addiction is a Choice* (Chicago: Open Court, 2000).

Spinelli, E. *The Interpreted World* (London: Sage, 1989).

—— *Tales of Un-Knowing* (London: Duckworth, 1997).

Walters, G. D. *The Addiction Concept: Working Hypothesis or Self-fulfilling Prophesy?* (Needham Heights: Allyn & Bacon, 1999).

10
Working With Young Offenders

Karen Weixel-Dixon

Introduction

Every relationship, every encounter, has the potential to be therapeutic or not. Relationships can be healing, profound and/or educational to varying degrees; they can also be demoralising, undermining and generally threatening on a variety of levels, including, of course, the physical dimension. These descriptions of the qualities of relating are not exhaustive or exclusive: every relationship comprises aspects deemed desirable as well as elements that are less favoured.

Every human contact challenges each of us with these possibilities. At that first moment of contact we cannot be certain as to how this particular engagement will play out; we are assessing the risk and safety factors from the first instant. The attendant anxiety that is inherent in these engagements is rarely laid to rest; even in the most intimate relationships we are often 'surprised' by attitudes or behaviour that seem anomalous with respect to the person we believed we knew so well. If one remains at all sensitive or aware, these tremors persist in every relationship.

The strategies that we employ to provide an illusion of safety in the human encounter certainly do not refer to the corporeal aspect alone. There is a crucial aspect other than that of the physical: that of one's own desired image of oneself. '... existential-phenomenological theory proposes that the self is the *product of*, or that which emerges from, relational experience ... it views the self as indefinable other than in a relational sense' (Spinelli, 1994: 342).

Being-in-the-world With Others

'Relational' can certainly refer to objects as well as people: we can distinguish ourselves as something we are *not*, as in 'I am not a chair'. Implied in this statement is that to some very great extent to 'be' experienced as I would like to be experienced, I need an Other's confirmation. '... human relatedness is a primary "given"... we find ourselves always in the world with others, never as separate entities but defined by others, as we define them' (Cohn, 1997: 25).

121

Frequently, in an effort to actualise my expectations of who I want to be I attempt to woo the Other into seeing me as I wish to be seen. If I want to be seen as intelligent I might enhance my vocabulary; if I want to be experienced as caring I bring flowers to an ailing friend. However, it takes little effort to imagine the less salubrious extremes to which this principle could be applied.

The illusion is that when we do seemingly achieve the desired validation of self it is not the complete, static, permanent perspective that we really wish it to be: it is always subject to change at the caprice of the Other. This lack of stability in one's perceived image can provoke a sense of powerlessness and anxiety about how one is ultimately characterised and evaluated. This 'dance' between and amongst us, of seeking and giving and withholding the affirmation that each of us requires is also evidence of the co-constitutionality of all relationships: the quality of any given encounter is the responsibility of (all) the participants. The responsibility is not necessarily in equal measure, nor is the value assigned to the characteristics of the relationship necessarily concordant, but each person makes a contribution to the creation that is the encounter.

As other authors have already argued in this text, most, if not all, human dilemmas manifest in this relational realm of existence and there are implications for others both far and near: our difficulties have an effect on those that inhabit our social, familial and even cultural milieu. One could even make the point, as Sartre (1969) does emphatically, that our responses to our situation(s) have an impact on all human existence at some level.

The recognition that these anxieties, these concerns, are ineluctable in every human contact can be a powerful source of empathy and understanding between individuals. We are all subject to living in a world where, as Sartre (1989) so succinctly noted: 'Hell is other people', for precisely the reasons delineated here. (It should be noted here that understanding, getting to know another's perspective is not the same as condoning it). Additionally, we are all struggling to come to terms with aspects of existence that are arduous, if not downright absurd.

Once it is made explicit that we are all struggling for some semblance of safety and a mitigation of these anxieties it may become more readily apparent that each individual's way of being with another, of being-in-the-world, is a reflection of this intention. The significance of this discussion cannot be lost on the reader: both the practice of psychotherapy and that of supervision occur in the context of relationship. The effects of these encounters are directly relevant to the quality of the engagement. Furthermore, as all relationships are themselves set in broader contexts, the consequences of these meetings can affect multiple milieus, thereby extending our responsibility indefinitely.

This principle certainly extends to my role as a supervisor. As a supervisor, as in life generally, I hope to be recognised as credible, reflective and supportive. Similarly, the supervisee harbours their own desires to be experienced as the person and practitioner that they aspire to be. When some or all of these ambitions on both sides are *not* realised, it can provide an opportunity to explore how we are in-the-world with each other and how this manner of being-with contributes to the frustration of our desires. Additionally, it can be highly productive to consider how this encounter is the same as and different to other relationships, thereby clarifying what is particular to this situation and what is more generally the case in our meetings with others, including that with our clients.

The Same and Different

It is hoped that the therapist will, much as the supervisor does, make a timely enquiry as to how the client experiences the relationship between them: to what extent does the client feel valued, understood and confirmed as a person. If a divergence in viewpoints is experienced as a critique and a deterrent to how one wishes to be experienced it can be informative to consider how this threat is met. This exploration can clear the way for both parties to consider what each has brought to the encounter that serves to characterise it. In so doing, each may recognise that they are to some extent responsible for the situation, a realisation that can be empowering, if also anxiety provoking: one can change how one engages with another, but one will never be totally in control of how one is experienced.

Such an exploration may also elucidate just how fundamental these dynamics are for those who have endured the most aggressive encroachments to their bodies and souls. Almost without exception, the young women who are the focus of this chapter, had from an early age been objectified, tyrannised and deployed as weapons and tools in the service of their caretakers, who were themselves involved in deplorable and illegal activities. The young women were acutely aware of the nature of this abuse in its most malevolent sense: the attempted negation of their humanity.

These abuses did affirm them in some ways: they experienced themselves as useful, efficacious and consequently they had some sense of belonging. However, for those that turned to criminal activities, their endeavours produced worthiness in an extremely limiting way. Their microcosmic social order could validate their utility and provide some sense of value but the community with the greater political power could deprive them of their liberty. The actualisation of some values demanded a high price and a great many other values were compromised.

It seemed that much of society perceived these adolescents as irredeemable misfits, devoid of positive possibilities. It was generally considered by most of the 'professionals' involved that any hope of a better life for these women was irretrievable. Once criminalised, these young women became 'units' assigned to a set category: again their subjectivity and their possibilities were denied. They were seen in terms of their behaviour, which could be violent towards themselves and others and seemingly necessitated them being under strict control.

In this respect the therapeutic encounter could offer these women an opportunity to consider how they contributed to the quality of their lives and relationships. The limitations imposed by their criminalisation could not be denied: their options were curtailed by cultural and social precepts but rarely had they been challenged to refer to their own agency within these constraints. The therapist could challenge the assumption that these women's futures would be solely dictated by their histories. Additionally they were given the opportunity to explicitly reflect on how they participated in their relationships, a discussion that was most often prompted by the encounter between themselves and the therapist. This exploration could then be broadened to include any of the engagements external to the therapeutic one: family, lovers, friends and even prison officials.

These young people were strikingly different to most of us with respect to the severity of the traumas they had endured at a young age. However, these adolescents faced the same challenges encountered by all of us: given the limitations produced either by the facts of their history or by erroneous choices, they were confronted by the possibilities still available to them. The same and different: we all struggle with the consequences of our own mistakes as well as the contingencies of our situation. It is due to the awareness of this universal predicament that we are able to work therapeutically with people from divergent backgrounds. In many cases it seems to be the only way to invoke awareness and the potential for change. The broad sweep of existential supervision allows us to recognise and work with the tensions of both similarities and differences.

Worldviews

The strategies we construct and employ to keep us safe from the risks inherent in relationships are one aspect of each individual's worldview. Our worldview is comprised of our attitudes towards Self, World (Cosmos) and Other, which includes our values in relation to these dimensions. The realisation of these values and perspectives serve in part as the foundations for our choices and actions. Emmy van Deurzen has formulated a practice of value clarification '... as a basic task of existential therapy ... (it) is for the client to determine what values he or she lives for ...' (Deurzen & Arnold-Baker, 2005: 240). It is the worldview that existential therapists seek to clarify and reflect on with their clients. It is also the intersecting of worldviews of the client and the practitioner in the therapeutic context and additionally those of the supervisor and practitioner in the supervisory setting that is the appropriate focus for consideration.

When the assumptions and values of the practitioner and the supervisor coincide there may be some risk of collusion as the viewpoints remain unchallenged. It is important to note this convergence and acknowledge that our biases can obscure and limit our perspectives. It is equally important to note the divergence of worldviews: 'truth' and 'knowledge' can be recognised in relation to their contexts, thus precluding exclusive possession to either of these positions. Such a discussion may help us realise where we are rigid or flexible in our approach to life and to others and that these strategies result in benefits and losses. Making assumptions explicit can provide a clearer under-standing of our choices and actions.

The therapist/supervisee will issue the same kinds of challenges to their clients in the clarification of their worldview. This is most readily prompted by the encounter between the therapist and their clients, where the expect-ations and needs of the client are sometimes thwarted or neglected, a situation that is likely to occur in every human relationship. In existential supervision, as has been stated before, it is of fundamental importance to clarify the client's/supervisee's worldview. Clearly without some understanding of a client's way of being we cannot enable them to make choices and decisions in line with their values. This is particularly important when supervising therapists who work with young people who are vulnerable and who may not be aware of their choices and possibilities.

The Aims of Existential Psychotherapy and Supervision

Being-in-the-world with others is an existential given. It is therefore not sur-prising that one of the aims of existential psychotherapy is to reflect on how we engage with others and how others engage with us. Additionally reflection on one's worldview and how one engages with the givens of existence may provide some insight into the purpose underlying our choices and actions. It has been suggested that all choices are purposeful: to acknowledge the values and assumptions that we strive to actualise can help clarify the basis for our decisions and behaviour.

These are the fundamental concerns of the existential psychotherapist who accompanies, challenges and supports their client through a philosophical enquiry that requires a great deal of courage, on the part of both parties: truly 'being-with' an other as they carry out this process requires one to confront one's own engagement with difficult aspects of living, to be open to question-ing one's own choices and beliefs about these matters. We can expect no less of ourselves than we do of our clients.

These declared aims of the practice of existential psychotherapy are relevant also to the practice of supervision: these intentions display the fundamental similarities between both practices. This work, the development of a reflective life and practice, can be progressed via dialogical engagement. It is hoped that in dialogue with the supervisor, the practitioner can reflect on the relationship they have with their client and consider how they themselves contribute to the quality of the engagement. This might include difficulties in relating to the client, as well as the nature of the encounter when it is deemed therapeutic, or conversely unhelpful. It can also be useful for both parties to consider how and what is useful or not in their own relationship and how these aspects are the same as, or different to the relationship between therapist and client. This also holds true for the other dimensions of the worldview previously outlined: the ambiguities and inconsistencies of our beliefs and value systems are disclosed on every occasion. Even when our assumptions and values are reviewed and revised, novel equivocations appear. The exploration of these seeming discrepancies is relevant to both the practitioner and client.

The practitioner reviews with the supervisor their own worldview and how it colours their work and relationship with the client; the client is encouraged to conduct the same manner of reflection on their own perspectives and actions. This last proposal summarises the fundamental responsibility of the client: the willingness, to the best of their ability, to question and consider their own worldview. This expectation should be clearly communicated to the client; difficulties that emerge by virtue of this challenge are certainly crucial to the work.

For psychotherapists who, in the philosophical tradition, endeavour to maintain a perspective of enquiry with respect to working and living, there would appear to be a great many similarities between the projects of psychotherapy and supervision. It is relevant to note these semblances: the existential attitude is not something that is applied rather it is something that is lived. It is a perspective that serves as the foundation for all engagements with the world and with others.

Verbatim Illustration

The following is a recalled account of a supervisory session. The practitioner works as a therapist to young women in prison. This session takes place via telephone, while I, the supervisor, am at home in my consulting room.

> **A.** I am writing a report for the police and court. I have been talking it through with the client, so she has known all along what is in it and how it might be helpful for her. I have stated in the account that her principle problem and topic while she was seeing me for therapy was the sexual and emotional abuse suffered at the hands of her father since she was a child. We have covered these aspects (she reviewed a short list of relevant points) and as you know a bit about court proceedings and such. I wondered what you thought and if there is anything else we might include, or that I might have missed …

As A. was relaying this I felt a tightening in my stomach and a growing irritation. As it was a telephone session, I was free to pace the room; obviously A. was not aware of how perturbed I felt at this point. I immediately began to consider: what is it that so bothers me about this action and the attitude it displays on the part of the practitioner? How is it that my reaction is so forceful? What is being threat-ened here that I feel so defensive? There was a long pause at both ends of the line. I was considering where to begin, A. was awaiting my comment. It took only a few seconds for her to realise I was not favourably impressed.

> A. queried tentatively: What are you thinking? (She was obviously anxious about my response).

> S. I am thinking about the reaction I am having to your decision on this occa-sion. The first thing that comes to mind, even as I am speaking, is that this could put you and your client at risk. I will develop that thought further but first, do I recall correctly that this kind of report is in fact part of your contract with the institution? And is that the primary motivation for your writing it?

> A. Well, yes, I am obliged to make a written account in the event of a court case. Admittedly, this one is eight pages long, whereas the others were very brief and I knew they would not be used anyway. I have included a lot of information about how I work so they do not confuse me with the other kind of therapists ... But this one is more important because I may be called to testify and I want to have something prepared ... but what do you mean that it could be dangerous?

There was a bit of a waver in her voice and she spoke in a whisper. I knew that at this moment we were both feeling vulnerable and that this vulnerabil-ity, for my part, characterised to some degree both my personal and profes-sional life. Additionally, I was not certain that I was justified in my censure or that I could rationally explain it. I also realised that A. felt exposed, as it was a rare occasion when I did not respond favourably to her interactions with her clients and this anomaly was upsetting for her; neither was I happy to be the one upsetting her as the work was certainly difficult enough! I was thinking, feeling and pacing as I attempted to clarify my experience.

> S. For one thing I am feeling protective of you: I know you are anxious about appearing in court, as you yourself are aware, so preparing is a good idea. But if you give the interrogators a lot of material beforehand they have plenty of time and opportunity to discredit your report, as well as the position of your client as represented there.

I paused – I did not feel that we had really touched on the heart of the matter. I decided to put the challenge over to her.

> S. What is it A.? What is it that is really upsetting for you about this?

The reply could have been related to several possibilities: she was bothered by my impending critique, she was worried about the court appearance or about her client's well-being, she was having a bad day; or there was something I did not anticipate or intuit at all.

> **A.** No one else believes her, no one! Just me and her social worker … Her voice trailed off, she was crying quietly.

I remained silent, absorbing the significance of her comment. I suspected there was more and that she would proceed when ready.

> **A.** It is just so difficult for her and for me! No one believes her, not her mother, not her friends or the rest of her family and I must show that I do believe her, to the whole world if need be! And on top of it all, we both know the bastard is going to get away with it and is probably going to do it again, if he hasn't already started! It is just so unfair, it happens this way time and time again …

I waited.

> **A.** And therapy is *just not enough*!

Ah, this was it – this was the contention that had surfaced on previous occasions: my supervisee was always inclined to a more practical approach to her work than myself. I am firmly rooted in a tradition that proposes that 'interference' actually undermines the client's agency. I had never failed to challenge this tendency in her and she had often conceded, to the extent that her contractual obligations allowed.

However, this exchange and the discussion that followed clarified things even further: A. was having difficulty, as was her client, with the injustices of life – indeed serious injustices incurring extreme suffering. However, even in such dire situations I would be disinclined to take practical action on behalf of my client because it was likely to be futile and I prefer to concentrate on a more philosophical approach to the topics of fairness and suffering. In my view this is more effective in empowering the client to choose their attitude and actions with respect to this inevitable 'injustice' (and indeed to other ineluctable aspects of living). The suffering and pain that dominated the lives of these young women never failed to touch us both deeply. As was often the case, I was also moved and impressed by A.'s passion, and caring. By comparison I felt somewhat cynical and cowardly.

Eventually, I was candid about my reservations and musings. We went on to discuss whether and how this action on the part of A. might be helpful and to whom: to what extent this report was a gesture that served to assuage A.'s feeling of powerlessness. Additionally, I reconsidered my reticent perspective in light of my own fears around the same issue, namely: powerlessness and how this might lead me to a rather passive position in my work and life; I may well have communicated this negative expectation to my own clients.

Our discussion produced the foreseeable result: neither choice was intrinsically right or wrong. There were possible consequences whichever path was chosen. A. modified her report to a minimum of factual material but was prepared to defend her position and she also felt she had more clarity about the basis for her choice. For my own part I returned to a familiar, disturbing question: am I doing enough about the suffering in the world?

Further Repercussions and Reflections

The recalled verbatim reported above can serve to demonstrate a number of the issues discussed earlier in this chapter. I believe it represents what might be described as therapeutic dialogue: both parties were available to each other and to the possibility of change; the exchange demonstrated the processes of review and reflection that were realised by virtue of the attitude of both parties. The supervisor was the party that was approached to occupy the role of facilitator: this did not preclude the opportunity for both parties to benefit from the engagement.

It was immediately apparent that I, in the role as supervisor, felt circumscribed by some of the expectations I had of myself, as well as those I harboured with respect to A. These expectations were not related exclusively to this occasion, or to my role as supervisor, they were assumptions that were relevant to my self-concept as a whole. For example, I was wary of exposing my uncertainty with reference to my opinion: I might appear to be lacking in the wisdom that should be my domain. My desired self-image was at risk. Similarly, there is evidence that A. too held a perspective on herself which comprised her image as an advocate or champion. A. was proud of being seen in this role and was willing to consider how this affected her relationship with the client; it could promote both desirable and adverse outcomes.

These self-images were not wholly inappropriate but it was helpful to notice and acknowledge them and to become aware of how they might be restrictive: they were consequently reviewed, modified and rendered more malleable, allowing for a wider range of options in *how to be*. These realisations were the outcome of this encounter.

In this short extract existential dilemmas were manifest: freedom and choice, meaning and meaninglessness, relatedness of self and Other, time and the demise of possibility (when one option is realised and another lost). The common problems of living were evidenced: injustice, powerlessness, evil and inequity. The more laudatory possibilities were also illustrated: hope, determination, change for the better, humanitarianism and certainly a profound caring and sense of responsibility.

The Client Group

'It doesn't really hurt, doesn't hurt me anymore ... see?'

This brief excerpt illustrates some of the extreme difficulties that trouble the group of young people to which the supervision under discussion refers. This group is made up of young women, aged 14 to 17 years old, incarcerated for some of the most serious legal and violent offences. A great majority of them had themselves been victims of severe, almost unimaginable, abuse and exploitation. Most of these teenagers were inclined to extreme self-harm and suicide attempts.

The circumstances particular to this group were not only their deplorable personal histories and incarceration, but their situation as adolescents: old enough in many cases to bear the full responsibility assigned to an adult, young enough to be without the resources that experience and maturity can bestow. In spite of this contradiction, these young people were faced with precisely the same existential dilemmas as any one of us. These were clearly demonstrated in the problems they brought to therapy.

Many struggled to make sense of the hardships and inequities that were visited upon them, and how to differentiate between what they could change, and what circumstances were beyond their reach. Did they dare to dream of becoming a pre-school teacher, when their criminal records were likely to exclude them from this occupation? Possibilities and limitations were continually revealed.

Many wrestled with the regrets, even at this young age, of poorly considered choices and the consequences that would haunt them for the rest of their lives. Had they really given 'informed consent' (a much debated notion amongst this group) to their involvement in drug trafficking, coerced as they were by their own family? On what basis did they make choices and how was it that even the 'right' decision sometimes incurred further suffering, for which they were also (in part) responsible? Freedom and choice within constrained circumstances.

'They can't make me stop, no matter what they do ...'

Suicide was an option and a possibility, even in cases where there was 24 hour surveillance. Rosary beads served as a ligature, the metal coil from a toilet fixture could be employed as a cutting edge: but what purpose would the act serve? Who would 'win'? Who wielded the 'power'?

'She's not a *real* cutter, not like *me* ... just look at this!'

They struggled with self-esteem issues: most shockingly, there was a 'hierarchy' in terms of 'cutting' or other forms of self-abuse. It proved a useful exercise to challenge them with this manifest desire for respect and approval.

'The next time I come back in here, it's gonna be for something – special!'

Almost to a person, they each considered the nature of responsibility, the complications and implications of existing in a world of other beings whose wills were so often in opposition to their own. They queried: had they been deserving or responsible for the sexual and emotional abuse they endured, even as teenagers, or could they acknowledge that in making some concession to the domination by others they often saved their own lives or protected the lives of others? Were they really destined to be the product of their personal histories, totally circumscribed by events and circumstances beyond their control? And most definitely all of these young people raged over and reflected on the nature of love, and of caring. Could they offer the kind of love that they sought, did they extend to others the same frailties and ambiguities that they came to appreciate in themselves?

They usually did not realise it but they were doing philosophy, accompanied by an individual courageous enough to listen, challenge and sometimes just be with them in their suffering.

The work carried out by the therapists was grounded in existential perspectives: an appreciation of the vulnerability and power that co-exists within and amongst us and a healthy respect for each person's agency. The dialogue proceeded like a dance of veils: revealing and concealing, approaching and retreating. There was no total exposure or absolute discretion: the encounter provided a stage for the display of defences, aspirations and worldviews. Both parties to the engagement participated in these ways.

Through the challenging and supportive supervisory process the existential dilemmas apparent in these women's lives (and shared by us all) were brought to the fore. Possibilities and limitations; meaning and suffering; freedom and choice; relatedness and its implications; death and transience. These were their issues, the same and different as for every other 'client group' and every other human being.

Conclusion

The existential perspective lends itself to all aspects of life: it directly refers to the issues that concern us all. It is therefore relevant to psychotherapy and supervision (the parallels of these practices have been discussed here). It has also been noted that each of us encounters the 'givens' of existence, which are the common factors of all human life. However, it has also been noted that the manner in which we engage with these aspects creates the individual contour to our being. It is in this way that we are all the same and different.

The reflective consideration of our engagements with these existential conditions and how they manifest in our worldview can lead to a more powerful and responsible engagement with life. This philosophical style of enquiry can be a potent process when conducted in dialogue. The repercussions can extend to any or all of the many interpersonal contexts of those involved. The responsibilities therefore range beyond immediate situations: from supervisor to supervisee, from supervisee to client, from client to family, from family to cultural and global networks.

These struggles never cease but to live an 'examined life' can be a profound and gratifying process.

Special Thanks to Niki D. for her contribution.

References

Cohn, H. W. *Existential Thought and Therapeutic Practice* (London: Sage, 1997).
Deurzen, E. van & Arnold-Baker, C. (eds) *Existential Perspectives on Human Issues* (Hampshire: Palgrave Macmillan, 2005).
Sartre, J-P. *No Exit and Three Other Plays.* Trans. S. Gilbert (New York: Vintage Books, 1989).
—— *Being and Nothingness.* Trans. H. Barnes (London: Routledge, [1943] 1969).
Spinelli, E. *Demystifying Therapy* (London: Constable, 1994).

11

Existential Supervision in the NHS

Digby Tantam and Brijesh Kumar

Introduction

The United Kingdom National Health Service (NHS) remains one of the biggest employers in the country. Many of these practitioners use counselling and psychotherapy techniques, and receive supervision from a line manager, if not a denominated supervisor. Few of these supervisors are, as yet, identified as having an existential background although an increasing number are interested in this perspective. This chapter will therefore consider how existential supervision can be applied to the NHS rather than reflecting a current reality.

There are several reasons to consider the existential perspective as particularly applicable in the NHS. One of them is the proximity of many NHS practitioners to death which means that their supervisor needs to have a good understanding of issues around death and dying. Although there is a robust private sector in the UK, most emergency care is provided by the NHS. Sudden death and fatal illness are a regular occurrence in every NHS hospital and the acute psychosis or suicide (Bergsma *et al.*, 2007) of a client have to be dealt with by most NHS mental health practitioners on a regular basis. Rather than avoiding these issues existential practitioners provide a route to living with the anxiety they raise (Deurzen, 2001). Avoidance leads to personal psychological problems and through these to reduced work effectiveness (Arndt *et al.*, 2005) including denial of the suffering of others (Goldenberg *et al.*, 2001). Psychotherapy supervision in the NHS is mainly provided as a component of the general training of psychologists and psychiatrists.

The atmosphere of many NHS psychotherapy departments is deliberately kept friendly and safe, unlike that of the admission ward or the emergency unit. But trainees who feel they can avoid their anxieties about death and other limit situations when they work in the psychotherapy department also run the risk of shutting out their client's fears about death, dying and going mad. It is the job of the supervisor to prevent this from happening and the

133

existential supervisor knows this better than most. Some of these points will be illustrated in the 'case study' of a man with panic disorder and a fear of dying.

A substantial proportion of NHS psychotherapy and supervision is provided in groups and the existential perspective may be particularly valuable in group psychotherapy and group supervision (Frankel, 2002; Tantam, 2005). An existential perspective is particularly relevant to the supervision of psychiatrists and psychologists whose professional training and working practice is increasingly dominated by neuroscience. Their task is to comprehend what might be happening in a person's brain but at the same time keep track of what is going on in their mind and in their being.

Phenomenology, one of the pillars of existential psychotherapy as practised in the UK (Deurzen, 1997), has the potential to bridge this gap although this potential is still not fully realised (Mishara, 2007).

Existential Thinking and the Realities of the NHS

One of the challenges of health services based supervision is the high drop out rates in therapy. A study of a psychology training clinic in Canada found that less than 40% of clients thought that they had achieved their therapy goals and 31% stopped attending because they were no longer interested in therapy, wanting a break, or just leaving without giving any reason (Hunsley *et al.*, 1999). Similarly supervisees who are busily employed in NHS work are often involved in emergencies and can easily cover up an unwillingness to attend supervision by citing conflicting duties. Non-adherence to supervision is therefore difficult to estimate but in our experience is a significant problem made worse because other NHS staff may be able to control supervisees' time and block their attendance at supervision. Consultant psychiatrists may, for example, schedule a ward round at a time that they know their trainee normally attends psychotherapy supervision. It is therefore the values and emotional flavour of the NHS itself that influence all of the parties involved in supervision and it is important that the supervisor takes this into account by concentrating on helping the supervisee to focus primarily on the preoccupying concern of the client – at the same time recognising that context cannot be ignored.

Existential Supervision within the NHS

Many existential practitioners might argue that both the values and the emotional flavour (Tantam, 2006) of the NHS are inimical to existential psychotherapy. For them the straight jacket of evidenced-based practice interferes with the existential attitude of facing up to the aloneness and meaninglessness of life. They value an attitude of acceptance, even encouragement of feeling anxious and of daring to be uncertain without flinching. In apparent contradiction to these ineffable considerations, measurability is a key NHS value. Aloneness is an immeasurable quality of experience weakly if at all correlated with its measurable proxies like social network size. Measurability is equally irrelevant to meaning. In fact some therapists would consider that to measure something is to cut it down to size and in doing so, to destroy it.

NHS practitioners and managers value measurement because it provides the most indubitable, or apodictic, evidence about effectiveness. Psychotherapists, including supervisors, rarely have access to this kind of evidence but this is not to say that no adequate evidence is available. Existential psychotherapists with their roots in phenomenology know that Husserl has demonstrated methods of providing evidence that involves phenomenological and transcendental reduction rather than measurement. It is unlikely that many NHS staff will want to master Husserl sufficiently to be able to evaluate this kind of evidence (Lee, 2007), but many will recognise the kind of evidence that Husserl's focus on intentionality leads to. This is the kind of evidence that we use when we see a stick in the water and know that it only *looks* bent but it is really straight. It is evidence based not on appearance or even description but on something that transcends this. Noe (2004) argues persuasively that this knowledge comes from knowing how the stick would handle. It is literally about 'grasping' things.

This knowledge is based on consciousness: we interrogate the schema involved in acting on the object that are immanent in seeing the object (Gallese & Metzinger, 2003). But this kind of evidence is the kind associated with 'knowing just what to do' rather than 'knowing that'. It is not based on measurement but on experience.

Practical knowledge of this kind is actually very familiar to NHS staff. A good manager understands a complex organisation if and only if she or he knows what to do to achieve a goal, not because she or he has statistics about the organisation at her or his fingertips.

Of course NHS supervisors do have to provide regular evidence of their effectiveness in order to fit in with a fundamental NHS value. However, we think that supervisors and psychotherapists can adduce other evidence than that obtained by measurement and still be seen to be upholding NHS values if they apply phenomenological principles. We have suggested that the spirit of Husserlian evidential procedures can be retained by using the language of action and intentionality, rather than the language of perception.

For example, in the particular situation of supervision, supervisees however acculturated to quantitative or scientific methods, will in our experience accept as evidence of the effectiveness of a method that an action within the supervisor-supervisee relationship produces a demonstrable and intended change in the supervisee-client relationship.

The Flavour of Hospitals

Most of us are only too aware that hospitals and clinics do have an atmosphere, often dominated by scuffed carpets, an odd choice of decoration and unusual smells. But we are referring in this section to the emotional atmosphere or flavour of the institution, of its methods and of its individual practitioners. If one emotional flavour is dominant in the NHS it is positivistic optimism. Few existential therapists would consider this emotional flavour particularly attractive or palatable. Existential therapists do not encourage can-do optimism but something different, which is how to tolerate and work with what Jaspers called limit situations (Jaspers, 1951), where optimism is irrelevant. Must existential therapy therefore confine itself to those limited areas of the NHS which deal with unremitting or fatal conditions, where other emotions than optimism and hope have to be foregrounded? We do not think so, although we do think that existential practitioners have to demonstrate an emotional register that is palatable to other NHS colleagues if they want to work in the NHS. The successful existential supervisor will need to respect the importance of optimism, but to shift it from optimism about physical or even mental recovery, to optimism about the client's capacity to be spiritually aware and to take the kind of leap of faith that Kierkegaard spoke about. It requires faith to open oneself up to who one really is, rather than to what one fears or what one desires. This brings deeper satisfaction than either the avoidance of fear or the pursuit of desire (Kierkegaard, 1983).

Phenomenology Applied to Supervision

Much of NHS psychotherapy has to be short-term, not just because of financial exigencies but also because this is what many NHS users expect. In order to meet this demand, one of us (Tantam, 2002) has developed a short-term method of therapy and supervision which is based on such evidence as is currently available about therapeutic change, without drawing on any particular modality. The origins of the approach lie in Frank's (1961) theories of 'remoralisation' and the focal psychoanalysis developed by Balint *et al.* (1972) for NHS work. The method is based on the repeatedly reconfirmed finding that practitioners of differing orientations have similar results (Stiles *et al.*, 2008), indicating that outcome is not determined by psychotherapy theory but by some other aspect of the therapeutic endeavour. This is an extremely important finding for supervision which favours an existential perspective.

Lambert and Ogles (2004) conclude their review of the outcome literature by emphasising the importance of early therapeutic alliance, ongoing therapeutic relationship and therapist skills, which cannot be attributed to training or modality of psychotherapy. Persistence in therapy is also an important factor (Tantam, 1995), which can be increased by feeding back client dissatisfaction to therapists early on (Whipple *et al.*, 2003), possibly enabling the therapeutic alliance to be strengthened. Feedback helps to ensure that the therapist is focusing on what matters to the client. This is an important determinant of persistence in therapy (and the persistence of a supervisee with a supervisor) along with congruence in values and palatability of emotional flavour (Tantam, 2002).

We have been arguing that an existential perspective incorporates values that can be shown to be congruent to those of NHS managers and colleagues and emotional flavours that can be made palatable to NHS clients. But there is a third element which has, so far, been missing: 'meaning'. We believe that the repeatedly used jargon word, 'meaningful', applied so often to relationships, events, activities and therapy, has to be taken seriously. The existential emphasis on 'meaning' is not simply another dogma but is an accurate reflection of and a guide to the actual concerns that preoccupy the client. Meaning cannot be prescribed to the client but has to be discovered by the client and the phenomenological method is a kind of blueprint for helping them do this. We illustrate this by an extended case example.

Illustration

George first presented to his general practitioner complaining of poor sleep. This was of particular concern to him because he was a window cleaner. When he had a bad night, his coordination was affected and he was afraid that he would fall off his ladder. He had already lost his job as a computer programmer because he could not concentrate. George lived with Sara who had children by a previous relationship. George said that he and Sara got on well, but that she had begun to sleep in another room as he kept her awake with his not sleeping.

His general practitioner established that George had difficulty in getting off to sleep and often woke in a panic in the night; that he was having trouble with his memory and with his concentration and that he often felt his heart pounding. The general practitioner prescribed a beta blocker for the heart pounding and explained to George that a tablet to help him sleep would only be of short-term value. He would quickly become tolerant of it and it would therefore be of little help for his long-term sleep problem. There was also a risk of dependence. His GP thought that George would benefit from anxiety management and gave George some self-help books and referred him to the community psychiatric nurse. She noted that George had not improved and attributed this to his disturbed childhood. She thought that he had a post-traumatic stress disorder and that he would need specialist help. George was therefore referred to the local psychiatrist and was initially seen by a trainee who took a history before discussing the case with the consultant. George confirmed the account of his anxiety symptoms that he had given to the GP. He could have attacks up to eight times in a night and sometimes had to give up trying to sleep because of them. His shortness of breath could get so bad that he had once or twice gone to Casualty to get checked out in case he was having a heart attack.

George said that his parents were both alive and well, and that he had three younger sisters. He thought that his parents were closer to his sisters than to him. His mother had rejected him, he thought, when his younger brother had died of a cot death at the age of four weeks, when George was only two. After that his mother had not really coped well with the children. The family were frequently seen by psychologists and psychiatrists and the children placed in temporary care by social services. George had begun to wet himself (enuresis) and had also developed severe constipation leading to overflow soiling (encopresis). His mother punished him severely whenever he wet himself or the bed and whenever he soiled himself. Sometimes she did this by locking him into his bedroom with a bucket for a toilet. There were two investigations of physical abuse but no action was taken until he was nine, the year that his mother did not celebrate his birthday, when he was placed in foster care. He was physically punished in the first foster family, too, but was then fostered by another, kinder, couple. His encopresis had resolved long before he was fostered and the enuresis stopped shortly after he joined his second foster family, when he was 12.

It often happens in NHS supervision that the background is not fully available to the supervisor. For those supervisors who work solely with the supervisee and their reactions in the supervision, it may be more important to know about the supervisee's background than the client's. One difficulty about this 'counter-transferential' approach in the NHS is that supervisors and their supervisees often have multiple relationships: for example supervisors are also trainers who are required to report on their supervisee's training progress and not just on their competence as therapists. It may be inappropriate for an educational supervisor to have the level of personal knowledge about a trainee that a counter-transferentially orientated supervisor might want to have about a psychotherapy supervisee. Focusing on the biases in the emotional reactions of the supervisee has another disadvantage. It encourages the supervisee to focus on the emotional biases, or transferences, of their client. Since psychoanalytic ideas remain dominant in the NHS, despite the inroads made by Cognitive Behaviour Therapy (CBT), many supervisees are only too ready to do this.

The supervision described in many other chapters in this book is focused on the supervisee, since its focus is on training or personal development. Training NHS staff, such as psychiatrists, who do not intend to become counsellors or therapists start from a different focus; these staff need to master the basic skill of identifying and attending to the preoccupying concerns of their patients or clients. Our method (or rather that of one of us, DT) to achieve this is to use a process similar to that of phenomenological reduction. In supervision, this means that the supervisor helps the supervisee to apply a reduction to the supervisee's memory of what happened in the session or sessions being reported. The outcome of this reduction is that the supervisor encourages – sometimes even challenges – the supervisee to bracket out their own assumptions about the social and psychological world of their client. The second step is for the supervisee to be open to all of the client's experience and not just those experiences that the supervisee has assumed are relevant or important. It is only when supervisees are too caught up in their own phenomenological world and they cannot undertake this reduction that the supervisor's attention needs to switch to the supervisee him or herself as the focus of the supervision.

One consequence of obtaining a wide range of information is that it supports many different approaches. Behaviour therapists, object relations therapists and attachment theorists would all have found much to support their own approach in George's history. Some might have concluded that his background was so traumatic that short-term therapy provided by a trainee would be inappropriate. The supervision seminar (three psychiatrists in training in supervision with an experienced consultant psychiatrist/psychotherapist/supervisor) considered this, but it was concluded that, so long as George was clear about the limits of what was available, some therapy was better than no therapy. However, the supervisor noted that both he and the therapist had an additional responsibility which was to safeguard George from the effects of further disappointment or abandonment.

In the next session George said that he was a hard worker and that in his early 20s (he was currently 27) he had saved up enough to take out a mortgage on a two bed roomed flat, where he currently lived. He lived there with his girlfriend for two years. She was in her late teens and had psychiatric problems. George had come home one day and found she had taken an overdose. The trainee asked him if that had contributed to his anxiety and George said that he could never be sure when she would repeat it. The trainee wondered if that was connected with his difficulty in sleeping and George said that he would sometimes lie awake wondering if he would find his girlfriend dead in the morning.

The instincts of the supervisee were to search for meaning, but as we have mentioned meaning cannot be prescribed, only uncovered. The supervisor therefore remained agnostic about the relevance of George' fears about his girlfriend and urged him to remain at a descriptive level. He did however note that George was resolute: he had continued working despite everything that had been happening to him. George described his symptoms in the following way. He might feel uneasy during the day but was rarely overtly anxious if he had slept well the day before. About one day in two he would lie down in bed to prepare to go to sleep when the anxiety would flare up. Once that happened he knew that his symptoms would increase to the point where he sometimes thought that he would die, he would toss and turn all night and not sleep. His relationship was suffering as a result.

The consultant concluded that George was suffering from a panic disorder, probably due to his fear of his girlfriend's unpredictable self-harming. She prescribed an anti-depressant, and referred George for CBT. The trainee who was in supervision asked if he could work with George under supervision and this was agreed.

This is so far a typical NHS case which is one reason that we have chosen it. Psychotherapy and medication are often combined in the NHS and CBT is considered to be the treatment of choice for anxiety related disorders. Although there might have been rare cardiac conditions that could have caused George to feel anxious when he lay down there was nothing in his history to suggest these and little indication for further physical investigations. The link with his fear about his girlfriend is plausible but George did not seem to resonate to it: it was obviously not his preoccupying concern. The supervisee thought that there were some missing elements in George's story and he was encouraged to take a further history.

NHS practitioners, particularly doctors and psychologists, are taught repeatedly to assess before they act. This leads to an instrumentalist conception of psychotherapy, sometimes shared by patients. The idea being that a detailed assessment can be followed by a specific targeted intervention which cures: the psychological equivalent of Ehrlich's 'magic bullet'. Phenomenological enquiry proceeds differently. Actions – comments, observations, provocations – lead to more accurate perception, not the other way around and so the supervisee was shown how to keep exploring along phenomenological lines instead of suggesting a solution or making an interpretation.

George said that although his relationship with his father had always been good, his father was under his mother's thumb. George said he did not get on well with his mother and she seemed to resent him being there. She would constantly tell him he was a nuisance and find any excuse to send him to his room. The supervisee asked what sending him to his room entailed. 'Well, I had to stay in there till she let me out. She would lock the door, you see. It could be from before teatime till the following morning'.

At the next supervision, we discussed the terror of being locked in at night, alone. This seemed to have some phenomenological relationship to George's current symptoms of feeling panicky. There was a debate about the importance of past events on current anxiety. It was clear to the supervisee that the client wanted help with his anxiety now and not with his past. The supervisee was not so familiar with psychoanalytic theory that he assumed that childhood experience was the main determinant of psychopathology in later life. If anything, he was impressed by his client's pluck and determination in overcoming his past.

Psychiatry trainees are expected to obtain supervised practice of psychotherapy in three modalities: psychodynamic, CBT and systemic. The supervisor was acting as a CBT supervisor and was happy to countenance CBT methods since they are consistent with NHS values and provide an explicit framework of procedures that structures the therapy hour and therefore reduces trainee anxiety. But the supervisor used an existential-phenomenological approach to provide a philosophical horizon to CBT interventions and to help the supervisee to understand what was actually happening.

The supervisee asked George to keep a diary of his symptoms and any associated events or thoughts. Although many trainees request this, many of their clients do not comply. The supervisee had formed a good therapeutic relationship with his client and he did comply. When the diary was reviewed it bore out what the client had said previously: that if he did not sleep well one night, he would sleep well the next. The diary entries also showed that George's first anxiety attack always began as he was falling asleep. The diaries demonstrated what the supervisee had already feared: that the anxiety attacks had become more common since the start of therapy.

That the client's anxiety began as he was falling asleep was a surprise in CBT terms, since this assumes that either a somatic symptom of anxiety or a negative automatic thought initiates an anxiety attack and that other thoughts then enter in to drive the anxiety to the level of panic. But falling asleep, that is entering phase 1 sleep, is associated with a reduction of sympathetic tone and therefore with a reduced likelihood of palpitations or shortness of breath. There is also a reduction of directed thinking and an increase of dreamlike thinking. Phase 1 sleep should not therefore be associated with anxiety symptoms or negative automatic thoughts. The supervisor asked other members of the supervision group to come up with phenomena that might be linked to anxiety and which might occur during phase 1 sleep and several medical possibilities were suggested. The supervisor knew from his own experience that the symptoms that are particularly associated with sleep induction are hallucinations (typically hearing one's name being called out) and myoclonic jerks – the latter consisting of spontaneous jerks of several muscle groups which are sometimes strong enough for people to dream that they are falling and to be 'jerked' awake. Though the client was not experiencing hallucinations, perhaps he was having a kind of myoclonic jerk.

Further phenomenological description of the client's actual experience was needed. George said that he would be drifting off and not particularly anxious, when he would feel a thump which he automatically associated with his heart. He would then think that his heart had missed a beat, or otherwise malfunctioned and that it might be going to stop altogether. He would immediately think that he had better not fall asleep because if he did and his heart malfunctioned badly he might not be aware of it or able to get help. So he would deliberately stop himself falling asleep, all the time worrying about what had caused that awful 'thump'.

The supervisee wondered if it could be a kind of jerk rather than a thump, that is a contraction of his chest wall and not a sensation transmitted from the heart inside the chest. The client agreed that this was possible because it actually did feel like a thump *on* his chest and not *in* his chest. The supervisee explained about muscular, myoclonic jerks, their association with sleep induction and their essentially harmless nature. The client took it all in and asked why it only happened some nights. As it happened there was a good physiological explanation for this as well, which we discussed in the supervision group, so that this too could be conveyed to George at the next session. When a person is sleep deprived they may skip sleep stages 1 and 2 and directly fall into phase 3 sleep within seconds after sleep onset. So when the client was tired he was not entering the stage of sleep associated with myoclonus. The client was even given an explanation for the jerk reflex taken from evolutionary psychology, after we had discussed this in supervision: when monkeys sleep, they find a flat place to lie down on, but if they nap in the day they risk losing their grip on a branch or of the fur on their mother's back and risk falling down. The jerk on falling asleep means they grip tighter rather than lose their grip: a useful reflex for their survival. George liked this explanation and apparently took it to heart.

At the next and last psychotherapy session George reported that he had some more jerks but they did not bother him now that he knew they were not due to his heart and they no longer stopped him sleeping. He had not entirely believed the therapist at first but had looked up myoclonic jerks on the internet and had discovered that lots of people had similar experiences to him which had finally convinced him. His girlfriend and he were now sleeping in the same bed again and he had returned to window cleaning.

Conclusion

Our case example may be an unusual choice for a chapter on existential supervision. At first sight, it seems like a triumph of medical diagnosis and not an illustration of existential practice at all. We would argue that working in the NHS does often mean that discourse about clients is appropriately carried out in the language that is familiar to other NHS staff. We do not think that George improved because of a medical intervention but because of an existential one. There were almost too many explanations for his symptoms and therapy could have been long and arduous, for he felt in the dark about his symptoms and the reasons for them and it might have taken a therapist many months to explore all avenues, without getting anywhere. But phenomenologically it was fear of not knowing that kept him awake. His fear, or rather anxiety, was existential in that it was concerned with his own death. It might have been possible to work with this productively, although it would have taken more than the four remaining sessions. However, we do not think that it was the awareness of his own mortality that made the client anxious for he was in many ways a resolute, even intrepid man. It was his inability to find any meaning in his predicament that unsettled him. It would have been easy to provide him with meanings, for example that he was traumatised by his childhood or that he associated being in bed with being punished. But an important point of the supervisory process was to hold off on explanations and to tolerate not knowing, until description was complete.

Although the therapy was very brief, its emphasis was continuously on description rather than on prescription or interpretation. It proceeded by a process of bracketing of irrelevancies to leave the client's preoccupying concern starkly exposed: was he feeling the thump of his heart going into spasm, or was it really a muscular jerk in his chest wall?

It is of course rare for a preoccupying concern to be so overtly physical, or for there to be a simple and rapid resolution. Often, concerns need further elaboration although, in our experience, once a preoccupying concern has been made manifest, many clients do feel able to face up to it in a new way, sometimes by using their concern as the spur to find a new meaning in their situation which canalises the energy of their anxiety in a new and less destructive direction.

Therapy ended when George was able to let go of one meaning that he had fearfully put on his experience, which was that his heart was bursting. He found another meaning for his experience in what the supervisee had said about evolutionary psychology and this meaning was not anxiety provoking and allowed him to feel at ease in life again.

On the way out of the third and penultimate session, the supervisee heard George say to one of his friends who had come with him: 'the doctor thinks I become a monkey at night', this was followed by relieved laughter.

References

Arndt, J., Routledge, C., Cox, C. & Goldenberg, J. 'The Worm at the Core', *Applied and Preventive Psychology* 11(3) (2005) 191–213.
Balint, M., Ornstein, P. & Balint, E. *Focal Psychotherapy* (London: Tavistock Press, 1972).
Bergsma, A., Liefbroer, A. & Poot, G. 'Happiness in the Garden of Epicurus', *Journal of Happiness Studies* (2007).
Deurzen, E. van, *Everyday Mysteries* (London: Routledge, 1997).
—— *Existential Counselling and Psychotherapy in Practice,* 2nd edn (London: Sage, 2001).
Frank, J. *Persuasion and Healing* (Baltimore: Johns Hopkins University Press, 1961).
Frankel, B. 'Existential Issues in Group Psychotherapy', *International Journal of Group Psychotherapy* 52 (2002) 215–31.
Gallese, V. & Metzinger, T. 'Motor Ontology'. *Philosophical Psychology* 13(3) (2003) 365–88.
Goldenberg, J. L., Pyszczynski, T., Greenberg, J., Solomon, S., Kluck, B. & Cornwell, R. 'I am not an animal', *Journal of Experimental Psychology* 130(3) (2001) 427–35.
Hunsley, J., Aubry, T., Verstervelt, C. & Vito, D. 'Comparing Therapist and Client Perspectives on Reasons for Psychotherapy Termination', *Psychotherapy: Theory, Research, Practice, Training* 36(4) (1999) 380–8.
Jaspers, K. *The Way to Wisdom* (New Haven: Yale University Press, 1951).
Kierkegaard, S. *Sickness unto Death* (Princeton: Princeton University Press, 1983).
Lambert, M. & Ogles, B. M. 'The Efficacy and Effectiveness of Psychotherapy'. In *Berger and Garfield's Handbook of Psychotherapy and Behavior Change*, 5th edn (New York: Wiley, 2004).
Lee, N. I. 'Experience and Evidence', *Husserl Studies* 23(3) (2007) 229–46.
Mishara, A. L. 'Missing Links in Phenomenological Clinical Neuroscience', *Current Opinion in Psychiatry* 20(6) (2007) 559–69.

Noe, A. *Action in Perception* (Cambridge: Massachusetts Institute of Technology, 2004).

Stiles, W. B., Barkham, M., Mellor-Clark, J. & Connell, J. 'Effectiveness of Cognitive-behavioural, Person-centred, and Psychodynamic Therapies', *Psychological Medicine* 38(5) (2008) 677–88.

Tantam, D. 'Why Select?', *The Art and Science of Psychotherapy Assessment*. In C. Mace (ed.) (London: Routledge, 1995).

—— *Psychotherapy and Counselling in Practice: A Narrative Framework* (Cambridge: Cambridge University Press, 2002).

—— 'Groups'. In *Existential Perspectives on Human Issues* E. van Deurzen & C. Arnold-Baker (eds) (London: Routledge, 2005).

—— 'The Flavour of Emotions', *Psychological Psychotherapy* 76(1) (2006) 23–45.

Whipple, J. L., Lambert, M. J., Vermeersch, D. A., Smart, D. W., Nielsen, S. L. & Hawkins, E. J. 'Improving the Effects of Psychotherapy', *Journal of Counselling Psychology* 50(1) (2003) 59–68.

Part III
Questioning and Developing Existential Supervision

Introduction

Emmy van Deurzen and Sarah Young

In this final part of the book the concept of supervision, as it is usually defined, is questioned. Consideration is given to the future of existential supervision and the possibilities for change in the field. The first chapter (Chapter 12) begins with a discussion of four commonly held assumptions about supervision and how these do not fit within supervision informed by existential-phenomenology. It is suggested that these assumptions can inhibit the openness which is so essential to existential phenomenology. The expectations inherent in certain work contexts are also challenged. These encompass issues of responsibility and it is shown how these relate to existential supervision, particularly given the move towards registration and regulation. The possibility of redefining supervision in the light of existential thinking and perhaps re-naming it as 'reflective discussion' is considered. The limitations of the notion of 'clinical' responsibility are highlighted and this is taken up further in the next chapter.

In this chapter (13) the issue of responsibility, perhaps one of the most important issues in existential thinking, given that we are all seen as ultimately responsible for how we live our lives whatever the imposed limitations, is opened more fully and considered from the standpoint of both the supervisor and the supervisee. The author digs deep into the supervisory relationship and challenges some firmly held beliefs about the extent of the supervisor's responsibilities. In contrast to the experience of online existential supervision here the emphasis is on 'leaping ahead' and handing responsibility back to the supervisee. As was shown in the preceding chapter the supervisor cannot know for certain what happens between the supervisee and their client. The idea that a more experienced therapist is necessarily a 'better' therapist is questioned as is the assumption that trainees need more monitoring than qualified therapists. The contradiction between encouraging the supervisee to provide their client with a safe, non-judgmental space and yet not providing it in supervision is brought to the fore.

Perhaps in slight contrast to the above the author of Chapter 14 suggests that in becoming a supervisor the therapist takes up another level of responsibility. More importantly, this chapter underlines the argument of the present

text that existential thinking has universal relevance in the field of psychotherapy and counselling and that therefore existential supervision is relevant
for all supervision whatever the orientation of the participants. The wheel of
supervision provides an accessible and clear framework for practice which can
be employed by supervisors from a wide range of backgrounds and in a
variety of contexts. In a simplified diagrammatic form the wheel encompasses
the 'givens' which emerge from existential philosophy. Helpful examples of
supervision in practice demonstrate the efficacy of the thinking along such
existential lines.

The fourth chapter in this section (Chapter 15) takes us into the realm of the
'evocative' and epitomises the theme of transcending narrow modalities. The
evocative brings us back full circle to the theme of spirituality described in
Part I of the book. It resonates strongly with the existential sexuality and embodiment discussed in Chapter 6. Existential supervision is taken forward to
explore an aspect of existence often overlooked by supervisors, including
those who might describe themselves as existential. The author questions the
use of the word 'clinical' and its implications for practice. While the word may
be inimical to therapy informed by existential philosophy it is surprising how
frequently this word and all it implies (that is the medical model and the client
as a passive patient who is sick and needs treatment) is bandied about in existential settings. Sensitivity to the evocative is shown to invigorate and enliven
supervisory relationships bringing a welcome vibrancy to these encounters.

In the final chapter of the book (Chapter 16) we draw together all the
themes that have been discussed throughout these pages and we summarise
what we mean by existential supervision. We will sketch out a possible way
forward for the process of existential supervision, particularly in light of the
current move towards evidence-based practice, statutory registration and regulation. It will be clear however that our intention is not to systematise existential supervision and reduce it to one form of practice, when the diversity of
different perspectives and varied and multiple forms of practice remains the
hallmark of an existential approach to supervision.

12

Supervision As We Know It: An Existential Impossibility

Martin Milton

Introduction

This chapter explores the concept of 'supervision' and the contexts within which it is practised. It questions the meaning of the term 'supervision'; asks whether a thing such as 'supervision' is possible for existential practice or not; and ponders whether existential practitioners need to claim the activity as their own and redefine the practice if we are to develop, resource and support the meaningful encounters that enable the therapist and potentially facilitate existential psychotherapy.

Before we consider the nature of what 'existential supervision' might look like or be experienced as, it is important to consider the contexts in which we work, because regardless of what the individual supervisor and supervisee might desire from the relationship, the expectations of others can often have an influence on what the supervisory relationship *can* be. The previous chapter on supervising in the NHS clearly described the sort of constraints inherent in that particular context. From there the chapter will look at some of these contextual influences and explore the ways in which these can assist or hinder 'supervision' in general and 'existential supervision' more specifically. The chapter ends with thoughts on the nature of a supervisory practice that facilitates the work of the existential practitioner rather than inhibits it.

What Do We Know?

The wider field of supervision boasts an ever-growing set of theoretical models (see Carroll, 1996; Hawkins & Shohet, 1989, 1993; Holloway, 1999; Langs, 1994; Mason, 1993; Page & Wosket, 1994), an enormous number of research papers (see volumes of *The Clinical Supervisor* and the APA *Journal of Counselling Psychology*) and of course, many of the professional bodies have statements on supervision that apply to practitioners (see British Association for Psychotherapy and Counselling (2007) and Division of Counselling Psychology (2005, 2007)). In addition to this, training courses often have requirements for supervision as do policy makers and employers (Carroll, 1999; Henderson, 1999; Tholstrup, 1999).

Despite this, there has been a dearth of literature that explicitly focuses on 'existential supervision' (see du Plock, 2007; Mitchell, 2002; Wright, 1996). This is interesting as it begs a couple of questions. Firstly, whether existential therapists are simply not interested in the practice of supervision. Or, secondly, whether this lack of a literature indicates a particular difficulty for those working from an existential perspective.

With regard to the former question, my own sense is that, while it is true that existential practitioners have not been very evident in the literature, there are, at least, the beginnings of an engagement. Some have tackled it descriptively as a demonstration of their work (Strasser, 1999) or more directly in a conceptual manner (see du Plock, 2007; Mitchell, 2002; Wright, 1996) and of course the present volume is also testament to this interest.

When we consider the second question, it is clear that there are a number of difficulties that need attention before we can be clear on the ways in which supervision can be of support to the existential practitioner. It is these difficulties that this chapter focuses on in more detail.

Definitions and Assumptions

As with many human phenomena, there is an issue of language to consider when we explore the nature of supervision. The term 'supervision' is problematic if it explicitly refers to a process whereby the supervisor 'oversees and directs the performance of, the one who manages, controls, is in charge of, or is responsible for' the practice of another (Mitchell, 2002: 92). This definition implies that the relationship will be based on an authoritarian stance and that this is both possible and desirable (Strasser, 1999).

As well as this definition, the language used to discuss 'supervision' is often problematic as it contributes to a lack of critical thinking which has meant that the supervision literature has, at times, conflated what theory and policy say supervision *should* be with what those involved need or want it to be. Or maybe that it *can* be. Some expectations of supervision may be at odds with the worldview held by psychotherapists of all persuasions. In these circumstances the influence of the employer or policymaker can be a factor in therapists ignoring or misreading the implications of empirical evidence and also conflating political instruction with evidence. When this happens we assume policy directives are doable, ethical and just without investigating whether this is actually the case. This acceptance can mean we fall into bad habits of settling for assumption rather than knowledge; taking headlines as entire stories and saying 'Yes' when maybe we should be saying 'No' – or at least, 'Hang on, lets have a think about that'! But more about that later, for now, lets have a look at what the different stakeholders are saying that supervision is.

In line with a stance of un-knowing (Spinelli, 1997) it is helpful to continually question the meaning of taken for granted phenomena, and to do this, the chapter focuses on four functions that are often associated with the concept of supervision. As well as clarifying potential clashes in viewpoint between the different stakeholders, such an approach might also contribute to a process whereby existential psychotherapy can elucidate what 'existential supervision' needs to be, the way it is distinct from other stances to 'supervision' and the ways in which mainstream supervision might be fruitful regardless of its allegiance to existential philosophy.

The four assumptions are the idea that supervision is a means to facilitate a) the development of the trainee therapist (Carroll, 1996), b) the learning of theory (Shipton, 1997), c) ongoing personal development (Henderson, 2001; Thomas, 1997; Zorga, 1997) and d) 'quality control' (Carroll, 1996; Wheeler, 1996).

Four Functions – and Many Dilemmas!

Assumption 1: Supervision is a means to facilitate the broader training of the therapist

Supervision is seen as a core aspect of the ongoing development of the therapist (Carroll, 1996). It is not just that the literature suggests this, in the United Kingdom supervision is also an *expected* part of our ongoing continuing professional development (CPD) as it is meant to be (and for many therapists is) a place or a process, where therapists open themselves up to new knowledge and ideas, gain support in their attempt to be as open as they possibly can be with their clients and feel supported and challenged as they undertake the considerable personal development that the profession requires of us (Milton & Ashley, 1998; Tholstrup & Shillito-Clarke, 2007; Thomas, 1997).

While supervision can offer such a sense of development, this is by no means guaranteed as it is of course reliant on the relationship between the supervisee and the supervisor. Because of the dependence on the relationship and the wider factors that affect the relationship, it may not offer this all the time. One particular factor to consider is the power of the supervisor over the supervisee's progression. The supervisor is instrumental in the trainee's 'passing' or 'failing' the course. This can mean that the urge towards an inauthentic style of relating exists and this can create problems. While both participants might, as Strasser (1999) suggests, attempt the most open relationship possible, there are significant dangers to the self-concept of both the supervisee and the supervisor and to their professional progress. While in some respects it might be appropriate that both are invested in a particular outcome (that is success, or passing) it can inhibit the pair in attending to the complex processes that psychotherapy and supervision are.

The evaluative role that permeates the developmental function of supervision can mean that as well as trying to hear what is *actually* experienced in therapy and supervision, both are likely to have an idea as to how it *should* be – sometimes these coincide and sometimes they do not. Supervision affected by this evaluative agenda can run the risk of moving from a space of exploration to a place where the supervisee can be pressured into adopting a cloak of 'bad faith' (Sartre, 1995; Mitchell, 2002) – doing what they 'should' rather than what they 'feel' is right or, in today's view of 'evidence-based practice', sticking to the manual rather than staying with the client. This is not just an issue for trainees either, I certainly made decisions about *not* using one supervisor as a referee because, regardless of my actual talents or limitations, the fact that I did not share their *core* professional background, meant that I was *de facto* 'sub-optimal'. So all the while that evaluation *of* the supervisee *by* the supervisor is a core requirement of supervision, it is important to consider the impact of this and whether it allows the openness so crucial to intimate encounters such as existential psychotherapy and supervision.

Assumption 2: Supervision is a means to teach theory

Teaching of theory seems to be one of the main functions of supervision particularly for those new to the profession or engaged in CPD training. It can be an important forum for understanding the theory or philosophy upon which practice is based as it can be a safe place to 'play' with theoretical concepts and to experience the ways in which this knowledge and these ideas influence our way of being in the consulting room. This is the same no matter what approach people are studying and is certainly no different for those entering the realm of existential psychotherapy. In some respects the requirement may be experienced as *greater* due to the fact that very few people are taught philosophy or relational ways of viewing the world in their everyday lives or their other educational experiences and so supervision is the forum where the therapists might explore theory most fully.

As with the first assumption, this is not without its problems. Firstly, we have to recognise that this aim explicitly requires supervision to relate experience to existing theory. To limit ourselves, to some degree, to material that has already been *experienced, noticed and theorised*. While this may make sense at one level, it means that the supervisee and supervisor need to be able to articulate the experience and be aware of relevant theory. What about those uncanny experiences? The ones which are felt but hard to articulate? This assumption is also based on the understanding that the supervisor will be sufficiently *au fait* with the theory and its implications to guide the trainee. And we need to consider the question of how a supervisee accounts for experiences not yet considered by existential writers? The author of Chapter 15 addresses some of the 'uncanny', 'hard to articulate' experiences mentioned here.

It is also important to note that theory is another area where the supervisory dyad may be affected by the demands of the system. And many systems ask (or more accurately require or demand) us to declare an 'evidence-based model'. Rather than simply being an ethical and scientific stance, (one that an existential phenomenological 'model' is more than able to be), this directive is often high-jacked by very definite – and non-existential – views as to the nature of science, evidence and ethics. It often simply means Cognitive Behavioural Therapy (CBT) whether or not CBT has been assessed in light of the specific factors relevant to the client and the context (see Wilkes & Milton, 2008). This can influence the supervisory dyad as it is used to support an assault on anything non-manualised, so that practitioners experience significant hurdles as to how free they are to utilise all relevant theory – especially when the Department of Health (DoH), National Institute for Clinical Excellence (NICE) and even the British Psychological Society (BPS) have views about the theory which *should* be used, even before client and therapist have met. This stance means there is limited support for a truly scientific, open and phenomenological stance or a wide-ranging understanding of theory.

Assumption 3: Supervision is a means of support and personal development

Trainees look forward to the day when the training course is over, there are no more supervisor's reports or exam boards and now as an existential practitioner you can simply pick the supervisor you want and all will be wonderful, you will be supported and personal development will be facilitated in supervision. Right?

Hopefully yes, but not necessarily. My own experience, and that of many a graduate, suggests that as in the other areas, the experience of supervision is often more complex than our supervisory literature, policy and guidelines would lead us to believe. I say this for several reasons. Firstly, work may not endorse or pay for the supervisor you feel is most suited to you so you may have to 'make do' with whom you are assigned to. So already there's a dilemma – you either take the supervision provided or organise your own supervision and swallow the expense. The former option raises questions as to how to safely identify and manage your personal needs? This may not be an issue if the supervisee and supervisor find that they work well together. But what if there is no spark between you and the allocated supervisor? Or if the relationship has the cold, harsh, emotional connection characteristic of many well known literary characters – including Harry Potter and Severus Snape (Rowling, 2007). While this characterisation is (hopefully) an exaggeration – it is an exaggeration to make a point. In other areas of human relating it is perfectly possible to *fail* to find intimacy with people. It happens with family members and romantic partners, and it happens between therapist and client – so surely we have to consider the possibility that some supervisory pairings may simply be unable to offer a sense of support and care. While these pairings may allow us to 'tick the CPD box', would such experiences warrant the term 'existential supervision', or even simply 'supervision'?

Assumption 4: Supervision ensures quality

Many of us will have experienced supervision as helpful (Milton & Ashley, 1998; Strasser, 1999; Wright, 1996) and this experience is sometimes elaborated into policy based on the idea that supervision inevitably 'corrects' or enhances practice. While the psychotherapy professions (or at least their regulatory structures) work on the basis that it is helpful, there is literature that suggests there is no evidence that client satisfaction and improvement are linked to the nature or frequency of supervision (Green & Sherard, 1999).

On the surface of it, maybe there is nothing to be concerned about as we all want to ensure that we work as well as we can. However, the view that supervision enhances the quality of our work should be 'read' in relation to today's cultural fetish for ever increasing efficiency which assumes significant problems exist in the current practice of workers. This is evident in government policy on health, social care, education and agriculture where everything is subjected to 'modernisation', 'rationalisation' and 'standardisation'. When thinking of psychotherapy specifically, du Plock notes 'we teach and practice in an environment increasingly (and I would say often detrimentally) in thrall to quality assurance agendas, and to the neurotic "evidencing" of educational aims and learning outcomes which frequently stifles the artistry of therapy' (2007: 33).

Another implication of the assumption of quality is that there are now systems that hold the supervisor to be 'clinically responsible' for the therapy of the supervisee's client. A fair question is: 'so what?' What's wrong with that? Firstly, it is simply just not possible. For this rather lofty assumption to have any real meaning we have to assume the supervisor knows *what* is going on and has the power to direct it. But is it really possible for person A to know what happens between persons B and C? It's difficult enough when people live together all the time – but even parents are often clueless as to whether Johnny smacked Mary, or whether Mary hurt Johnny first! And even if it were possible, as Mitchell notes 'I find it hard to imagine that an existential-phenomenological therapist would assume it is possible to "over-see" and objectively judge what was happening within their client's different relationships' (2002: 94).

There is another problematic assumption and this is that the supervisee (whether deliberately or accidentally) is, on probability, going to do harm. To hold this assumption means the supervisor *assumes* the presence of malpractice or ineptitude (or another version of weakness) and goes looking for it. Or at least, does not challenge the ethos of the work context. If this is accepted, we have to ask about the impact that this has on the relationship. A stance like this veers away from the value base of existential psychotherapy which does of course attend to the relational struggles but also recognises the importance of positive regard, hope and faith in human life. This stance may also 'impede successful training [*and development*] because it can increase the possible feeling of defensiveness of the supervisee' (Strasser, 1999: 119).

Such a stance can eat away at the supervisory relationship. The imperative to oversee and be responsible leads to a hermeneutic of suspicion – and this may well create a 'less than optimal' relationship. If this does occur it should not surprise us that the supervisee, who in relative terms may feel emotionally dependent and less powerful, may find it very difficult to open up fully, to trust the supervisor and to let go of their own natural suspicion, no matter how much our western, rational, legalistic mind accepts the argument provided. It would be naïve to think that this evolutionary safe-guard would be any less potent simply because policy or practice says it *ought* to be so. The complexity of this relationship needs greater recognition in the workplace of all psychotherapists rather than the simplistic view that permeates many discussions of supervision today. When applied to existential psychotherapy and its 'supervision' it becomes very urgent indeed.

Where Now?

Because of the challenge that existential practice makes to the assumptions inherent in current policy around supervision, existential-phenomenological practice is vulnerable to concern and suspicion from outside. This is exacerbated by a lack of understanding of an existential-phenomenological world-view and often results in a lack of support for the existential project. This gives the existential-phenomenological practitioner a dilemma. It might be that existential psychotherapists can simply accept this state of affairs and limit our therapeutic contributions to those who find us wherever we are. Alternatively we might want to think about other, more inclusive possibilities. For instance, can we discuss our approach and our stance to supervision in ways in which others can understand without 'dumbing-down', or losing, the meaning of our project? In its entirety, this volume is of course an attempt to do just that. My own thoughts on the matter are that we need to consider the ways in which existential principles are engaged within the practice of that thing we call 'supervision'. And it may be no surprise to readers to realise that the first of the suggestions to follow is to do with definitions.

A New Definition?

As noted above, 'Supervision' is a term that risks becoming meaningless because too many people have loaded it with too many different meanings. The few existentially oriented authors that have tried to discuss supervision all seem to be moving away from talking of 'supervision' as if it were a single concept and encourage us to consider 'existential supervision' specifically (du Plock, 2007; Mitchell, 2002; Wright, 1996).

In light of this, we might simply want to stop using the term and discuss what *kind* of supervision do I need? What *focus* would be useful? *Which* supervisor will assist me with *that* issue? What person, structure, format do I need in order to experience enough safety to engage with the anxieties, risks and challenges that existential practice throws up for us? This reflection might mean that we also consider appropriate ways in which to rename the types of relationship we need at different times and in different circumstances. Must it be called 'supervision' or might the struggle to name it lead us to new and creative terminologies? Or would a term such as 'Reflective discussion' suffice and be more honest?

Relational Qualities

Whatever the field ends up calling the reflective and supportive endeavour that we currently call supervision, one key principle of an existential approach to supervision is its focus on a relational understanding of life and practice. Du Plock suggests this when he notes that 'notions of relationship, encounter and meaning-making are central to the existential-phenomenological therapeutic alliance' (2007: 35) and 'we need to find ways of ensuring that they occupy a similar position in the supervisory alliance' (du Plock, 2007: 35). Thus the therapy discussed might be one that attends to relational issues, as might the therapist and colleague when they consider how best to understand the client, the therapeutic relationship and the encounter that is being considered.

Focus

To be explicitly existential we have to reflect on the relational nature of Dasein and the implications this has for relationships and of course these may be many and diverse. This does not mean that it is hard to pinpoint the appropriate core focus for reflective discussions between a therapist and their colleague. Mitchell notes that one way to distinguish an existential approach to supervision is to compare it to existential therapy and notes:

> The difference between existential therapy and existential supervision lies not in the particular way of thinking, but in the agreed project between the therapist and the client and the supervisor and supervisee. The focus and intention in supervision and in therapy are different. Supervision is concerned with facilitating a certain kind of exploration that is concerned with themes and issues that emerge in the therapeutic relationship. Whereas in therapy there is a joint exploration of whatever the client chooses to talk about (2002: 91).

Du Plock is also very clear that the ultimate focus of an existential approach to supervision is 'to engage with the client in a piece of co-research to clarify the way the client creates meaning' (2007: 33). Strasser seems to support this idea when he states that 'the purpose of supervision is to talk specifically about difficulties concerning particular clients and to discuss theoretical issues that might emerge' (1999: 139). Therefore, the supervisee's needs, the development of theory and the quality control agenda all fade into the background – only to be attended to in service of an understanding of the client. Having said this, du Plock is also right to note the 'absurdity of the notion that it would be possible to "fix" the nature of this aspect of existential work' (2007: 32) and so, in the language of public sector management, the therapist and supervisor should retain the 'right' to their creative freedom as well as to their ethical responsibility.

To be attuned to existential principles, the reflective discussions that therapists and their colleagues undertake need to be collegial and egalitarian, focusing on the relationship between the client and their therapy and may result in a variety of different structures, formats and conversations. The issue of responsibility is clearly held by the individuals concerned for their part of the work. It is now time to briefly consider the contextual factors that are helpful for an existential approach to supervision.

Contextual Factors

Existential therapists and their supervisors may need to discuss and contract issues related to the context as these may facilitate or hinder attempts to be open and disclose all aspects of their practice, whether perceived as talents or as difficulties. Clarity about the role of the context is important (as discussed in Chapter 7) since the reflection on therapy may call the therapist to discuss and review delicate aspects of their very being and may sometimes challenge 'sedimented' beliefs that are impacting on the practice in therapy. For example, it may become apparent that the psychotherapist objects to the neurotic 'risk assessment' focus of many public sector settings. This may affect the supervisor and supervisee in a variety of ways. But as well as the supervisory dyad discussing these issues, it may be useful for discussion to take place, within the particular system within which the dyad are located, as to what occurs when such differences in values are apparent.

By initiating conversations between the supervisor, supervisee and other stakeholders too, incompatibilities between perspectives can be identified and considered so that the nature of the reflective process is understood as much as possible before any party feels too involved. Some obvious, specific issues to discuss in National Health Service, Prison or training settings might include freedom, responsibility and focus – the core issues for existential psychotherapists and clients.

Discussion is often very useful but of course it may also lead us to difficult and un-resolvable situations which may be disturbing for all concerned. For instance, the existential view that: 'the general rule is to aid the supervisee to realise their own issues and then it is their responsibility to explore their personal worldview' (Strasser, 1999: 139).

This may be difficult for some settings to accept and may lead to reflections on an experience of bad faith or for some existential psychotherapists the need to change work contexts so that clients and therapists are responsible for the therapy and as independent of state interference as possible.

Conclusion

It is clear that there is some useful support available already in what we term supervision. Greater clarification and debate may well lead us on to develop concepts and language that make the different roles and expectations clear. As others have written there is urgency to this as there are currently some significant changes happening in the way that the psychotherapies are constructed and regulated. This provides a time and a place to contribute our understanding of human experience and we need to be as clear and persuasive as we can be.

References

British Association for Counselling and Psychotherapy *Ethical Framework for Good Practice in Counselling and Psychotherapy* (BACP: Rugby, 2007).

Carroll, M. *Counselling Supervision: Theory, Skills and Practice* (London: Cassell, 1996).

—— 'Supervision in Workplace Settings'. In M. Carroll & E. Holloway (eds) *Counselling Supervision in Context* (London: Sage, 1999).

Division of Counselling Psychology *Professional Practice Guidelines* (Leicester: British Psychological Society, 2005).

—— *Qualification in Counselling Psychology: Candidate Handbook* (Leicester: British Psychological Society, 2007).

Du Plock, S. 'A Relational Approach to Supervision', *Existential Analysis* 18(1) (2007) 31–8.

Green, D. & Sherard, C. 'Developing an Evidence-base for Post-qualification Clinical Supervision', *Clinical Psychology* 133 (1999) 17–20.

Hawkins, P. & Shohet, R. *Supervision in the Helping Professions* (Milton Keynes: Open University Press, 1989).

—— 'Approaches to Supervision of Counsellors'. In W. Dryden and B. Thorne (eds) *Training and Supervision for Counselling in Action* (London: Sage, 1993).

Henderson, P. 'Supervision in Medical Settings'. In M. Carroll & E. Holloway (eds) *Counselling Supervision in Context* (London: Sage, 1999).

—— 'Supervision and the Mental Health of the Counsellor'. In M. Carroll & M. Tholstrup (eds) *Integrative Approaches to Supervision* (London: Kingsley, 2001).

Holloway, E. 'A Framework for Supervision Training'. In E. Holloway & M. Carroll (eds) *Training Counselling Supervisors* (London: Sage, 1999).

Langs, R. *Doing Supervision and Being Supervised* (London: Karnac Books, 1994).

Mason, B. 'Towards Positions of Safe Uncertainty', *Human Systems: The Journal of Systemic Consultation and Management* 4 (1993) 180–200.

Milton, M. & Ashley, S. 'Personal Accounts of Supervision: Phenomenological Reflections on "Effectiveness" Counselling', *The Journal of the British Association for Counselling* 9(4) (1998) 311–14.

Mitchell, D. 'Is the Concept of Supervision at Odds with Existential Thinking and Therapeutic Practice?', *Existential Analysis* 13(1) (2002) 91–7.

Page, S. & Wosket, V. *Supervising the Counsellor: A Cyclical Model* (London: Routledge, 1994).

Rowling, J. K. *Harry Potter and the Deathly Hallows* (London: Bloomsbury, 2007).

Sartre, J. P. *Being and Nothingness*. Trans. H. E. Barnes (London: Routledge, 1995).

Shipton, G. *Supervision of Psychotherapy and Counselling: Making a Place to Think* (Milton Keynes: Open University Press, 1997).

Spinelli, E. *Tales of Un-Knowing: Therapeutic Encounters from an Existential Perspective* (London: Duckworth Press, 1997).

Strasser, F. *Emotions: Experiences in Existential Psychotherapy and Life* (London: Duckworth Press, 1999).

Tholstrup, M. 'Supervision in Education Settings'. In M. Carroll & E. Holloway (eds) *Counselling Supervision in Context* (London: Sage, 1999).

Tholstrup, M. & Shillito-Clarke, C. *Supervision: A Secure Base*. A workshop presented at the Division of Counselling Psychology Annual Conference (2007).

Thomas, S. 'Supervision as a Maturational Process', *Psychodynamic Counselling* 3(1) (1997) 63–76.

Wheeler, S. *Training Counsellors: The Assessment of Competence* (London: Cassell, 1996).

Wilkes, R. & Milton, M. 'Therapists' Experience of Evidence Based Practice: Towards a Grounded Theory', Unpublished Doctoral Thesis, University of Surrey (2008).

Wright, R. 'Another Personal Approach to Existential Supervision', *Existential Analysis*, 7(1) (1996) 149–58.

Zorga, S. 'Supervision Process Seen as a Process of Experiential Learning', *The Clinical Supervisor* 16(1) (1997) 145–62.

13
Responsibility in Existential Supervision

Diana Mitchell

We may be able to evade a particular choice, but we cannot avoid responsibility, as a denial of response is in itself a response

(Cohn, 2002: 110).

Introduction

Responsibility and how we cope with responsibility affects how we are in the world and all our relationships. The focus of this chapter will be on responsibility within the context of existential supervision and the supervisory relationship. I will show how responsibility, as experienced by the supervisor and the supervisee, can alter and I believe enhance the practice of supervision.

For Heidegger the concept of 'care' (*Sorge*) is our most fundamental mode of Being-in-the-world. Heidegger (1962: 156) refers to two 'ontic' or experiential modes of care: one is concern, which is how we relate to objects or things; the other is solicitude, which is how we relate to human beings. As we have seen in previous chapters, Heidegger describes two modes of solicitude: the first is 'leaping in' solicitude (*Einspringende Fürsorge*) where 'the other is relieved of responsibility or the ability to respond to his/her own Being in his/her own way' (Karban, 1995: 8); the second is 'leaping ahead' solicitude (*Vorspringende Fürsorge*), 'instead of disallowing responsibility it is a relating which facilitates the responsibility of the other and his/her ability to respond to Being' (ibid).

We can choose to take responsibility for the other (leaping in) or we can choose to allow and enable the other to trust in his or her *response-ability* (leaping ahead) – breaking up the word responsibility in this way emphasises that as human beings we always already have the ability to respond. Inevitably we respond to the world and the situation we find ourselves in. We find ourselves responding to other people, objects and all that we see in our own particular way. As human beings-in-the-world-with-others it is impossible not to respond, but we can and do choose how to respond. To ignore a person or turn away in silence is a chosen response. The response-ability that comes with being human, which is always part of our interconnectedness with the world, can be referred to as our ontological Responsibility with a capital **R**, while the responsibility that we can choose is our chosen ontic responsibility with a small **r** (private discussion with Jyoti Nanda, 2008). Both modes of responsibility are of course not separate: the ontological Responsibility and the ontic responsibility are always related and connected.

Heidegger shows us that there can be no such thing as an individual. Each person is seen and can only be understood in the context of others, the world, history and time. He states that: 'conscience, in its basis and its essence, is *in each case mine* … the call (of conscience) comes from the entity which in each case I myself am' (Heidegger, c.f. Cohn, 2002: 99). Our personal responsibility and the choices we cannot escape from making confront us with our 'mineness' (ibid: 99). There is no such thing as an individual who is a separate being outside the world. However, in that moment of choosing, we experience 'being alone': the choice is mine and mine alone. Sometimes making a choice can feel very risky because we can never be completely certain that the choice we make is the 'right' one. This touches on the desire to 'make' another person responsible for our choices, rather than to face up to our own responsibilities.

Existential Supervision

I would love to find a new word for supervision, because the word supervision already implies a relationship where the supervisor is expected to monitor and correct the person who is being supervised in how best to 'practice therapy'. This further implies that an outsider (the supervisor) can see and know what is really happening between the therapist/supervisee and his/her client and that what is happening can be seen by the supervisor and possibly corrected. Super-vision means to 'oversee' and suggests a particular kind of relationship where one human being is 'above' the other.

When I refer to an existential therapist or existential supervisor I always mean 'existential-phenomenological therapist or supervisor'. As an existential therapist and supervisor I am aware of the existential dimensions of being (ontological) but it is the phenomenological dimension (ontic) of the situation that becomes the focus in therapy. I would say that both dimensions of being: the ontological and the ontic, are discussed and explored in existential supervision.

I agree with du Plock (2007: 34) that it is indeed 'bizarre' that existential-phenomenology, which prides itself on questioning and challenging our taken for granted assumptions about the practice of therapy, has to a large extent, overlooked the practice of supervision. This book goes a long way towards addressing this oversight.

The term and the concept of 'clinical' supervision clearly came into being without the contribution of existential-phenomenological thinkers. As we will see later in Chapter 15 the term 'clinical' is inimical to existential thinking. Gilbert and Evans state there is a general agreement that:

> supervision is a learning process in which a psychotherapist engages with a more experienced practitioner in order to enhance his skill in the process of his ongoing professional development. This in turn, promotes and safe-guards the well-being of his clients (2000: 1).

In supervision the person who is a more experienced therapist is expected to watch over, guide and teach the other therapist, in particular the trainee thera-pist. However, the supervisor cannot control the supervisee's way of being within his or her therapeutic relationships. The same point was raised in the previous chapter in relation to one of the possible functions of supervision – that of ensuring quality. It makes sense that a less experienced therapist would prefer to talk to a more experienced therapist about his/her client work. One would also think that the more experienced therapist with many client hours would be better at what they do than a therapist with very few client hours, the more often we do something the better we are at doing it: 'practice makes perfect'. But is there an assumption here that experience nec-essarily equals good or better? Perhaps the answer is yes and no.

'Yes' in that what we learn and take from our life experience plays an important part in what we as therapists and supervisors have to offer our clients and supervisees. As therapists we use who we are in relation to our clients. This is why it is so important, with the help of another therapist, to hear and see ourselves in ways that we could never do on our own. But also 'no' because, in some circumstances, experience can lead to complacency, over-confidence and even arrogance on the part of the therapist/supervisor. I believe that the more experienced a therapist becomes, the more difficult it can become to 'un-know' (Spinelli, 1997, 2007) some of the knowledge we have gained in order to truly hear what our clients are telling us. There is an assumption that less experience equals 'less competent' and more experience equals 'competence'. And yet we all know that as therapists we will repeat-edly find ourselves feeling confused or out of our depth, no matter how long we have been practising therapy and as supervisors we will be faced with supervisees who seem to be 'naturals' and yet they may have spent very few hours with clients, far less than a 'qualified' therapist.

To assume that a more experienced therapist is a better therapist is a form of linear thinking, a step-by-step progression from inexperienced (less com-petent) to experienced (competent). This implies that trainee therapists have not yet evolved into responsible and trustworthy therapists who are good at the practice of therapy. Existential therapists in training cannot be 'trained' to perform skills or to develop techniques that can be applied at will to benefit their clients. The skills of a therapist develop from their own personal qualities and sensitivities. If something therapeutic happens, it happens between two human beings, emerging from their particular unique relationship (Mitchell, 2002: 94).

Assumptions in Training Supervision

Underlying supervision there are, from the existential perspective, several questionable assumptions. One of them seems to be that there are different categories of therapists and that each category should be supervised in a particular way. Therapists are split into different groups, depending on their qualifications and their level of experience. The manner in which the supervisor approaches responsibility may vary depending on the particular group or category she is supervising. Three groups of supervisees can be distinguished: trainee therapists, qualified therapists and experienced qualified therapists. In order to take these categories seriously we would have to believe and accept that it is possible to generalise and approach a group of adults in a particular way, depending on the group they belong to. Knowing the, in my view artificial, status of a supervisee tells me nothing about that person as a therapist.

Let us first consider the trainee therapist group. Here, the general view appears to be that therapists in training are not yet capable of being 'good enough' therapists. This assumption follows most trainee therapists throughout their time at college. I have noticed how some trainee therapists collude with this view that they have a lot to learn before they become 'proper' therapists, regardless of their qualities as human beings. And yet we also know that trainees are made up of a wide range of adults from different cultures, of different ages, life experiences, social and family backgrounds, sensitivities, strengths and weaknesses. Emmy van Deurzen implies that the training of therapists is not about clocking up the 'right' amount of therapy and supervision hours because: 'some people will not reach the necessary perspective and depth with any amount of therapy. Others will be well ahead by having engaged in a discipline of self-reflection for years' (Deurzen, 2007: 208). Therefore it does not necessarily follow that a person becomes a better therapist because they have years of therapy and supervision hours, it 'is the quality that will be judged instead of the quantity' (ibid: 208).

The level of responsibility on the supervisor's part will be seen to vary with the 'category' of the supervisee. With trainee therapists, the supervisor might be required to carry some of the responsibility for the therapist's practical work, at times even taking responsibility for 'the safety' of the therapist's client, depending on the role of the supervisor, the experience of the therapist and the policy of the organisation where the therapist and the supervisor work. It is generally accepted that the trainee therapist needs to be monitored in a more rigorous way than the person who has finished their training and graduated. Does this imply that experienced therapists do not need supervision, just because they are experienced? This is an assumption that I cannot go along with because, in my view, we all need to be 'co-monitored', regardless of the number of years we have practised therapy. This 'need' varies and depends on our ever changing personal lives and the particular client we have a relationship with.

Nevertheless everything seems to change when a person becomes a qualified, experienced therapist. The suitably qualified and experienced person is trusted enough as a therapist to see another qualified experienced therapist for peer-supervision. This supervisory relationship is bound to be less hierarchical and more equal than the relationship between the less experienced therapist and supervisor.

However as an existential supervisor I am aware that we now live in a culture where it is increasingly unacceptable to make mistakes and where ways of measuring client's symptoms, needs and treatments are being introduced all the time. It is very important for the supervisor to be aware of, accept and work with the context in which his or her supervisees work as therapists. In the previous chapter we saw how important it is that supervisors take account of the constraints imposed by the particular context in which a supervisee works.

My view is that it is not the inexperience or the experience of the therapist/supervisee that is important, rather it is my perception of the supervisee as a human being and how the supervisee talks to me about him/herself in relation to and with his/her clients. I also take into account the possibility that the supervisee might want to please me, as I have a role as an evaluator. Supervisors are expected to encourage openness and free expression in order to facilitate a different and new understanding by the therapist in supervision, but that very same supervisor from the point of view of the trainee can be seen as judge and jury, the person who assesses and judges the capability of the therapist/supervisee. How can I as an existential supervisor combine these two qualities and perform these two requirements?

The supervisor, particularly in a training situation, is expected to guide trainee therapists towards becoming sound existential therapists. This teaching and guiding is not something I would set out to *do*. However, teaching and guiding may emerge if the supervisory relationship is mutually respectful, open and creative. Teaching and guiding is often a two-way process – I continually learn from my supervisees.

I have noticed a pattern in group supervision where someone talks about their relationship with a client while everyone listens. Gradually everyone in the group starts to respond with questions and observations, often opening up new and unexpected areas to contemplate and explore. I believe that it is often in this chaotic and creative interaction that something new and surprising can emerge. This is when the process becomes spontaneous and unpredictable. As an existential supervisor I try to embrace uncertainty and resist the temptation to jump in and create order and bring clarity for myself and my supervisees. Existential supervision should ideally mirror existential therapy. Just like the therapist, the supervisor is responsible for his/her way of being as a supervisor. This way of being hopefully facilitates something 'new' that might be useful and significant for the supervisee and his/her therapeutic relationship. Learning is mostly about reconfirming and clarifying, by throwing a different and brighter light on something perhaps already known. The word 'discover' means just that: to take the cover off something that already exists. Both supervisee and supervisor are affected by the relationship. However, the supervisor cannot be held responsible for what the supervisee takes from supervision, nor how the supervisee is influenced by what happens in supervision.

No matter whom we are to each other: supervisee and supervisor, client and therapist, friends or lovers, the relationship is intersubjective – two subjects each with his/her own needs and worldviews. There will, of course, be times when each person comes away with a different understanding to that intended by the speaker.

An Existential Attitude by the Supervisor

The existential supervisor can never with certainty know how the supervisee is in relation to her client because this is a relationship in process. This process happens within a certain context, between two people. It does not belong to the therapist or to the client and it can never be fully captured, bottled and brought to supervision. I believe that one of the responsibilities of a supervisor is, through her way of being, to convey the same listening and being-qualities that we aspire to as therapists (Spinelli, 2007: 135). This, of course, can be seen as a form of teaching that is not didactic. By 'setting an example', I most certainly do not mean that the supervisor tries to achieve a kind of perfectionism (ibid: 128–9). In my experience many therapists in training appear to have the idea that once they have graduated and are experienced therapists they will stop making embarrassing mistakes and that they will become finely tuned, self-aware, confident and capable therapists. The supervisor is in danger of perpetuating this myth if she is always perceived as all knowing, unflappable and confident, with a clever or wise comment for every dilemma.

I try to encourage supervisees to find their own answers and to come up with their own understanding and solutions to their dilemmas. Supervisors are likely to be seen as role models by some of their supervisees, so I believe that another of the supervisor's responsibilities is to have the courage to show themselves as real human beings (rather than super-inhuman beings) who are also capable of making mistakes with their supervisees and with their clients. The supervisor is first and foremost an imperfect human being who, like the therapist, is a facilitator and enabler who needs to trust him/herself to take responsibility for inevitable mistakes, misjudgements and insensitivities and then to try to learn from those mistakes. Emmy van Deurzen could also be referring to the supervisor when she states that our clients need to know we are human and that we too can 'fall short' and struggle as well. Perfection is not what is required of us, 'Being real in the end is what it is all about' (Deurzen, 1998: 113). It seems to me if supervisors approach their responsibilities in this way it is more likely that they will encourage their supervisees to trust themselves as responsible adults – *even* when they are in training. Trainee therapists should be encouraged to accept and learn from their mistakes, but also learn to trust themselves and never lose sight of their strengths.

What happens in supervision will occasionally come across as 'advice' from the supervisee's point of view. As long as the supervisee understands that it is possible to: 'Take all the advice that is offered, but act on your own judgement' (Judas, 2005). This line, taken from Rasputin's notes, shows that 'advice' can be thought provoking, it is after all another point of view. However, when supervisees are back with their clients they must trust their own judgement and their ability to take up their responsibility. A supervisory relationship, where the supervisee understands that the supervisor's perception is not intended to be understood as the 'right way', but simply another point of view, will be a relationship that is bound to be more respectful and trustworthy.

'The client you meet as a therapist is the client who meets you. There is no client *as such*. If two therapists meet the same client, it is not the same client' (Cohn, 1997: 33). This deceptively simple statement could equally well apply to supervision: 'The supervisee you meet as a supervisor is the supervisee who meets you. There are no supervisees as such. If two supervisors meet the same supervisee, it is not the same supervisee'. From the moment supervisee and supervisor meet they will each be responding to each other. Each person will be judging, assessing and trying to make sense of the other, within the context of supervision. The supervisor, like the therapist, will try to understand and get to know the supervisee and the supervisor will give the supervisee a chance to get to know him/her. This 'getting to know' and 'knowing each other' will of course have a different feel with each supervisee. I tend to reveal more of myself as a supervisor than I do in my 'role' as therapist. I am more open about my limitations, judgements and personal feelings, because that seems to be one of the ways to make myself useful as a supervisor.

As I said previously, in the context of training supervision the supervisor will be asked to act as a teacher, facilitator and assessor. The existential supervisor will know that his or her response to each person in the group will be unique and subjective, never objective or detached. Merleau-Ponty reminds us that it is not possible to 'stand outside' our situation: 'We are caught up in the world and we do not succeed in extricating ourselves from it in order to achieve consciousness of the world' (Merleau-Ponty, 1962: 5). Any assessment by the supervisor will come from within the relationship he or she has with the supervisee and the context in which it happens. A different supervisor working with the same group will be left with different impressions of each member of the group.

The supervisor or perhaps better named the facilitator is responsible for her way of 'being-in-relation' and for trusting in her 'being-qualities' (Spinelli, 2007) rather than performing her 'doing skills'. This can be mistaken for 'doing nothing', which is far from the case. As supervisors our way of being and how we think about something (our theory) is also expressed in what we do and what we do not do in the supervision session. If these are the skills that we use as therapists, then these are also the skills to be nurtured in supervision. This relationship will be unique and full of changing possibilities and limitations, like any other relationship. Any assessment by the supervisor will also be informed by the supervisor's response to the supervisee-in-relation to each member of the group. Every time the supervisee 'brings' a client she 'brings' herself. Merleau-Ponty shows that when we talk about others we can only do so through ourselves: 'I borrow myself from others; I create others from my own thoughts. This is no failure to perceive others; it is the perception of others' (Merleau-Ponty, 1992: 37). The supervisee(s) will also be responding to the supervisor (and the group) in a certain way, which will also play a part in what is revealed and not revealed in their client presentation.

Challenging in Supervision – Existential Supervision in Practice

My approach to challenging is that I try not to challenge a supervisee before we have established a certain level of mutual trust and understanding. To challenge a supervisee too soon without understanding can be counter productive and possibly close down, rather than open up possibilities and self-understanding for the supervisee. The following example shows how I became concerned about Mary, a therapist who came to me for one-to-one supervision.

Mary wanted to talk about a client she was finding difficult. It was not long before Mary started to look angry, flustered and upset as she told me that it was 'not right' for her client to have a young family and wife and yet to be having an affair while at the same time expecting his wife to be a good wife. Mary then told me that she had challenged her client by asking him how he felt about how he was treating his family. I asked her what his response to her challenge was. She thought for a moment and then told me that her client promptly changed the subject, which she saw as a sign that he probably felt guilty, but did not want to face up to his responsibilities. I became more worried as I listened to Mary, for she could not see what might have been happening between her and her client, how her personal views had prevented her from helping her client to understand himself and his situation. All she could see was 'her right way'. I was getting concerned, not because her values and worldview differed from that of her client, but because she seemed unable to 'step back' and see that her view was just that: her point of view.

At this point I told her that as I listened to her I was feeling more and more uncomfortable and that I was getting a strong impression that she seemed caught up in her personal views. We were then able to discuss and clarify what might have been happening. Mary started to see how her client's behaviour was too close to her own situation and how it clashed with her values. After talking about her personal situation it seemed easier for her to see how she got swept away into her own world, leaving her client with his experience and way of being unexplored. My response came from my concern for Mary and for her client, not just because it was my duty as her supervisor, but because my whole being compelled me to respond in the way I did at that moment. Clearly a supervisor always has in mind care and concern for the client.

Martin Adams put it this way: 'As people, as supervisors, we have a responsibility to ourselves and to others to communicate our perceptions about the matter in question, which in supervision is the supervisee's practice' (Adams, 2002: 207). What we choose to communicate and how we communicate it will be influenced by our response to the context we are in (supervision) and how we see our role within that context. Mary seemed to get caught up in her personal response to her client, this response was not wrong as such, what was 'wrong' to me was that she did not seem to be aware of the implications of her personal views within the context of the therapeutic relationship.

As a person and as her supervisor it was my responsibility to help her to become aware of something she seemed unable to do on her own. I exercised my responsibility in order to facilitate a new understanding, which might enable Mary to take up her responsibility in a different way. I was also grateful that Mary had spoken so honestly about her feelings because it gave me a chance to help her to think about 'herself in relation' to her client. I was possibly looking after her client's well-being, however, there was absolutely no guarantee that she would feel and act differently the next time she saw her client, which is something I have no control over. Some supervisors might suggest that Mary should explore her issues in therapy but this is not something I would automatically do in this type of situation. It would all depend on how often this sort of situation arose and the level of the supervisee's self-awareness. My responsibility as supervisor is to try to make myself, my assumptions and my views available to my supervisee, while at the same time, respecting and trusting the supervisee as a fellow adult who is already experienced in relating, in living and negotiating relationships. Adams reminds us that it can be painful to live in a world with other autonomous beings, but that: '… each of us has a responsibility to acknowledge both our own view and that of the other' (ibid: 208).

A Safe 'Enough' Non-Judgemental Space

It seems that sometimes tutors on training courses believe that the trainee should first be deskilled and then (hopefully) be put back together again. This approach is for me the opposite of an existential attitude towards another human being. From an existential-phenomenological perspective there is no 'right' or 'wrong', 'healthy' or 'unhealthy' way to be. I try to accept and work with the person as 'presented' and perceived by me. It is not my job to change that person and their worldview rather it is my job to facilitate new possibilities and self-understanding in the hope that this will ultimately be helpful to the supervisee in his or her work as therapist. This in turn might very well change the therapist/supervisee's worldview, as it were by default. The supervisor is in a sense disrespecting the supervisee and undermining their response-ability if he or she 'leaps in' before a respectful and trustworthy relationship has been established and an understanding that can only come through getting to know another person.

> It is ironic how we aim to create a safe and non-judgemental space for our clients but at the same time, those who need that almost more than anyone – those trainees who are soon to have the huge responsibility of creating that space for their clients – are denied it themselves (Hall, 1997: 310).

The quote above demonstrates what can happen when training supervision goes wrong, where the experience of supervision contradicts what the supervisees are trying to create with their clients. Therapists in training are usually practising therapists seeing 'real' clients on their own. It seems to me all the more important to question and challenge some of the assumptions and judgements that follow trainee therapists throughout their training. Why not assume that the trainee therapist is already experienced in life, relationships and 'being skills' that can be identified and celebrated?

I am speaking here from my personal experience, not just as a trainee therapist, but also as a classical ballet dancer in training. I really started to express myself when I had the good fortune to work with a highly gifted teacher. Most ballet training focuses on the dancer's weaknesses and most dancers are very tough and critical of themselves and their ability, in much the same way as therapists in training are. This teacher taught us to trust ourselves and to value and make the most of our strengths. She also encouraged us to be responsible and take responsibility for our own training. We discovered a new self-discipline, rather than the usual experience of being disciplined by our teachers. We 'listened' to our bodies and paced ourselves accordingly. We were treated with respect and treated ourselves respectfully. This did not stop us from being aware of our weaknesses, which we still battled to overcome. Our newfound confidence and ability to 'stand on our own feet' and own our strengths opened us to new possibilities as human beings and dancers.

This is also what we do as therapists: we use who we are, from moment to moment in relation to and with another person. Supervision is a place where our many, sometimes contradictory, qualities and emotions can be expressed and where differences can be tolerated, acknowledged and celebrated. It is also a place, like a dance studio, where the supervisor is responsible for holding up a mirror in order to help the supervisee to see him or herself more clearly.

The Political Context of Supervision

The existential perspective always includes an awareness of the context in which we live – from the ontological to the immediate every day context. Working as therapists or supervisors in organisations, particularly in the NHS, may entail protecting ourselves and the organisation against the possibility of being sued for malpractice. Training organisations are under more and more pressure to conform and to fall in line with universal guidelines for trainees, trainers and supervisors. I am very aware that this new reality is something that existential therapists and supervisors have to accept and find a way to work with.

I am at times faced with a situation where, in a sense, I am also supervising for a third party. I see an existential therapist for supervision who works for an organisation where the therapist is required to conform to a system that is at odds with existential-phenomenological thinking. The contract states that the therapist first sees their client for an 'assessment' session which requires taking a detailed history and this will be followed by identifying an area for the client to focus on. Finally the therapist will be asked to predict when and what the outcome will be. In my role as supervisor we discuss the context in which the therapist works and together we look at the different possibilities and choices that the supervisee feels she has: my responsibility is to help the supervisee to find her own answers. I cannot take responsibility for her choices but I am responsible for trusting her to exercise her own responsibility.

Conclusion

I have tried to show how the supervisor's use of and attitude towards responsibility can be one of the important factors in creating a more equal, open and mutually respectful relationship. I believe that an existential supervisor will be acutely aware of his or her response-ability as a human being who is in the unique position of having confidence in the supervisee's ability to take up his or her responsibility. This very same therapist/supervisee will already know that s/he can never take responsibility for his or her client's way of being with others: that is the client's responsibility.

References

Adams, M. 'Reflections on Reflection', *Existential Analysis* 13(2) (2002) 204–13.
Cohn, H. W. *Existential Thought and Therapeutic Practice* (London: Sage, 1997).

—— *Heidegger and the Roots of Existential Therapy* (London: Continuum, 2002).

Deurzen, E. van *Paradox and Passion in Psychotherapy* (Chichester: Wiley, 1998).

—— 'Existential Therapy'. In W. Dryden (ed.) *Dryden's Handbook of Individual Therapy* (London: Sage, 2007).

Du Plock, S. 'A Relational Approach to Supervision', *Existential Analysis* 18(1) (2007) 31–8.

Gilbert, M. & Evans, K. *Psychotherapy Supervision* (Buckingham: OUP, 2000).

Hall, M. 'Stepping Off the "Game Board": A New Practitioner's View of Accreditation'. In R. House & N. Totton (eds) *Implausible Professions* (Ross-on-Wye: PCCS Books, 1997).

Heidegger, M. *Being and Time*. Trans. J. Macquarrie & E. S. Robinson (Oxford: Blackwell, [1927] 1962).

Judas, E. *Rasputin, Neither Devil Nor Saint* (California: Life & Liberty Publishing, 2005).

Karban, B. 'Leaping in' and 'Leaping ahead': An Exploration of Heidegger's Notion of Solicitude' (unpublished paper, 1995).

Merleau-Ponty, M. *The Phenomenology of Perception*. Trans. C. Smith (London: Routledge & Kegan Paul, 1962).

Merleau-Ponty, M. Quoted by Michael Yeo. In T. W. Busch (ed.) *Merleau-Ponty, Hermeneutics and Postmodernism* (New York: State University of New York Press, 1992).

Mitchell, D. 'Is the Concept of Supervision at Odds with Existential Thinking and Therapeutic Practice?', *Existential Analysis* 13(1) (2002) 91–7.

Spinelli, E. *Tales of the Un-Knowing* (London: Duckworth, 1997).

—— *Practising Existential Psychotherapy: The Relational World* (London: Sage, 2007).

14
Givens of Supervision: A Cross-Theoretical Framework

Alison Strasser

Introduction

Becoming a psychotherapist is a personal journey. Identifying the philosophical and theoretical direction for this journey is where our supervisor and our experience of supervision are so important. Supervision is a vital part of the learning cycle – one in which the supervisor should be able to match their supervisee's needs by creating an environment that is supportive, facilitative and evaluative. Growth and learning comes about through the encouragement of personal awareness and critical contemplation which is all part of the 'reflection on practice' that lies at the heart of supervision.

Becoming a supervisor is also a journey that demands a quantum leap from that of working as a therapist. It requires a different framework, additional skills, a broader knowledge and the willingness to take up another level of responsibility. Although supervision is now advisable for psychotherapists and counsellors in most countries, what actually constitutes supervision, or rather how we develop our own model of supervision has been less clearly defined.

As an existential psychotherapist and supervisor it is important to develop a framework and a professional identity that is congruent with existential thinking. This means abandoning a strict developmental model and focusing more on the supervisee's individual and personal expectations. Since existential-phenomenology is steeped in the relationship realms, any framework needs to allow for the multi-faceted aspects that emerge between supervisor, supervisee, client and the situational context. An educational component is often required by both the supervisee and the contracting organisation; and as supervision is often conducted in groups, the skills of a group facilitator are also essential. It is usual for a training programme for supervisors to be cross-theoretical and all encompassing.

This chapter is the outcome of my own journey. It involved the completion of a professional doctorate during which I developed a framework: 'The

Wheel of Supervision'. The concept of the wheel emerged from *Existential Time-Limited Therapy* (Strasser & Strasser, 1997) and is a diagrammatic representation of the givens of existence. In *Existential Time-Limited Therapy* we proposed that the wheel aids therapists address client issues and simultaneously allows them to remain cognisant of the interconnected nature of human existence. In a similar fashion the 'Wheel of Supervision' provides a framework for both supervisors and supervisees to examine and explore all aspects of supervision relevant to their particular working contexts. In this chapter I will describe how each of the wheel segments is a 'given' to all practice of supervision and also illustrate how it can be used specifically within an existential frame. This overview of the 'wheel of supervision' only highlights some of the key points to demonstrate how it may be used as a cross-theoretical framework.

The givens described are as follows (see Figure 14.1) the relationship between:

- supervisor and supervisee
- supervisee and client
- self of the supervisee/supervisor
- supervisee/supervisor and outside agencies
- the significance of emotions and self-esteem
- the identification of theories, values and assumptions
- the awareness of choices and meaning
- the setting up of the frame and contract

At the centre of the wheel is the worldview, that aspect connecting all the givens. In the outer circle are the givens which encompass existence:

- Uncertainty
- Time
- Anxiety
- Choice
- Safety
- Interpersonal Relationship

Use of the Wheel

The wheel is used as a backdrop for both the supervisor and supervisee to explore all aspects of supervision, bearing in mind that all segments are interconnected. Since these segments are described as being universal to all theoretical paradigms, the wheel allows for each person to work within their own modality and to develop their own relationship alliance as suited to their theoretical approach.

The phenomenological method of enquiry is fundamental to existential supervision and therapy. It is imperative to 'tune in', to suspend personal

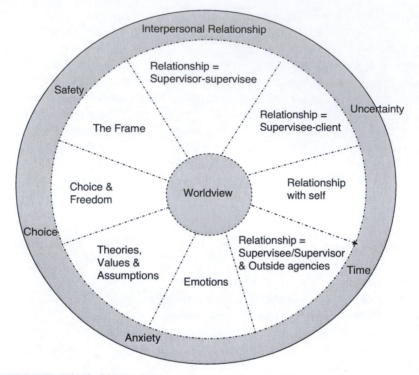

Figure 14.1   The Wheel of Supervision

assumptions and judgements as much as possible in order to expand understanding of the client's world. It is the same process when working in supervision. In other words the supervisor attempts to get as close as possible to experiencing and describing the phenomena as lived by the supervisee in their world (including the context in which they work), and to understand their sense of being with their client. In agreement with Mitchell's remarks in the previous chapter, only when the supervisee feels supported by the supervisor, is it appropriate to challenge or ask the harder more didactic, thought provoking questions that bring about the 'reflection-on-action, or indeed, reflection-in-action to result in reflection-for-action' (Carroll, 2007: 36).

Existential Givens

The inner circle of the wheel is built up of segments (or givens) that are the characteristics of supervision and are intrinsic and fundamental to the process, regardless of theoretical model, developmental stage, situational context or type of supervision. Each of the segments of the wheel is interconnected, allowing for fluidity and change. A change in one segment will have a knock-on effect on all the other segments, giving the wheel a systemic flavour. For example the frame co-exists with all the other givens in the sense that it is shaped by the relationship between the supervisor, supervisee, client and the context of the supervision. In turn the theories, values, and assumptions of each of the parties will influence the relationship and approach to supervision. How each reacts to these givens is part and parcel of their emotional attitude, self-concept and general approach to supervision.

A fundamental concept of existential philosophy is that of the ontological 'givens' of existence: these being aspects of living which are universally true and inescapable. For example we cannot choose where and to whom we are born and none of us can choose to live forever. However, where we do have choice is how we each respond to these givens. In other words we each have the capacity to create our own individual meaning in relation to living and to dying.

In the outer circle of the wheel are some of these existential givens or paradoxes of existence, those aspects of living that lie in the background of our everyday being. For instance, we all live within the paradoxical realm of trying to create certainty (or safety) in an uncertain world; of creating meaning to living within our time-limited existence; of being born in a world of relationship and yet seeking to illuminate our own sense of identity. Attempting to live within these paradoxes is anxiety provoking. To cope with this abundance of unease we create a certain sense of safety by choosing to live within certain beliefs, assumptions and attitudes thus providing a cushion against the world. This is our worldview.

Worldview

At the centre of the wheel is the worldview or 'the expression of the sum total of our particular way of being with or engaging in the world' (Strasser, 1999: 11). In other words our worldview, whether this is that of the supervisor, supervisee or client is intrinsic to the supervision process. It encompasses all the segments of the wheel and seeks the connections between all these aspects.

Our worldview is not static. It is in constant change as we confront the uncertainty of living in the world. Sometimes we see everything as a limitation and we lose meaning while at other times the world becomes one of possibilities and new meanings. This is concurrent with the way we might see supervision, our work with supervisees and our work with clients. Our worldview is a current expression of who we believe we are; how we make sense of the world at this particular moment and is all embracing of our values, beliefs, attitudes, emotions, self-esteem and so on. It includes the four worlds (physical, public, private and spiritual) as initially described by Binswanger and elaborated by van Deurzen (2002).

The Frame

As noted, one of the existential givens that human beings continually face is that of uncertainty and in supervision, as in therapy, we need to establish a secure frame. This is equally important within the supervisory setting in order to reduce the level of uncertainty and anxiety for both the supervisor and supervisee. Although, it is inevitable that anxiety will still exist.

The frame is essentially the contract made between the supervisor and supervisee or supervisees in a group setting, but may well include third parties such as an educational institution, manager, agency and other external parties. Additionally the theoretical style of the supervisor will inform these parameters. Hence, the agreement will vary according to the setting and nature of the supervision but will include the frequency of meetings, the fee (or not), the purpose, nature and style of presentations of clients, confidentiality and other aspects that might arise determined by the individuals concerned. The frame will include any potential dual relations and how these are best handled.

As in therapy, the supervisory contract will have explicit (sometimes implicit) expectations or goals, dependent on the nature and context of the supervision. It has been cogently argued that:

> bringing the supervisee's goals into the supervision spotlight provides a coherent structure within which other aspects of supervision, such as supervision effectiveness, the supervision alliance, and the experience of the supervisee can be more clearly understood (Lewis & Carey, 2007).

Although the concept of goals is often seen as anathema to working existentially, exploring expectations allows for fluidity and change. Starting with an exploration of expectations allows both supervisor and supervisee to reveal their worldview and what is important for them, thereby introducing more transparency into the relationship. Additionally unrealistic expectations can be discussed and put into the context of the wheel. For example, Joanna had just begun working with clients and in her opening statement said her role was to help others, even though she knew from her training that this was not the purpose. This led us to examine her definition of helping, why it was so important to her and leading ultimately to the realisation of her own particular fear of being stuck and feelings of being trapped.

The Relationship Realms

In the 'wheel of supervision' I have identified four levels of relationship: that established between the supervisor and supervisee; that between the supervisee and client; the relationships that the supervisor and supervisee have privately with themselves (self-to-self) and the relationship they have with the outside world. In addition, if supervision is conducted in a group, there are the multiple levels of relationship between all participants.

Relationship between supervisor and supervisee

The degree to which the multiple levels of relationship are discussed in supervision will depend in part on the model of supervision, but also on the individual participants and their willingness to participate in self-disclosure. Developmental models of supervision might argue that new therapists will need to focus on their skills rather than on the interpersonal levels of enquiry. Other models believe that the self of the therapist remains in the domain of personal therapy and not supervision.

From the existential perspective, supervision has a predominant focus on the relationship for: 'people are seen as existing in relationship with themselves, with others and with the world. Each individual and his or her world are said to co-constitute one another' (Valle & Halling, 1989: 7). I explore the relationship realms of 'I focus, You focus, We focus and They focus' (Spinelli, 2007) which allows for the exploration of the interconnections in all their complexity. In practical terms this entails gaining an understanding of the worldview of the supervisee and the client and what is happening in the supervisory relationship. For instance, I am curious about how the client presents in the session and what impact this mode of being has on the supervisee. Does the supervisee like or dislike their client and how does this impact on or have any resonance with the issues being presented?

Unsurprisingly all the supervisees I interviewed talked about the significance of the relationship or the lack of a meaningful one. Trust appeared to be the linking feature at all levels of relationship but obviously how each person develops trust and what they mean by trust is unique and personal. For instance one supervisee talked about the relationship with his supervisor as: 'like a meeting of two souls'; yet in another supervisory relationship in which honesty, trust, and safety were absent, he felt disempowered and angry, resulting in his withdrawal. Another therapist described the supervisory relationship as trusting in the sense of it being safe to hold different opinions; another used the metaphor of a policeman to describe the inherent power dynamics which may be used at certain times to ensure ethical practice.

The issue of power between supervisor and supervisee is another area to be explored from each participant's perspective. Supervision starts when a student is in training and integral to this type of supervision is a formal assessment process – hence this awareness will influence the supervision process. It can also be argued that some form of assessment process is intrinsic to all supervisory relationships. This would be particularly so if the supervision is a requirement of working within an agency.

However part of the supervisor's responsibility is to be a guardian of the legal and ethical codes under which we all work and as such the supervisor remains in a position of power. It is a fine line between allowing the supervisee to explore and assume responsibility and when and how the supervisor might become accountable. The previous chapter provides a fuller discussion of these issues of responsibility within the supervisory relationship.

How both the supervisor and supervisee respond to each other's status is part of the supervisory journey. Indeed Lawton (2000) noted that most supervisees needed to imbue their supervisor with more experience and status. This could be for a variety of different reasons including that of wish-fulfilment where supervisees: 'need to regard the supervisor as a dependable expert who contains their anxieties and proves infallible when they felt vulnerable' (Lawton, 2000: 34). It would appear to be part of our cultural indoctrination that both the word and the institution of supervision have an element of the teacher-pupil relationship ingrained within. This refers back to the problematic nature of the term supervision already discussed in Chapters 12 and 13.

Relationship with self

When a trusting relationship occurs, then the supervision is more likely to include personal issues as they relate to the client. Again, how this aspect of the private world is explored, or whether it is indeed part of the contract, is dependent on the mode of therapy. The question of where supervision stops and therapy begins is one that is continually asked. It would seem largely a personal decision and one that is negotiated in the contract. Sometimes supervisors will suggest that a personal issue that emerges for the supervisee in supervision should be 'taken to therapy'. Though of course from the existential perspective there is no clear dividing line between the 'personal' and the 'professional' since everything always involves what is personal.

For existential supervisors, and for many from different orientations, self-awareness is an essential component of supervision. Beatte talked passionately about how in supervision: 'she met herself for the first time' and described how she used her self-awareness to work with her clients. Kristie would arrive for supervision knowing that the two or three clients she presented with whom she felt stuck or blocked would, when further examined, be linked to her personal 'stuckness'. Once, we were able to establish this self-connection, Kristie would acknowledge greater clarity and would often report that the issue discussed in supervision disappeared with the clients. In other words, as expected, personal awareness appears to have a direct effect on work with clients.

Additionally, if a supervisee feels stuck with a client or feels that they cannot find any means for tuning into their worldview, it can be useful to find a situation or a feeling within the supervisee that may draw parallels with the client's being-in-the-world. Margaret talked about Rupert who, at the beginning and end of each session, demanded solutions, thereby giving the impression he was not pleased with the way the therapy was proceeding. Yet, during the session itself, it appeared that he gained clarity and awareness and was beginning to make changes in his life. In supervision, I asked Margaret to imagine she was Rupert and as I continued to ask her questions, she realised that she felt the fear of losing control. Initially, she had felt a connection with me but as the end came closer, it dawned on her that the potential ending and subsequent loss of this connection made her panic and feel totally alone. In the following session with Rupert, Margaret explored their relationship where he revealed issues around intimacy.

Relationship between supervisee and client

This section has its own separate segment on the wheel to acknowledge its paramount importance. In my view the primary function of supervision is the commitment to the development and well-being of both the supervisee and client. Once again, there are the interconnections between all aspects of the wheel such as the contract and the assessment process between the supervisee and client.

From an existential perspective the relationship which emerges between the therapist and client is often reflective of other relationships that the client holds in their wider world, sometimes described as the 'other-construct' (Spinelli, 2007). For example Jane presented her client as angry and continually testing their relationship by either walking out of sessions or by writing letters explaining how she felt abused by statements that Jane had made. This was mirrored in the client's world of work where she described how she felt undervalued by her manager and reacted by ignoring the rules, until she was eventually sacked. Jane began to explore the similarities in attitude with the client who over time revealed her self-loathing, realising that she needed to prove this repeatedly by getting others to dismiss her. The dilemma for the client was that Jane refused to be dismissed, resulting in a different kind of relationship for the client, one in which she was able to talk about her fear of abandonment and rejection.

Although perceived differently by existential therapists, most practitioners would be working with the therapeutic relationship, though not referring to this, as discussed in Chapter 1, as 'transference' or 'countertransference' but rather simply in terms of relationship issues between the client and their therapist and in terms of their bias. However described, this relationship realm is an important component to explore in supervision and can offer valuable insights into the multiple levels of parallel relationships as discussed above.

Relationship between supervisee/supervisor and outside agencies

Obviously supervision does not occur in isolation but always within a set of different contexts including the setting, such as in a training institution, an agency, a business or a government organisation. This segment includes external controls such as the legal requirements of reporting, the professional code of ethics and the organisation's vision and mission. Included in this context are the specific codes of practice the supervisor and supervisee will have to abide by which are a component of the frame, such as boundaries, dual relationships and specific rules about contacting clients. Working within an organisational setting may entail the necessity of working with a specific model, time limitations and with a specified supervisor. It is therefore paramount that the supervisor understands the particular context and rules so that the supervision can reflect these dimensions.

The relationship with outside agencies is inclusive of the broader context of the various professional bodies that the therapist belongs to as well as the legal constitutions of the particular state or country. It covers the dimension of ethical practice and the necessity of working through scenarios of 'what is right' and 'what is good' in relation to the client, for society, self protection, the profession as a whole and any organisation involved. Though clearly there is often no certainty around right and wrong, it is not surprising my research highlighted this as an area where both supervisors and supervisees felt vulnerable and open to scrutiny. Supervisees felt very strongly that it was important their supervisors were cognisant of the legal parameters and the ability to ensure that they were working within an ethical framework.

Theories, Values and Assumptions

In supervision both the supervisor and supervisee will bring to the relationship their own particular theories about life, therapy and supervision that they perceive as integral to their work as a therapist. Under this segment or given, are included each person's values in relation to their morals, ethics and their attitude towards their code of ethics and legal entities.

These theories, values and assumptions are both the espoused theoretical framework of the supervisor and supervisee and the personal worldview that they both bring into the multiple relationships embodied in the supervisory process. Usually, the psychotherapeutic theoretical model of the supervisor will be the guiding basis for the direction and purpose of supervision in terms of the setting of the frame; the theory behind their understanding of client work; the interpretation of what the relationship constitutes and how this is worked with both between the supervisor and supervisee and between the supervisee and client. It is one of the tasks of the supervisor to explore and, to the extent that this is possible, understand each supervisee's perspective. Indeed, it is often the case that a supervisor works with a supervisee from another modality: the challenge being to accept difference and still allow for the reflective learning to take place.

Within the existential field there are as many ways of interpreting the philosophy and theory as there are therapists and each will have their own particular ways of working and exploring with their supervisees (Cooper, 2003). Some may focus on the four worlds; some may explore the philosophy; while others will emphasise the dimensions of relationship. Similarly, as is high-lighted in the Existential Time-Limited Therapy wheel, exploring and gaining an understanding of our worldview in terms of our beliefs, values and assumptions, with regard to how they affect our sense of self, behaviours and coping mechanisms is fundamental to our work. The same examination and understanding is used in supervision to explore the beliefs of the client, those of the supervisee and supervisor, how they intersect and what, if any, impact this may have at all the levels of relationship.

In supervision, Penny spoke about a client who worked in risk manage-ment. After six sessions he unexpectedly revealed that this would be the last session. In supervision we explored how Penny had reacted to this client, how he had related to her and how he might relate to others in his world. The overall theme that emerged was about his need to control his environment. I suggested to Penny that in their next (and last) session she attempt to stay more attuned with the client, to say less and trust that the issue of 'controlled' or 'not in control' would emerge. In the next supervision Penny voiced her surprise when, during the silences of the last session, the client remembered that as a boy he would have sleepless nights fearing that his father was going to kill him. Controlling his environment, including the therapy, became his way of shielding against his anxiety around lack of safety. Interestingly, Penny recognised that her own assumptions included the belief that creating a safe environment was an essential part of therapy. Penny's sense of safety and that of her client were quite different.

Emotions

We are never without emotion and 'in emotion ... we can rediscover the whole of human reality, for emotion is the human reality assuming itself and emo-tionally – directing itself towards the world' (Sartre, 2002: 10). Emotions are inherent in all aspects of our being such as our values, our behaviours and ultimately our sense of self or self-esteem. Emotions do not exist in isolation, they are linked; so for instance anger may be associated to sadness or the feeling of joy may relate to jealousy. Concurrently, emotions are always directed towards something, such as love of another person or love of food.

Other people's opinions are interwoven into how we view ourselves which in turn affects how we value ourselves and how we relate to others. From an existential viewpoint anxiety is intrinsic to our self-concept and self-esteem. These emotions can manifest themselves in supervision around feelings of self-worth, self-expression, validation, support, evaluation, personal and pro-fessional competency and so on.

The supervisor needs to understand how each supervisee experiences the relationship between self and other in terms of their view of themselves, the supervisor, the client, and at the organisational level. As previously mentioned since most, if not all, supervisory relationships have some element of formal or informal assessment, it is important to explore the emotional impact this has on the supervisory relationship. While one supervisee might perceive a question as judgemental, another may recognise the same question as life enhancing. Naturally, the supervisor also needs to be aware of these aspects in terms of their own reactions to criticism and how they affect their self-esteem.

As with all these concepts, each therapeutic tradition has their own understanding of how emotions assimilate into their working methodology. For example cognitive behavioural therapists believe that changing our thought processes will transform our emotional state while many therapists in the humanistic tradition will focus on emotions believing that until these are expressed, understood and assimilated, a true sense of self will remain elusive.

Regardless of our position, emotions reveal our worldview which in turn helps to clarify the intention in our emotion. In supervision this can bring a richer sense of what is occurring for the client, therapist and supervisor. Jason discussed how for personal reasons he had to cancel a client at the last minute and how this made him feel guilty for being 'unprofessional' in disappointing the client. On further reflection, he realised that the same client was prone to cancelling and for a moment felt a sense of vindication until we explored what might be keeping the client away from therapy. At that point he understood that a few months before the client had come to an acute realisation and had undertaken to do things differently. Now he was living in shame for not sticking to these promises. In relation to the therapy this client did not want to disappoint the therapist, the same emotional sense that the therapist had felt in the cancellation process. Disappointment, commitment and the fear of the client letting herself and others down emerged as the theme for further exploration.

Identifying Choices and Meaning

Although choice and meaning are broad concepts, they are an important dimension when thinking about supervision. Firstly, they allow an exploration into the way we choose to view supervision. One supervisee might embrace supervision as a way to learn skills and theory, another as an insurance against bad practice, another as a means of self-reflection, yet another as a mandatory requirement and so forth. Understanding the position of the supervisee highlights the feelings and attitudes towards their supervision and supervisor. From an existential position we all have, whatever the limitations, a choice of attitude. So even when supervision is viewed as limiting we are choosing to behave in a certain way. Hence this theme is linked to responsibility for self, others and the organisation.

Laura was one of the supervisees in group supervision as part of a Masters' programme. From the first week she was sullen, making it very clear that she had no wish to be a member of that group. In the third week, answering a challenge by another group member, Laura admitted she was only doing the Masters for the 'piece of paper' and did not expect to learn anything new. Although her essential attitude did not change over the course of the programme, she admitted to the group that she felt excluded. Her way of coping with her vulnerability was to appear as if she did not care. In remaining separate to the others in the group she was not taking responsibility for herself and her negative attitude impacted on each of the supervisees in different ways.

Such attitudes can be extended to all types of supervision. David, for example, talked about revealing different aspects of his work depending on the agency he was working with, while Ian decided to join a peer supervision group as he was unable to find a supervisor who matched his expectations of a spiritual leader. In essence, this theme includes the supervisee's attitude towards the role of supervision and their relationship between other supervisees, supervisor and outside agency. It is closely tied with the notion of responsibility towards self and others already discussed in the previous chapter.

The supervisor too is also included under this given, in the sense that he or she will strike a particular attitude about their role at all levels of the relationship – between themselves as supervisors, the supervisee, the agency as well as the broader ideas of ethics and professional responsibility.

Conclusion

Although the wheel of supervision was conceived as a cross-theoretical framework for training supervisors in the counselling and psychotherapy field, it is intrinsically flexible and can be adapted to any context. I have modified it to train supervisors specifically from an existential perspective and have used it as a way of teaching supervisees the art of supervision. Working as a supervisor, I retain the wheel in my awareness to ensure that all the segments are covered in an interrelational way.

Supervision is establishing itself as a distinct profession. Hence a supervisor can supervise across a range of professions, be it psychotherapy, counselling, coaching or mediation; in different spheres as in the medical world or social work as well as across the breadth of theories. The wheel of supervision is an all inclusive and flexible means of embracing the complexities of supervision permitting supervisor and supervisee to advance their journey in their unique way.

References

Carroll, M. 'One More Time: What is Supervision?', *Psychotherapy in Australia* 13(3) (2007) 34–40.

Cooper, M. *Existential Therapies* (London: Sage, 2003).

Deurzen, E. van *Existential Counselling & Psychotherapy in Practice,* 2nd edn. (London: Sage, 2002).

Lawton, B. 'A very Exposing Affair: Explorations in Counsellor's Supervisory Relationships'. In B. Lawton & C. Feltham *Taking Supervision Forward: Enquiries and Trends in Counselling and Psychotherapy* (London: Sage, 2000).

Lewis, I. & Carey, T. 'Supervisees' Goals: Often Forgotten but Never Lost', *Australian Psychologist* (2007).

Sartre, J-P. *Sketch for a Theory of the Emotions* (London: Routledge, 2002).

Spinelli, E. *Practising Existential Psychotherapy: The Relational World* (London: Sage, 2007).

Strasser, F. & Strasser, A. *Existential Time-Limited Therapy: The Wheel of Existence* (Chichester: Wiley, 1997).

Strasser, F. *Emotions: Experiences in Existential Psychotherapy and Life* (London: Duckworth, 1999).

Valle, S. & Halling, S. 'An Introduction to Existential-Phenomenological Thought in Psychology'. In S. Valle, M. King & S. Halling (eds) *Existential Phenomenological Alternatives for Psychology* (New York: Plenum Press, 1989).

15

Evocative Supervision:
A Non-Clinical Approach

Greg Madison

Introduction

As an existential supervisor, I try to create an environment that sustains the 'humanity' and mutuality of the supervisory relationship, combining respectful collegial rapport with moments of profound experiential depth similar to therapy itself. Alongside a sensitivity to power dynamics, existential supervisors exhibit a general willingness to question much of what passes unquestioned in contemporary therapeutic practice. As has been stated in earlier chapters, the humility of un-knowing is not sacrificed in order to claim authority based solely upon years of experience or psychological 'evidence'. Although such attributes pose the existential supervisor with certain professional dilemmas, I believe that they are increasingly important traits as the profession and the species as a whole hurtles towards technological, and increasingly biotechnological and cybernetic, solutions to human problems.[1]

Contrasting this existential stance with current trends in the psychological professions will highlight 'the evocative' as an essential though unexplicated aspect of existential supervision. 'Evocative' supervision connotes an *experiential-existential* stance that prioritises *implicit* experiencing and by its nature is not quantifiable. *Anything I say is not 'it' but only an attempt to point towards 'it'*. The Canadian phenomenologist Max van Manen (2002), describes his phenomenological research as 'evocative', deriving the term from *evocare*, 'to call forth, to call out, and refers to the act of bringing to mind or recollection, recreating imaginatively through word or image, fastening a hold on nearness …'. Similarly, evocative supervision requires us to attend patiently to the depth of *now* by following the bodily flow of experiencing as it arises in shared understandings that are never solidified by explanation. I want to distinguish this form of encounter from what is typically called 'clinical' supervision.

---

[1]See Madison (2008a).

Defining the 'Clinical' in Clinical Supervision

Psychological professionals are currently faced with a significant culture shift in the provision of, and understanding of psychological therapies. Along with an increasing demand for experimental evidence come positivist and modernist assumptions in the form of 'manualised treatment'; these quasi-medical practices seem consistent with adjectives we have long used, such as 'clinical'. The dictionary defines 'clinical' as 'efficient and coldly detached', 'relating to the observation and treatment of patients' (OED, *AskOxford Website*, 2008). The etymology of 'clinical' is Greek, *klinike* and *klinikos,* meaning physicians practising 'at the sick bed' (Online Etymology Dictionary, 2008). So why do *we* preface many of our psychotherapy nouns with a term that seems inconsistent with the intention of existential practice: 'clinical counselling', 'clinical practice', 'clinical judgement' and so on? Is our use of the adjective 'clinical' simply an attempt, as 'human *science'* professionals in a 'hard science' world, to appear to possess the certainty of explanatory knowledge? Are we aligning ourselves with the claims of objectivity and expertise proffered by the medical profession, within which psychological therapies are increasingly subsumed?

Clinical supervision approximates a 'teaching laboratory' in which a technical expert oversees student mastery of proper diagnostic and intervention procedures, often incorporating live sessions with clients. This model seems to parallel medical education in which junior doctors are paired with senior consultants and mentored in medical procedures with live patients. It is not surprising then to note that North American psychology and psychotherapy are increasingly aligned with the underlying positivism of medical science. At least this ties the adjective 'clinical' to a consistent practice and theory. Such practice is spreading across Europe but arguably remains most prevalent in North America.

In contrast, British models of supervision for psychotherapists and counselling psychologists tend to arise out of a more relational stance to therapy (*Counselling Psychology Review*, 2008). Most emphasise the impact that the *person* of the therapist has on the process of therapy and *vice versa*.[2] Therefore personal attributes of the therapist and their unique life experiences are germane topics in ascertaining how they might be affecting the therapy. Continuing post-registration supervision is accepted as essential for the competent practice of all counselling psychologists and psychotherapists and it is a requirement in professional ethical codes (Bond, 1990). Within Britain there is little distinction between training supervision and post-registration 'consultation' and the term 'supervision' is typically applied to both.

---

[2]Personal therapy is a requirement for British counselling psychology trainees while it is not for North American psychology trainees.

In North America the expectation for regular supervision ceases when training is completed. Post-registration 'supervision', if it occurs, is voluntary[3] and is usually termed 'consultation' (Barnet, 2007: 272). This variance regarding the necessity for ongoing post-registration supervision reveals diverse assumptions about the nature of practice. If we assume that therapy is a *treatment* provided by well trained specialists in clinical technique, offering their expertise in order to diagnose and alleviate problematic symptoms, then why would this 'expert' require ongoing supervision? Once a plumber (or a medical doctor) learns his or her profession they do not continue to apprentice.

Of course the relationship between client and therapist is not entirely ignored in North America nor are therapeutic skill and knowledge irrelevant to British therapists. However, there is a prevailing distinction in emphasis between the professional cultures on these two continents and this has particular practice implications, including what constitutes supervision and the attitude toward post-registration continuing supervision. Below I will outline some aspects of a non-clinical approach to supervision in preparation for discussing the evocative dimension consistent with existential supervision.

The Person in Non-Clinical Supervision

Existential supervision invites the supervisor to be guided by 'the ontological rather than the technical' offering 'tentative hypotheses' over 'absolute truths' highlighting the potency of evoking '*personal* impressions, comments, thoughts, feelings...' (Jones, 1998: 912, *italics added*).

The family therapist Per Jensen cites ten years of research to demonstrate the pivotal role that the personal experiences of the therapist (and presumably also the supervisor) has on their 'clinical competence' (Jensen, 2007: 379–82). These studies support the assumption that increasing therapist competency is associated with the integration of the *personally evocative* into professional practice. This suggests that our training methods, including supervision, should encourage trainees to attend to what *feels important in their life experience and personal struggles* in the service of their professional development. This is in stark contrast to the 'clinical' perspective:

> According to the [clinical] practice perspective the therapist's job is to deliver the intervention. The principle is the same as when the physician gives the patient a pill. It is the active substance in the pill that works. It is believed it is the same in therapy, that it is the intervention that works and the therapist's competence is to deliver it the best way. From this perspective it is important that the therapist gets the necessary training to be a

---

[3]Some professional counselling bodies in North America require post-registration supervision.

scientist-practitioner in order to make the right interventions. When we ask about 'what works' in psychotherapy, we are reminded that psychotherapy is often compared with the effects of chemicals from the pharmaceutical industry. In other words, we are invited to use the same rhetoric about psychotherapy as we use to describe chemical effects (Jensen, 2007: 380).

According to the clinical perspective, any therapist who is expertly trained can perform the treatment and the treatment should remain the same with any therapist. However, by heeding Jensen's reminder of the importance of ther-apist biography, we open the possibility that each encounter requires its own therapy because it includes each therapist's unique being. By incorporating this interrelational sensitivity existential supervision embraces the embodied felt experiencing of the therapist/supervisee as it impacts upon the relational work of therapy. However, the evocative is not a clinical *technique*, it must arise authentically; we prepare an environment and then we wait. These moments are often quite poignant, simultaneously personal and professional, and their coming requires a supervisory culture of openness and acceptance.

Necessary Conditions for Evocative Supervision

Although *clinical* supervision emphasises the development of technical skill and competencies, research has consistently found that the *relationship* between supervisor and supervisee is an essential component of effective supervision: '... the supervisee must feel the supervisor's emotional investment, and a trust-ing and collaborative relationship must be present' (Barnet, 2007: 271).

Ineffective or undesirable supervisors do not attend to the supervisory rela-tionship and exhibit a tendency to be critical, inflexible and emotionally unsupportive (ibid). Unger (1999) reports a disturbing study in which 50% of supervisees reported inattention to the supervisory relationship as resulting in 'problematic' supervision experiences, while 15% also reported being trauma-tised in supervision (c.f. Ellis, 2001: 404).

From the *clinical* perspective, the relational environment is overlooked in favour of training micro-skills that are operationally observed and checked, for example knowledge of diagnostic systems, formulation skills and risk assessment (Falender *et al.*, 2007). Defining micro-competencies is overly reductive to existential supervisors who are concerned that the personal and interpersonal realms within which any skills develop will not be adequately nurtured. It becomes clear that the definition of 'competency' is entirely dependent upon the corresponding definition of therapy. Existential therapy emphasises the 'being qualities' of the therapist (Spinelli, 2007; Todres, 2007). I would like to suggest that awareness of the evocative dimension is one 'being-based' competency that could be further nurtured within existential supervision.

Evocative Supervision

A trusting supervisory relationship is a necessary prerequisite in order to attend sensitively to the *personal* experiencing of supervisees as they present their dilemmas with clients. These dilemmas are explored by attending to the supervisees' *present embodiment*. The evocative is bodily, a *feeling* of being moved, an *experience* of being carried along in a specific direction without a predictable outcome. This does not arise from theory or interpretation. It requires an experiential environment that *feels* open to ongoing development of therapist *being-qualities*. Guided by bodily sensing supervision sessions can include moments of deep connection amongst those present. The deepening connection, from personal dilemmas to universal existential dilemmas, can allow a bodily felt poignancy – this is the evocative. A feature of this aspect of human living is that it can never be encapsulated; it remains a *fecund no-thing-ness*.

The evocative interweaves personal and existential strands.[4] We are always already participating in an implicit dimension of experiencing that we do not often pay attention to. It rumbles along diffuse until our turn in attention invites it to arise fully as the unfinished and elusive, but *clearly felt evocative*. In our supervision sessions why do we focus so exclusively on substantive explicit narratives rather than the implicit source from which they arose?

The work of philosopher and psychotherapist Eugene Gendlin addresses the level of implicit experiencing. Gendlin saw therapy as a unique place where the process of bringing unformed experience into language could be investigated. Gendlin discovered that the ability to stay with an unclear (but clearly felt) bodily experience constitutes a natural form of self-reflection that he called 'Focusing' (Gendlin, 1981). Focusing guides us to the evocative. It allows us to witness how implicit feeling generates explicit content and how there is always a 'more than' hazily surrounding anything explicit. Reflecting upon bodily-felt experience in an open phenomenological way can lead to shifts in bodily comportment, often accompanied by insights into self and world. Focusing is a way of paying attention to our being-in-the-world.

Gendlin has a different conception of *the body* than one finds in clinical approaches (see Gendlin, 1997). The body is not locked within its essence like a rock. Nor is it a malleable lump of clay that needs a sculptor to give it form. The body is not just an electrical box that can be rewired to generate less heat or more light. Gendlin's conception of the body is always *more than* a physiological machine or a derivative of culture. The body *is interaction*. It is a space of open responding to one's environment so radically that what we call 'body' and what we call 'environment' is simply a matter of perspective. Bodily felt

---

[4]The word 'strands' suggests that the personal and existential could be unwoven and separated. Perhaps conceptually this is possible, however experientially they are 'in' and 'of' each other.

experience is an intricate interaction with the environment. Feelings are finely ordered relational events that are further elaborated when a word, phrase or symbol 'fits' the feeling, touching and moving the body *all the way in*, raising deep resonances that elicit the feeling of understanding, understanding as an unfinished process rather than understanding as a final achievement. Language, when it flows with the way the body is responding to a specific situation, carries forward that situation.

Focusing cannot be thought of as a 'competency' in the clinical sense. It is more like an orientation towards existence. It is the phenomenology of noticing how the *more than* social and cultural moves through us in each moment. What we feel is not inner content but the sentience of what is happening in our living with others. Gendlin calls this feeling a 'felt sense', a murky sort of feeling, usually generated in the trunk of the body. Life is not formed out of unrelated bits of perception or isolated internal objects: 'we humans live from bodies that are self-conscious of situations. Notice the "odd" phrase "self-conscious of situation". "Conscious", "self", and "situations" are not three objects with separate logical definitions' (Gendlin, 1999: 233). Situations *are* bodily process, and this is useful therapeutically and in supervision sessions.

Any speaking that evokes a felt sense and carries it along is very exact and not arbitrary; not just any word will do. I may not like what emerges but I am not free to just reframe it, to decide it is something else, to make it something nicer or more acceptable. Within an accepting supervision relationship we can acknowledge a 'felt sense'. Rather than interpreting content, attending directly to this process allows the unfinished body to flow forward. At any point the felt sense can seem like set content, but it is not discrete, it is a *process* that implies a next movement and this is clearly felt when we 'focus' on it: 'such sensitive phenomenological attention to an implicit speech which is "not yet formed" is precisely what is precluded by standard conceptual thinking about the body' (Wallulis, 1997: 277–8). We are so used to thinking in terms of set content and fixed inner subjectivities that it requires some reorientation to realise that the body *is* a sensing that can carry itself forward into novel reconfigurations of past-present-future.

Focusing enables the supervisee to directly access their experience of being with a specific client rather than just analysing themes from sessions or formulating interpretations according to psychological theory alone. The relationship co-created between therapist and client is available again, from the therapist's side, but now 'crossed' with the present environment of the supervision group. We do not assume that the therapist/supervisee's feeling is 'counter-transference', or purely related to their own subjective difficulties. The felt sense *is* that living therapeutic situation as a phenomenological process, unfinished, inconclusive and open. As the body opens the door to the evocative it often speaks poetically, turning words sideways in order to eek out a saying that will allow experience to flow further, even briefly.

An Example of the Evocative in Supervision

The following vignette occurs in a small group format of three supervisees, all nearing completion of a doctorate in existential psychology at a training institute in London. The group has worked hard to establish a respectful and trusting space into which 'mistakes' and insecurities are welcomed without judgement.[5] The supervisor, 'Paul', avoids being too didactic or prescriptive and instead takes an exploratory stance whereby supervisees find their own felt resonance for what might be helpful with their clients.

The presenting supervisee, 'Jean', is talking about a client, 'Rob', with whom she is halfway through a six month contract. Jean experiences this relationship with Rob as 'guarded' and she wants to understand this better. In the most recent session Rob begins to tell Jean in new detail about the death of his father 15 years ago. Rob feels he did not get a chance to grieve at the time as he had to look after his younger siblings and his mother. Rob has begun to express a somewhat surly attitude toward Jean at the end of their sessions. Jean fills in some more detail for the group by which time it is obvious that she too is feeling something about these interactions with her client, Rob.

The supervisor, Paul, influenced by Gendlin's philosophy, is attentive to the importance of evocative moments in supervision. Paul notices that Jean is beginning to feel something as she gets into the detail of her recent session with Rob, so he interrupts the narrative, *'Jean, I get the impression that you're beginning to feel something now as you tell us about your last session with Rob. Are you feeling something?'* Jean pauses and looks reflective, *'Yes, I guess … I think I feel angry. I'm sick of his little snipes at the end of the session but I don't know how to bring it up with him. It makes me feel I have to be on guard with him and I feel helpless to do anything about it'.*

This is the first instance of an invitation to notice what is being evoked in supervision. Rather than continuing with the narrative about the recent session, Paul invites Jean to pause and notice how the feeling of that session is coming again now as she talks about it. A moment earlier Jean was feeling something but not paying attention to it, now as she becomes aware, her body begins to change, simply in response to her attention on it. Her attending is the beginning of symbolising what was previously diffuse and only implicitly 'there'. In order for the feeling to stand out more so that it can be referred to concretely, Jean must bring to her own experiencing the same kind of open acceptance that the group has established with each other. The environment of Jean attending to herself and the group attending to Jean is connected as one relational environment.

As Jean quietly begins to sense the feeling in her body, the supervisor, Paul, offers a reflection, *'So there's helplessness about how to address this situation with*

---

[5]What comes in the body needs to be protected from 'knowing' or critical voices.

Rob and he's expressing something like anger at you and you're angry with him. And there's that guardedness between you'. Brief reflections invite Jean to check her own words back with what she is feeling in order to remain grounded in her experiencing as it unfolds – it is easy to get marooned back in concepts and descriptions that no longer have any evocative resonance. In response to the reflection Jean nods and replies, *'Yes, I guess that guardedness makes some sense if we're both angry at each other'.* Jean's body relaxes as she says this. She realises that up until then she had been judging her 'guardedness' as a failure to be open to Rob, but now she sees that it is an accurate feeling of their relationship at present. Jean now feels that she could address the relationship with Rob, something she's wanted but felt unable to do as long as she judged her feeling as wrong. Jean needed to understand her feeling for herself before she considered disclosing it to Rob.

The supervisor, Paul, next asks, *'Jean, what are you feeling in your body as we talk about this now'?* Jean notices a feeling in her shoulders and upper chest. She searches for a word that would fit this sense she has, *'I'm feeling a kind of cloudiness across the top of my body, my chest and shoulders'.* As Jean stays with this feeling the rest of the supervision group is quiet, fully engaged in what is spontaneously unfolding. *'I feel fear in this. I think I'm afraid of us being angry with each other, like it could be explosive and messy and I'm supposed to be the therapist!'* As Jean says this she sighs deeply and nods her head. *'Yes, it's a fear of losing my role with him, failing him'.* Paul reflects this back and then offers an interpretation that he hopes Jean will not take unless it continues to evoke bodily responses of rightness. *'Maybe it feels like you're supposed to contain your anger so that you can help process Rob's anger? [Jean nods yes, "exactly"]. Like Rob did with his family, holding onto his own experience in order to look after the needs of others?'*

As Jean ponders this, Paul begins to feel this comment was mistimed. It was not 'in' Jean's present feeling and perhaps not 'experience near' enough to be evocative. Paul is concerned that his comment may now take them off into *making* links rather than *sensing* them. During the silence Jean is checking the words to see what resonates and what doesn't, after some time Jean again breathes deeply and with some emotion replies, *'Yes, we're stuck together like he's stuck in his family. And we're both scared but now I also feel closer to him and this makes me less scared. It feels like I can work with that. I feel less stuck. I'm beginning to feel differently towards him'.* Paul is relieved, *'OK, you can feel some new potential to work with this in your relationship. I'm glad to hear that, I was afraid I'd taken us off track there'.*

The rest of the group has also been sensing their bodily responses during this interaction. Now the dialogue is opened up to include the whole group and each supervisee is given space to share their experience – many of their specific feelings also carry along the process for Jean, creating an evocative interaction within the group. Later Paul asks the group, *'Rob's anger relates to having suffered the death of his father without the space to grieve. Do any of you have a feeling for what that would be like, grief with no space?'* This is another facet of the evocative, where an individual's unique experience offers an opening for each of us to reflect bodily upon the wider significance their experience may have for each of us. After some silent reflection the group begins to discuss their own experiences of loss, their need for time and space and their reactions to others' needs. The feeling of the discussion carries along each person's felt self-understanding. The atmosphere in the group remains poignant. By the end of Jean's time the group symbolised their experience as *'grief must reach out for its own connection'*. Our felt understandings of Rob and ourselves had changed. Jean would return to her next session with Rob as a changed body, offering him a new environment to interact with.

Focusing offers a phenomenological stance that arises from the supervisee's own embodiment rather than theory or convention. Of course therapy is more than just Focusing, but I would like to suggest that through its evocative impact, Focusing is as efficacious in supervision as it is in therapy (Madison, 2008b).

What does Evocative Supervision Contribute?

The evocative stance within supervision can be an overarching sensitivity for working existentially or it can constitute particular moments within a super- visory practice that integrates many different perspectives, including clinical modalities. In either case it may be useful to list some of the advantages that may ensue from working evocatively.

Evocative supervision:

1. Is attuned to each present moment, making supervision sessions feel alive and directly relevant to both our personal lives and to our current client work; the two are not separate because we have only one body – this was also referred to in the previous chapter, from an existential perspective the 'personal' and the 'professional' are not separate since everything is *personal*. The evocative dimension breathes life back into supervision sessions that can, even at the training level, too easily become an obligation or ritualised habit.
2. Offers a correction for our tendency to obsess over the minutiae of client stories and concentrate too much on the explicit presentation of the client's issues. If we focus on content alone we can perceive client problems as discreet, each needing to be addressed one at a time.
3. Reasserts the 'carrying forward' of experience in each moment as an intricate measure of 'evidence' of efficacy rather than a general outcome measure at the end of therapy.
4. Goes all the way in, from individual significance, to supervision group effect, to deeper existential levels, inviting exploration of the therapist in

their professional role, therapist as unique person *and therapist as example of human existence generally*. Such supervision benefits the client because it returns the therapist to an open philosophical attitude, where assumptions and conclusions about life can loosen and return to un-knowing.

5. Might for some minutes sound rather like therapy for the supervisee but the distinction between therapy and supervision can be simultaneously clear *and* flexible. It is usually apparent when someone is not bringing enough of themselves into the supervision forum or when they are using supervision solely to explore their own personal issues.

6. Fosters supervisor sensitivity to the feeling of the supervisory relationship. This includes acknowledging the phenomenon of 'parallel process' which is often ascribed to the unconscious 'pathology' of the client (Lees, 1999: 131) or as indicating that the supervisee is trying to *show* us a major issue in the therapy that they cannot yet speak about. Parallel processes are not especially mysterious phenomena when we recall that our bodies can create a holistic 'felt sense' of our life situations. It is not necessary to assume that someone is *doing something* to someone else when so called parallel process is experienced. It may simply be that in supervision our bodies form a felt sense of *being in* the session we are recounting, we live it again in a shared way. This shared experience inevitably implies human existentials beyond the particular individuals involved.

Conclusion

Evocative supervision is more 'process-centred' than content centred. From his experience as an existential supervisor Pett (1995) finds that while a supervisee presents their work with a client, 'very often this description will lead to a response "standing out" of the description, much in the way Gendlin's (1981) "focusing" leads to a "felt sense"' (Pett, 1995: 122). Neil Friedman, a Focusing-oriented psychologist, has suggested that 'Focusing is the way that the Heideggerian and phenomenological approach to the body enters the world of psychotherapy' (2000: 225).

Concentrating on the experiential process, as I have suggested, could give us forms of supervision that are *responsive* to the immediate needs of supervisees, keeping supervision challenging and relevant to our client work and our own personal lives. However, there are other supervision tasks which require a different quality of discernment or even an imposition upon the experiential-existential. These tasks may originate in part from the *context* of supervision – professional codes of practice and prescriptive policies of specific organisations. We must acknowledge the external authority, knowledge and judgement of the larger world of therapy, institutions and jurisprudence. This reminds us that discussing contracts, offering advice on professional development or practice, conducting annual appraisals and dealing with managerial concerns may also be appropriate aspects of supervision.

Several contributors have referred to the importance of the organisational elements that inevitably impinge on supervision, however limiting and constraining these cannot be ignored. For example in Chapter 13 the author acknowledges the need to work with the supervisee to find ways of working *within* these constraints despite their contradiction with an existential-phenomenological perspective.

At times there may be conflicts between the experiential-existential approach and what is accepted as professional convention. Becoming aware of the times when our felt sense unfolds in one direction while our professional duties pull in another can provide important information. It may be that Focusing not only enhances the efficacy of supervision, but that it assists in keeping us reflective regarding the professional accoutrements of supervision and psychotherapy. Attending to the 'more than' intricacy of our lived experience may guide us to develop unique formulations of supervision and psychotherapy in the future.

Evocative supervision offers to deliver us from the mundane and inspire us to work from the broadest possible life perspective. Such moments should sear away any accrued professional arrogance or defensive practice to reveal the humility of the moribund human. Evocative moments in supervision can feel spiritual, making the familiar dazzle with novelty and poetic expression. If existential therapy includes a 'spiritual' dimension (Deurzen, 2001) then so should existential supervision. The evocative is an understanding that 'embodies' just such a spiritual approach (Campbell & McMahon, 1985). Focusing on the bodily implicit can connect us to a self-responding infinity: '...*the edge of awareness. It comes between the conscious person and the deep universal reaches of human nature where we are no longer ourselves*' (Gendlin, 1984).

References

AskOxford Website Dictionary. http://www.askoxford.com/?view=uk: Accessed 2008.

Barnet, J. 'In Search of the Effective Supervisor', *Professional Psychology: Research and Practice* 38(3) (2007) 268–75.

Bond, T. 'Counselling Supervision – Ethical Issues', *Counselling* (1990) 43–5.

Campbell, P. & McMahon, E. *Biospirituality* (Chicago: Loyola University Press, 1985).

Counselling Psychology Review 'Bringing Psychology and Psychotherapy Together', 23(1) (2008).

Deurzen, E. van *Existential Counselling and Psychotherapy in Practice*, 2nd edn (London: Sage, 2001).

Ellis, M. 'Harmful Supervision, a Cause for Alarm', *Journal of Counseling Psychology* 48(4) (2001) 401–6.

Falender, C., Shafranske, A. & Edward, P. *Professional Psychology: Research and Practice* 38(3) (2007) 232–40.

Friedman, N. *Focusing: Selected Essays, 1974–1999* (USA: Xlibris Corporation, 2000).

Gendlin, E. *Focusing* (New York: Bantam Books, 1981).

—— 'The Client's Client: The Edge of Awareness'. In R. L. Levant & J. M. Shlien (eds) *Client-centered Therapy and the Person-centered Approach* (New York: Praeger, 1984).

—— *A Process Model*. Focusing Institute website. http://www.focusing.org/process. html (1997).

—— 'A New Model' *Journal of Consciousness Studies* 6 (1999) 232–7.

Jensen, P. 'On Learning from Experience: Personal and Private Experiences as the Context for Psychotherapeutic Practice', *Clinical Child Psychology and Psychiatry* 12 (2007) 375–84.

Jones, A. 'Out of the Sighs – An Existential-phenomenological Method of Clinical Supervision: The Contribution to Palliative Care', *Journal of Advanced Nursing* 27 (1998) 905–13.

Lees, J. 'An Approach to Supervision in Health Care Settings', *European Journal of Psychotherapy, Counselling and Health* 2(2) (1999) 131–41.

Madison, G. 'Futurist Therapy'. http://www.goodtherapy.org/custom/blog/ 2008/01/05/futurist-therapy-what-role-will-therapy-have-in-a-post-human-future/ *Good Therapy*. Featured Contributors (2008a).

—— 'Focusing, Intersubjectivity, and "Therapeutic Intersubjectivity"', *Existential Analysis* 19(1) (2008b) 58–72.

Online Etymology Dictionary: http://www.etymonline.com/: Accessed (2008).

Pett, J. 'A Personal Approach to Existential Supervision', *Existential Analysis* 6(2) (1995) 117–26.

Spinelli, E. *Practicing Existential Psychotherapy* (London: Sage, 2007).

Todres, L. *Embodied Inquiry* (London: Palgrave, 2007).

Unger, D. 'Core Problems in Clinical Supervision: Factors Related to Outcomes'. In M. L. Friedlander (Chair) *Psychotherapy Supervision: For Better or for Worse*. Symposium 107th Annual Convention of the American Psychological Association, Boston (1999).

Van Manen, M. *Inquiry: The Evocative Turn: Nearness* (2002). http://www.phenomenology-online.com/inquiry/20.html: April 15, 2008.

Wallulis, J. 'Carrying Forward: Gadamer and Gendlin on History, Language, and the Body'. In D. Levin (ed.) *Language Beyond Postmodernism* (Evanston: Northwestern University Press, 1997).

16

The Future of Existential Supervision

Emmy van Deurzen and Sarah Young

Introduction

What can we conclude about the future of existential supervision from the preceding chapters? First and foremost we can say that existential supervision is being formulated systematically for the first time but that it emerges out of the long established praxis of existential supervisors. While the articulation of this practice was long overdue it will undoubtedly lead to further debates and developments in the field. The intention is neither to stifle the creativity and freedom that are fundamental and necessary aspects of existential thinking nor to create a standardised form of practice. What stands out in these pages is the way in which existential supervision fans out across a wide range of views, which is a reflection of the broad and integrative nature of existential therapy and of existential thinking in general. This diversity and individuality has meant that a distinctive existential perspective on supervision has taken a while to take shape. The first attempt at formulation was probably that by van Deurzen and Spinelli in a short film on existential supervision, produced by Strasser in 1996, even in this training video there was a clear difference between their two approaches, the former philosophically based and the latter interactionally based. Besides this a small number of papers have appeared in the Journal of the Society for Existential Analysis (Pett, 1995; Wright, 1996; Mitchell, 2002; Adams, 2002; du Plock, 2007), each with a different emphasis.

To date then the literature on existential supervision *per se* is remarkably sparse and this volume is a first step towards remedying this situation. In some ways it is surprising that so little has been written since existential therapists are routinely in supervisory relationships as they value dialogue and discussion about practice. But perhaps the form these relationships take has not been examined because it has been assumed that there would be a large degree of congruence with existential practice itself. It is also undoubtedly, as several authors in this volume have remarked, because existential practitioners are generally wary of formulating their practice, reluctant as they are about accepting technique, methodology and formalisation, emphasising the aspects of *being with* rather than *doing to* the client.

As this text demonstrates, however, there are many elements of existential supervision practice that are shared and that can be clearly formulated without losing the crucial elements of presence and being-with. All authors in this book have spoken of the importance of tuning into the client's experience. All have mentioned phenomenology or implied the use of this descriptive rather than interpretative method for making sense of experience. Some have mentioned specific philosophers who inspire their practice, and all have shown that they value a philosophical exploration of the therapeutic relationship and the life issues clients are struggling with. Some specific themes have emerged from these pages.

Emerging Themes

Being-in-the-world

As we have indicated already, underpinning the existential perspective is an understanding of the human situation as described by phenomenologists such as Heidegger. Human beings are not seen as separate subjects isolated from each other. Rather they are understood as beings-in-the-world, always in relation to others and the world around them. This has profound implications for our work as therapists and supervisors. We cannot take up an expert stance and see ourselves as separate from our supervisees or clients. We are in this world together, as are our clients, facing the same 'givens'. What is created in our relationship we create together – the way I am with you is a direct response to you and only you – and we need to be aware of this and each take responsibility for it. This includes the situation we are in now in, the context of our lives, and it is informed by our individual past experiences and our hopes for the future. Each relationship is a new creation of the two people involved in that particular situation and in each relationship we respond differently and have a new opportunity to learn.

This fundamental understanding of the human condition as an *inevitable connectedness*, means that we cannot as existential supervisors be exempt from examining our own part in the relationship, or hold ourselves aloof; hence the stress that has been placed on collaboration between supervisor and supervisee seen throughout this book. This understanding is radically different from the Cartesian view that we are separate subjects – objects to each other. One of the difficulties facing those who attempt to describe existential thinking is the obtuseness of some of the writings that inform our understanding. Another difficulty is the fact that our language is embedded in this Cartesian split, so that we speak as if we were separate, whilst, at the same time, trying to understand our interactions as part of an open system and as a network of connections. Heidegger (2001: 3) demonstrated this profound understanding with an extraordinarily simple drawing:

$$(<$$

These symbols show human consciousness as an open system rather than as the usual encapsulated, isolated psyche. Consciousness is out there in the world through intentionality, open to all that it encounters and it is always less than the connectivity it opens itself towards.

Phenomenology

Throughout this book the authors have acknowledged the importance of approaching our clients and supervisees phenomenologically, that is from a position of unknowing or rather of bracketing our assumptions. If we follow the epoché we need to recognise and set aside, to the extent that we can, our prejudices, biases and presumptions about the world and each other. This allows us to attend more completely to what is actually there and describe it carefully. Of course we can never eliminate our bias or our assumptions. In the process of existential supervision these assumptions and the beliefs which inform them will be revealed and examined carefully and respectfully – hence the recognition that we are changed through the encounter in supervision because we learn about ourselves. The descriptive, hermeneutic unravelling which is the stuff of existential supervision is discussed by most authors in some shape or form and can be said to underlie all existential supervisory practice. It means coming to the supervisory encounter with an attitude of wonder and doubt, ready to be amazed by new discoveries but also ready to be confronted with our usual bias and blind spots. The aim is to shine light and clear our consciousness towards a greater openness.

Dialogue

This openness and attentiveness to the other is a fundamental starting point to the process of existential supervision, but it needs to be followed up by a particular quality of encounter. As existential supervisors we listen and give our full attention to our supervisees. This requires us to have the discipline to not become caught up with what we are going to say or with what we are expecting to hear or with our own worries and concerns. Buber's notion of the in-between is important in this respect: making us attentive to the atmosphere we co-create in the space between us. Again we must acknowledge this is not something we can achieve as a constant, for there will be many times when our attention will flicker and waver and we will inevitably fail to give the other our full attention. Throughout the book authors have stressed how important it is to keep working on this stance of openness and respect for the other. Existential supervisors will encourage therapists not to take their understanding of their clients for granted, but look again and again at what is actually being presented to them.

Love, care and respect

This leads to the recognition of the importance of care and respect for the other in existential supervision. Understanding and truly feeling into the client's way of being is foregrounded, whether we think of this as existential sexuality or as love. Being human is to be in a with-world and even when we are alone or isolated this is so in relation to the absent other. To understand the with-world that exists between client and therapist and between supervisee and supervisor is to start making explicit a whole dimension of being that may have become neglected. To do so not only means ameliorating the quality of the therapeutic and supervisory relationship and to bridge the gulf that may have existed but to expand one's capacity for being with others and thus for being itself.

Embodiment

Implicit and explicit in this idea and indeed in all of the chapters is the understanding of human beings as embodied beings. If Descartes' worldview separated mind and body, Husserl mended the split and provided us with the concept of intentionality and a worldview where mind and body were united. Existential supervisors are aware of the importance of our embodied presence in the flesh. They accept that mind and body are two aspects of the same being. These two aspects are not just linked, for linkage implies separation – they are two sides of the same coin. This puts a new complexion on the concept of 'psychosomatic' experience, since mind and body are inevitably both involved in human experience. Though sometimes our bodily/physical response may dominate and at other times our mind/psychological response, there can never be one without the other. Nothing is ever purely physical or purely psychological – any physical problem is accompanied by a psychological response and *vice versa*: the two are inextricably intertwined.

Worldview, spirituality and meaning

And so the existential worldview puts emphasis on the totality of being. Not everyone may agree with the distinction between different dimensions of existence, but existential supervisors will usually encourage therapists to explore the multiplicity of their clients' experience. They may use the fourfold world model and the emotional compass to do so, or they may use the wheel of existential supervision. They may, alternatively, simply be sensitive to the different layers of clients' experiences and tease out the different meanings that are generated in the clients and supervisees' worlds. But it would not be possible to do existential supervision without paying attention to the spiritual domain of beliefs, purpose and meaning.

To make room for the intangible, for the intuitive and for what remains silent is to make room for being and to reach out for new horizons. Some people refer to this as the evocative, others as the *Uberwelt*, others still may consider this to be the domain of love. But without some space and time for this core quality, existential supervision would not be worthy of the name. The spiritual dimension is where we create meaning and make sense of our experiences and existential supervision regards this as central in understanding both the client's and therapist's experience.

Responsibility and freedom

Several authors have also referred to responsibility and the extent to which we can be responsible for another's behaviour – as in 'clinical responsibility'. In this context several authors discussed the concepts of 'leaping in' and 'leaping ahead'. Although there is room for the occasional leaping in, existential supervision favours a leaping ahead, which means to hand responsibility back and allow the other to make their own decisions and choices. This also invokes Heidegger's description of 'thrownness', which Sartre called the facticity of our existence, aspects of our lives for which we cannot take responsibility. These simple facts of life are sometimes referred to as the givens, over which we have no control, but which we can take in our stride. Jaspers' idea of limit situations and Tillich's ultimate concerns also relate to these facts of life which limit us. The fact that we are thrown into a world at a time and place over which we have no choice, defines the setting of the ontic givens of our situation, including the culture, family and country we are born into and so on. How we respond to these givens is our area of freedom – and where we take up our responsibility.

Sartre emphasised our extraordinary freedom – a freedom we frequently deny. He showed how we limit our lives when we pretend, in bad faith, that we do not have choices and are not free. Existential supervisors will often refer to the paradox of freedom versus necessity. Freedom is always doubled edged. On the one hand it is wonderfully exhilarating: I no longer *have to* do my duty – it is my choice to do or not do what is expected. On the other hand it is utterly terrifying: I am free to leave my country, marriage, job my whole way of life, but ultimately I have to choose to do something and engage with it. Kierkegaard describes the anxiety created by this sense of overwhelming responsibility in the face of possibility beautifully as the 'dizziness of freedom'. For Sartre our freedom can be so overwhelming that it is nauseating. In the final analysis there can be no existential supervision without constant reference to this fundamental freedom and the tensions it creates. Our freedom brings with it responsibility along with other existentials – anxiety, guilt, uncertainty, isolation, failure and death. Existential supervisors help their supervisees to remember these fundamental struggles and show them how to enable clients to reclaim their lives and face these facts.

Organisational context

We have also seen several references in these pages to the contribution existential supervision can make when working within an organisational context, be it a therapeutic or an educational one. Existential supervision always takes the social, cultural and political context into account in the issues under discussion and so has a great deal to contribute in this situation. It is, in John Towler's words very aware of the 'invisible client' (Towler, 2008). This invisible client makes demands on the therapist and puts constraints on the therapeutic frame and objectives. Several authors have discussed the possible constraints inherent in working within various organisations, including the NHS, and they have also shown how flexible the existential approach to supervision is in adapting to the specific situation and context the supervisee is working within.

The Way Forward

This book has begun the process of formulating the theory and practice of existential supervision, in order to open up a whole new field. In making existential supervision visible – it has put it on the map, but without pinning it down to one specific location. Rather than restricting or confining existential supervision, this book is an invitation to further formulations and contributions and to more debate. There are many more avenues that need exploring before the territory of existential supervision becomes clearly visible and known. For the moment it will remain a place for adventurous explorations, experimentation and discovery, not just by a select elite of existential therapists, but by all those who are passionate about a supervision that is true to life.

Research

It is clear from current psychotherapy research (Wampold, 2001; Tantam, 2002) that dealing with issues of meaning is crucial to success in psychotherapy. The fact that it is the individual therapist rather than the method they use that predicts good results for therapy may say more about that individual therapist's capacity for contact, reality and vigour in searching for meaning than anything else. The finding that therapeutic outcomes are similar, whatever approach is employed, seems to suggest that the factors that create the best therapeutic relationships and the most curative effects are related to personality and charisma, which is tantamount to saying they are about having a personal impact on another person. Such personal impact is invariably based on the values we inspire in the other, in the beliefs and the confidence we help create in them and in the faith in life that results.

Therapy and especially therapeutic supervision has reached a stage where it is ready to go beyond technique and cognitive strategies, when even the research is pointing in a more personal, intense and intimate direction (Cooper, 2008). Perhaps this means that the time is ripe for existential therapists and supervisors to come out of the closet and clearly state what they do and believe. In these days of evidenced-based practice many existential thera-pists express the fear that attempts will be made to formalise and manualise existential perspectives. But, of course, if one tried to do so the vital ingredi-ents of existential thinking would immediately be lost and the real practice of existential therapy would have to transcend the formalisation of it. Freedom simply cannot be captured. For this reason many existential therapists and supervisors are equivocal about research as they believe that many of the inef-fable aspects of relationships, be they supervisory or therapeutic relationships, are what make a difference and enable the client/supervisee to bring about change. These invisible and ineffable aspects are, of course, immeasurable (whether you use the more sophisticated methods of qualitative research or not) and it may well be that the very act of measurement and formalisation that is required for measurement destroy the essence of such work and hinder its progress.

It is not for nothing that existential therapists clamour for freedom of prac-tice and that they value the individual variations that this entails. Those who seek to establish the approach in a dogmatic fashion, selecting certain ele-ments of practice that fit with manualisation confine the definition of existen-tial to their own particular interpretation of the approach. They are in fact working in contradiction with the spirit of existential thinking. True philo-sophical thinking requires flexibility and individuality and this leads to diver-sity of thinking. Long may this diversity last and flourish.

Nevertheless, despite these reservations and the limitations inherent in the research tools we have at present, now the challenge is to do the specific research that can pinpoint exactly how change in therapy and supervision comes about. Existential therapists have set up several research groups (EPCORN: Existential Psychotherapy and Counselling Outcome Research Network) in relation to the Universities that teach existential therapy and supervision. The future of existential supervision will be secured by doing this research and demonstrating what a wider vision in therapy and counselling can achieve.

Cross-theoretical appeal

Many supervisors who find themselves regularly confronted with existential issues may realise that all supervision is in some ways of an existential nature. We cannot avoid the life issues raised by therapeutic difficulties when we are supervising and we cannot avoid a certain amount of existential and moral speculation either. As existentially informed supervisors and therapists we know that most of the work we do goes well beyond the modalities we origi-nally trained in and that supervision needs to be able to occupy that higher ground, which provides the bird's eye view over the whole field of therapy – this is true for existential practitioners as much as for anyone else. And yet such an overview is not enough, for *theory* never captures *practice* and we have to return to the realities of the therapeutic interaction in order to acquire new understanding that is in tune with experience. In this sense supervision is always a journey. Perhaps the existential part of the journey starts when we realise we have to keep searching and cannot just follow well trodden paths.

The existential psychotherapist Hans W. Cohn described his journey thus:

> My original psychoanalytic orientation … increasingly failed to help me with the experiences I had with my clients … I moved gradually…to an existential-phenomenological understanding of our life as human beings … This was not a question of 'applying' Heidegger's concepts to the practice of psychotherapy – rather it was the realization that some of his understanding of the way human beings exist reflected my own and therefore underlies my therapeutic practice (Cohn, 2002: xvii–xviii).

This is often the way in which supervisors and therapists discover the existential perspective: it expresses and summarises the kind of issues and questions that we have to deal with no matter what theoretical orientation informs our practice. For this same reason the existential perspective provides a great advantage to supervisors who run supervision groups in settings where many of the therapists have different backgrounds and work with different therapeutic methods. When working in such a situation it becomes clear that we need a meta-model of some sort to do justice to all our supervisees. An eclectic model will not fit the bill, since it requires technical competency in many methods and we do not necessarily wish to espouse a model that allows for so much contradiction and internal tension. We need an integrative model, but one that has a theoretical discipline behind it that is capable of valuing, matching and challenging all the elements of the models used by the different members of the group. Where better to find an integrative model with philosophical clarity than the existential? Once this perspective becomes more defined, there will be many who see its advantages, especially in relation to the more complex demands of supervision.

The integrative potential of existential thinking has long been recognised, Flach (1989), in his introduction to Man as Process: Existential Aspects of Psychotherapy by Hans W. Cohn noted that:

> Even if not consciously acknowledged, all clinicians employ existential concepts in their approach to psychotherapy. After all, therapy assumes the possibility of change, and the existentialist vision centers on the issue of becoming, of movement from a particular, presumably unhealthy form of adaption to a more integrated and effective one (Flach, 1989: 170).

It is an advantage that many would include some forms of classic psychoanalysis within the ranks of existential practice. By the same token some cognitive therapists have great sympathies with existential therapy, as do third wave practitioners who practise mindfulness. Many humanistic approaches were founded on existential thinking and benefit greatly from existential supervision to remind them of their roots. But equally many approaches that are based in spirituality find themselves on existential territory, since they search for meaning. Jungian and Transpersonal approaches, including Buddhist ones, are closely enough related to existential thinking to thrive on existential forms of supervision. This has been well documented see for example Brooke (1991) and Zimmerman (2006).

There is indeed a great deal to be said for allowing the existential label (though, of course paradoxically, labelling is anathema to existential thinkers) to apply to anyone who wants to claim it. Inclusiveness rather than exclusiveness has always been one of the great strengths of existential philosophy. This is all the more reason for existential supervision to be compatible with the demands of the multi-disciplinary team in the NHS. Trans-modality and non-dogmatic based practice is increasingly in demand, both in settings like the NHS and in voluntary settings that draw their practitioners from a wide range of disciplines and backgrounds.

In spite of this compatibility and appropriateness of the existential perspective there remain a number of problems with the future flourishing of existential supervision. Firstly existential and philosophical practitioners tend towards hiding away in obscurity and like to keep themselves away from public scrutiny. They relish practising in the margins which afford them the maximum freedom they prize, but which also makes them seem like mavericks at times. Secondly in the wider world of psychotherapy there is a fair deal of suspicion for an approach that is based in philosophy and phenomenology rather than on a positivistic outlook. The jargon of much of its philosophical background remains enigmatic and idiosyncratic enough to repel many who have tried to find out whether the existential approach may have something to offer them.

If existential supervision is to thrive and become a serious contender for public health based supervision it will be essential for existential supervisors to practise in a manner that is as jargon free as is feasible. Similarly existential practitioners will have to accept the need to associate with colleagues from a multiplicity of backgrounds and dare to speak their convictions, rather than speaking only to the converted. If these conditions are taken into account the future of existential supervision is filled with promise. The work of those who have contributed to this book shows how many paths it can take and how many truths it will be called to uncover and explore.

Conclusion

In summary the book has demonstrated that it is possible to practise supervision from a coherent and consistent existential perspective, though this is by no means an easy option. Neither is the field so clearly defined that we can simply teach existential supervision by rote. There is no one form of existential supervision but many. To learn existential supervision is a philosophical and very personal as well as a professional challenge, which involves us in profound, sometimes disturbing but always exhilarating explorations. One of the indispensable elements of existential work is its dynamism and constant evolution, so we cannot delineate the existential approach in an essentialist way. Existential supervision is only as good as the individual practitioner who practises it and only as valid as the intensity, vitality and passion for truth with which he or she practises it at any one moment. It will always remain a diverse and multiply defined field, as was shown in these pages. For those who are willing to take the existential challenge to heart there is a field with tremendous opportunities here. In final analysis the existential perspective on supervision is a philosophy of life.

References

Adams, M. 'Reflections on Reflection', *Existential Analysis* 13(2) (2002) 204–13.

Brooke, R. *Jung and Phenomenology* (London: Routledge, 1991).

Cohn, H. W. *Heidegger and the Roots of Existential Therapy* (London: Continuum, 2002).

Cooper, M. *Essential Research Findings in Counselling and Psychotherapy: The Facts are Friendly* (London: Sage Publications, 2008).

Du Plock, S. 'A Relational Approach to Supervision', *Existential Analysis* 18(1) (2007) 31–8.

Flach, F. (ed.) *Psychotherapy*, Directions in Psychiatry Monograph Series no. 5 (New York: Norton & Company, 1989).

Heidegger, M. *Zollikon Seminars* (ed.) M. Boss (Northwestern University Press: Illinois, 2001).

Mitchell, D. 'Is the Concept of Supervision at Odds with Existential Thinking and Therapeutic Practice?', *Existential Analysis* 13(1) (2002) 91–7.

Pett, J. 'A Personal Approach to Existential Supervision', *Existential Analysis* 6(2) (1995) 117–26.

Tantam, D. *Psychotherapy and Counselling in Practice* (Cambridge: Cambridge University Press, 2002).

Towler, J. 'The Influence of the Invisible Client': A Crucial Perspective for Understanding Counselling Supervision in Organisational Contexts. Division of Counselling Psychology *Occasional Papers in Supervision* (August 2008, Leicester: British Psychological Society).

Wampold, B. E. *The Great Psychotherapy Debate* (New Jersey: Lawrence Erlbaum Associates, 2001).

Wright, R. (1996) 'Another Approach to Existential Supervision', *Existential Analysis* 7(1) (1996) 149–58.

Zimmerman, M. 'Heidegger, Buddhism and Deep Ecology', in *Cambridge Companion to Heidegger: Second Edition* (ed.) C. B. Guignon (Cambridge: Cambridge University Press, 2006).

Glossary
of Existential-Phenomenological Concepts Referred To in This Text

Authentic/inauthentic refers to Heidegger's recognition that human beings are inclined to let themselves be taken over by others in the way in which they think about the world and act. They are inauthentic in that they follow an external locus of reference until they become aware of the limitations and realities of their own existence. It is mainly in coming to terms with death that authentic living first becomes possible. But even after we become capable of authentic being we continue to waver between authentic and inauthentic ways of being.

Being with a capital B is an abstract concept and refers to the basic principle of Being that transcends us and that only humans can embody. Indeed humans provide the place for Being and are the guardians of Being. Human beings are, according to Heidegger, the only beings who are interested in Being, who are self-reflective and ask what it means to be.

Being-for-itself this is human consciousness as Sartre refers to it, utterly boundless and completely free. We have no 'human nature' as such – we are nothing other than consciousness. We can therefore become whatever we choose.

Being-in-itself this is Sartre's definition of all objects and it refers to living entities lacking in self-awareness. As human beings we become, being-in-itself when we deny our freedom and treat ourselves as objects.

Being-in-the-world is Heidegger's way of describing our inevitable involvement in the world, our unity with our world – we can get out of our car but we cannot get out of our world, we live in a web of interconnections from which we cannot extricate ourselves. In a sense we carry our world with us and when we die our world dies with us.

Being-with emphasises that we are always in relationship with others, even if we choose the life of a hermit we do so in relation to others. We are inextricably involved with others as they are with us.

Bracketing is literally to put in brackets – to set aside our assumptions in order to see what really *is* unclouded by our biases and prejudices. It is an attempt to remain open to all that we encounter. Of course what is put in brackets still has to be dealt with: it remains part of the equation.

Co-constituted/co-construct the reflecting being and the object of reflection are defined through each other, they are co-constituted. We are actively involved in any experience and what we experience is co-constructed by us *and* by the object/person we encounter – any experience of a relationship says as much about me as it does about the other, it is a co-constructed relationship.

Dasein literally 'the there of being' or 'being-there', this is the term Heidegger used to refer to human beings, sometimes translated as existence but this fails to capture the uniqueness of being human and all that it implies.

Dialogue is to talk through something in order to find the truth, this is not two 'egos' doing battle and taking it in turns to have their say in monologue, not really listening to each other but a talking through which is a joint exploration seeking clarity.

Embodiment summed up in the phrase 'I am my body', we are not considered to be separate bodies and separate minds rather we are embodied beings, mind and body are inseparable, a unity. One cannot affect the other since any change impinges on both body and mind. All our perceptions occur through our bodies and our minds.

Epoché literally means suspension. It is an aspect of phenomenological reduction often referred to as bracketing (see above). It is a withholding of assumptions in a spirit of 'not-knowing' in order to examine our experience in a fresh and new way.

Givens are the facts of our existence (sometimes referred to as our 'facticity') over which we have no control and cannot change, because they limit and constrain us. There are personal (ontic) givens such as the family, culture and time we are born into and there are universal givens (ontological) such as our mortality, that we live in time, we are always in relationship and so on.

Hermeneutic refers to a method of investigation or interpretation that encompasses context – 'the whole is more than the sum of its parts', both the parts and the whole are included. Hermeneutic exploration will include all that is presented and will attempt to penetrate its significance/its meaning. This type of analysis will not replace one phenomenon with another but will explore what is present.

In-between is the space between two people in a genuine encounter, a space of openness and mutuality where the other is regarded as a 'fellow traveller', each accepts the other in their full humanness and does not treat the other as a separate object.

Intentionality refers to the understanding that consciousness is always directed towards something, reaching out towards an object or a feeling, there is no divide between us and our world, consciousness is out there in the world through intentionality.

Intersubjective/intersubjectivity our experience is always intersubjective because we are inevitably in relationship with others and with the world, we are interrelated and can never be isolated subjects, all experience is relationally derived.

I-Thou highlights and complements our usual way of relating namely in an I-It fashion treating the other as an object, judging them and not recognising their humanity – using them. In an I-thou relationship we encounter the other in their full humanness and allow their freedom, we relate with our whole being and to the whole being of the other.

Leaping ahead another Heideggerian concept which encompasses a further concept, namely that of care or concern. Heidegger distinguished two aspects of care for the other: leaping ahead is when we give care back, we allow the other to be responsible for themselves, we do not impose or dictate rather we let them find their own way.

Leaping in is when we take care away, we make ourselves responsible for the other rather than letting them make their own decisions, we take over and impose our view. This can lead to a kind of dependence and to a lack of autonomy.

Ontic – Heidegger distinguishes between the ontic and the ontological dimensions of existence. Ontic refers to the concrete world, to particular beings and to our everyday, personal concerns.

Ontological (ontology is the study of existence or Being), ontological aspects of Being are those that are universal, true for us all – the essential conditions of existence, such as being-with, being-towards-death.

Sedimented or sedimentation refers to the notion that something is fixed, set in stone and cannot be changed – 'I am just like that' is a sedimented belief which limits our capacity for change.

Self-construct from an existential perspective there is no such thing as a fixed 'self', our self-construct is a work in progress, we are always in a state of becoming, we limit ourselves by seeing ourselves as solid and unchangeable.

Socratic dialogue is a style of questioning (developed by Socrates) which allows us to reveal our beliefs and assumptions. In a spirit of genuine and open enquiry questions are asked so that we can show ourselves what it is we actually know and do not know.

Worldview (*Weltanschauung*) refers to the sum total of our values, beliefs and assumptions. These inform how we lead our lives and bring a sense of stability and continuity, at the same time our worldview shifts and like our self-construct it is not a fixed thing.

For a comprehensive compilation of existential-phenomenological concepts and a more in-depth discussion of those above please consult van Deurzen & Kenward's *Dictionary of Existential Psychotherapy and Counselling* (London: Sage, 2005).

Index

211